The Domestic Politics of Negotiating International Trade

The Domestic Politics of Negotiating International Trade considers the issues surrounding intellectual property rights in international trade negotiations in order to examine the challenges posed to domestic policy-makers by the increasingly broad nature of Free Trade Agreements (FTAs). Throughout the book the author demonstrates the importance of domestic politics in understanding the nature and outcome of international negotiations, particularly as they relate to international economic diplomacy.

The book looks in detail at the intellectual property negotiations which formed part of the US-Peru and US-Colombia FTAs and analyses the extent to which public health authorities and other parties affected by the increased levels of intellectual property protection were integrated into the negotiation process. The book then juxtaposes these findings with an analysis of the domestic origins of US negotiation objectives in the field of intellectual property, paying particular attention to the role of the private sector in the development of these objectives. Based on a substantial amount of empirical research, including approximately 100 interviews with negotiators, capital-based policy-makers, private sector representatives, and civil society organisations in Lima, Bogotá and Washington, DC, this book offers a rare account of different stakeholders' perceptions of the FTA negotiation process. Ultimately, the book succeeds in integrating the study of domestic politics with that of international negotiations.

This book will be of particular interest to academics as well as practitioners and students in the fields of international law, economic law, intellectual property, political economy, international relations, comparative politics and government.

Johanna von Braun has been working in the fields of intellectual property, trade and development for over ten years. She currently lives in South Africa where she was based as a post-doctoral fellow at the University of Cape Town during the writing of the book.

Routledge Research in International Economic Law

Available:

Recognition and Regulation of Safeguard Measures Under GATT/WTO
Sheela Rai

The Interaction between WTO Law and External International Law
The Constrained Openness of WTO Law
Ronnie R.F. Yearwood

Human Rights, Natural Resource and Investment Law in a Globalised World
Shades of Grey in the Shadow of the Law
Lorenzo Cotula

The Domestic Politics of Negotiating International Trade
Intellectual Property Rights in US-Colombia and US-Peru Free Trade Agreements
Johanna von Braun

Foreign Investment and Dispute Resolution Law and Practice in Asia
Vivienne Bath and Luke Nottage (eds)

Forthcoming:

Improving International Investment Agreements
Armand De Mestral and Céline Lévesque (eds)

Trade Remedies
A Development Perspective
Asif Qureshi

The Domestic Politics of Negotiating International Trade

Intellectual property rights in
US-Colombia and US-Peru
free trade agreements

Johanna von Braun

Routledge
Taylor & Francis Group

LONDON AND NEW YORK

First published 2012
by Routledge
2 Park Square, Milton Park, Abingdon, Oxon OX14 4RN

Simultaneously published in the USA and Canada
by Routledge
711 Third Avenue, New York, NY 10017

Routledge is an imprint of the Taylor & Francis Group, an informa business

British Library Cataloguing in Publication Data
A catalogue record for this book is available from the British Library

Library of Congress Cataloguing in Publication Data
von Braun, Johanna.
  The domestic politics of negotiating international trade :
  intellectual property rights in US-Colombia and US-Peru free
  trade agreements / Johanna von Braun.
      p. cm.
  Includes bibliographical references and index.
  ISBN 978-0-415-60139-9 (hbk : alk. paper)—ISBN 978-0-203-
  15636-0 (ebk : alk. paper) 1. United States—Commerce—
  Colombia. 2. Colombia—Commerce—United States. 3. United
  States—Commerce—Peru. 4. Peru—Commerce—United States.
  5. United States—Commercial treaties—Colombia. 6. United
  States—Commercial treaties—Peru. I. Title.
  HF1732.C7V65 2012
  382'.973—dc23

                                                    2011021492

ISBN: 978-0-415-60139-9 (hbk)
ISBN: 978-0-203-15636-0 (ebk)

Typeset in Garamond
by RefineCatch Limited, Bungay, Suffolk

Printed and bound in Great Britain by
CPI Antony Rowe, Chippenham, Wiltshire

For my father.
With love and gratitude.

Author's note

The US-Colombia Free Trade Agreement was finally ratified by the US Congress in October 2011, five years after the negotiations between the US and Colombia were concluded. This latest development in US-Colombian relations took place after the editing deadline for this publication. While its ratification is significant in terms of the insight it provides on future US trade policy, it does not affect the purpose or argument of this book.

Contents

List of abbreviations

ACJ	Andean Court of Justice
ACTPN	US Advisory Committee for Trade Policy and Negotiation
AFIDRO	Colombian Association for Pharmaceutical Research-based Laboratories
AFL-CIO	American Federation of Labor and Congress of Industrial Organizations
AIPPI	International Association for the Protection of Intellectual Property
ALAFARPE	Peruvian Association of National Pharmaceutical Laboratories
ANDAs	Abbreviated New Drug Applications
ANDI	National Association of Colombian Businesses
ARVs	Antiretrovirals
ASINFAR	Colombian Association of National Pharmaceutical Industries
ATPDEA	Andean Trade Promotion and Drug Eradication Act
BATNA	Best Alternative To a Negotiated Agreement
BIO	Biotechnology Industry Organisation
BITs	Bilateral Investment Treaties
CAFTA	Central American Free Trade Agreement
CAN	Andean Community of Nations
CBD	Convention on Biological Diversity
CBERA	Caribbean Basin Economic Recovery Act
CBI	Caribbean Basin Initiative
CUFTA	Canada-US Free Trade Agreement
DAD	Decide, Announce, Defend (Approach in Negotiations)
DE	Data Exclusivity/Data Protection
DIGEMID	Peruvian Drug Regulatory Authority
EFTA	European Free Trade Association (includes Switzerland, Norway, Iceland and Liechtenstein)
EPO	European Patent Office
EU	European Union
FAO	Food and Agricultural Organization

FC	Full Consensus (Approach in Negotiations)
FCNs	Friendship, Commerce and Navigation Treaties
FDA	US Federal Drug Authority
FDI	Foreign Direct Investment
FICPI	International Federation of Intellectual Property Attorneys
FoD	Friends of Development
FTA	Free Trade Agreement
FTAA	Free Trade Area of the Americas
GAO	Government Accountability Office
GATT	General Agreement on Tariffs and Trade
GIs	Geographical Indications
GPhA	Generic Pharmaceutical Association
GSP	Generalized System of Preferences
HAI	Health Action International
ICC	International Chambers of Commerce
ICTSD	International Centre for Trade and Sustainable Development
IFARMA	Institute for Medicine-research in Health Systems
IFPMA	International Federation of Pharmaceutical Manufacturers & Associations
IGC	Intergovernmental Committee on Intellectual Property and Genetic Resources, Traditional Knowledge and Folklore
IGOs	Intergovernmental Organisations
IIPA	International Intellectual Property Alliance
IPC	Intellectual Property Committee
IFARMA	Foundation Institute for Research in Medicines and Health Systems in Colombia
IIPA	International Intellectual Property Alliance
ILO	International Labour Organization
IP	Intellectual Property
IPC	Intellectual Property Committee
IPRs	Intellectual Property Rights
ITAC	Industry Technical Advisory Committee
ITC	US International Trade Commission
JPO	Japanese Patent Office
LDCs	Least Developed Countries
MFN	Most Favoured Nation Principle
Mincetur	Ministry of Commerce and Tourism, Peru
MinComercio	Ministry of Commerce, Colombia
MNCs	Multinational Corporations
MPAA	Motion Picture Association of America
MSP	Ministry of Social Protection (including health), Colombia
NAFTA	North Atlantic Free Trade Agreement
NCEs	New Chemical Entities
OAS	Organization of American States
OTCA	US Omnibus Trade and Competitive Act (1988)

PAHO	Pan-American Health Organization
PCT	Patent Cooperation Treaty
PhRMA	Pharmaceutical Research and Manufacturers of America
PMA	Pharmaceutical Manufacturers Association
SACU	Southern African Customs Union
SPLT	Substantive Patent Law Treaty
TAA	Trade Adjustment Assistance
TPA	Trade Promotion Authority
TPP	Trans-Pacific Partnership Agreement
TRIPS	Trade Related Intellectual Property Rights
UNCTAD	United Nations Conference on Trade and Development
UNESCO	United Nations Economic, Scientific and Cultural Organization
UNICE	Union of Industrial and Employers' Confederations
USPTO	US Patent and Trademark Office
USTR	United States Trade Representative
WHO	World Health Organization
WIPO	World Intellectual Property Organization
WTO	World Trade Organization
ZOPA	Zone of Possible Agreement

Acknowledgements

This book is based on my thesis, submitted in 2008 at Queen Mary College, University of London. It was borne of my conversations with a broad range of policy-makers who generously offered their time and insight into their experiences related to international trade negotiations in general and IPRs negotiations in particular. Their stories included accounts of bargaining processes at the negotiation table as well as descriptions of the daily activities of capital-based policy-makers, civil society advocates and private sector lobbyists. Each is important in its own way and contributes to the heart of this book. I am humbled to these nearly 100 individuals in Geneva and Berne, Bogotá, Lima and Washington, DC, who had confidence in me to document their stories accurately while retaining the spirit under which they worked and who were incredibly generous with their time and wisdom.

I am equally grateful to those friends who hosted me during the many weeks that I stayed in Berne, Bogotá, Lima and Washington, DC, respectively, including Peter Beyer, Paulo Vergara, Jairo Alberto Hurtado, Alexander von Loebell, Mirtha and Emilio Castillo, Stephan Bachenheimer, Saswati Bora and Knowledge Ecology International, whose offices I used while in Washington, DC.

Through my interviews I had substantial exposure to the ongoing trade negotiations, but putting it all together into one framework took a lot of time and thought. Crucial in this process were discussions with my supervisors Graham Dutfield and Uma Suthersanen, who provided me with never-ending support and feedback. Without their loyalty throughout the entire process, this book would not have been possible.

Many of my ideas about the nature of negotiation processes were shaped by the years I spent at the International Centre for Trade and Sustainable Development (ICTSD) in Geneva. Not only did my work provide me with an invaluable proximity to the negotiations and to the stakeholders themselves, but my colleagues helped me to better understand these negotiations and place them in their wider historical and political context. Particular thanks in this regard go to Pedro Roffe, David Vivas-Eugui and Ricardo Melendez-Ortiz.

Turning the final thesis into a book took place when I was a post-doctoral fellow at the University of Cape Town's Intellectual Property Law and Policy

Research Unit to which I owe my thanks. In this transition process I received invaluable feedback to different chapters of this book, including from Natalia Angel, Trineesh Biswas, Jacques Gorlin, Arthur Hong, Bernard Maister, Christopher May, Teresa Mera, Alejandro Neyra, Chan Park, Dwijen Rangnekar and Luis-Guillermo Restrepo Velez.

Last, but not least, many people say that the hardest part of finalising a large piece of writing is managing the rest of your life while you are at it. The fact that I did I attribute largely to my friends and family who pushed me through this process, even at the lowest moments. While many deserve to be mentioned here, particular thanks go to Ashwin Vasan, who had to bear the brunt of it all. I am ever so grateful for their love and support.

Johanna von Braun
Cape Town, 21 April 2011

Introduction

The negotiation of the US-Andean Trade Promotion Agreements (free trade agreements, or FTAs, from now on) started on 18 May 2004 in Cartagena de las Indias, Colombia, and originally included Bolivia, Colombia, Ecuador, Peru and the US. Bolivia only participated as an observer until the 10th round of negotiations and Ecuador withdrew from the process during the course of the negotiations for domestic political reasons. The negotiations with Colombia and Peru were finalised on 17 February 2006 and 7 December 2005 respectively, in Washington, DC.

On 25 September 2005, after 12 rounds of negotiations, three employees of Colombia's health authorities, assigned as technical experts to the national negotiation team, wrote an open letter[1] to their Minister officially resigning from the team. They claimed that no advances had been made with respect to Colombia's public health concerns, as the US had maintained a position of absolute inflexibility in the intellectual property (IP) negotiations. They further claimed that their negotiation principals had declared the end of the 'technical negotiations' and the beginning of the 'political negotiations' phase that was going to see the final trade-offs necessary to conclude the FTA.

Because hardly any of the final public health 'no-go' areas were maintained after the last three rounds of negotiations, one of the three negotiators also resigned from his post in government. In his open resignation letter[2] he blamed the Colombian Ministry of Commerce for an 18-month charade arguing that

> . . . it would have been much more transparent to tell the country [. . .] that there really never were negotiations and that in order to sign an FTA with the US it is necessary to abandon an 'interest based-negotiation strategy', that the 'red lines' will have to be crossed, and that increased [IPRs] protection to levels that are similar or higher than the FTAs between the US and Chile or the Central American countries (CAFTA) will have to be accepted [translated by author].

On 7 November 2006, nearly a year after the FTAs with Colombia and Peru had been signed, US Congressional elections led to a Democrat majority in

Congress. A 'New Trade Agenda for America' resulted in May 2007. In addition to changes in labour and environment provisions it included some of the specific public health safeguards that the Colombian and Peruvian health negotiators had tried, but failed, to integrate during the FTA negotiations. In July 2007 these changes were retrospectively introduced into the finalised texts of the US-Colombia and US-Peru FTAs. While at the time of writing the US-Colombia FTA remains pending before the US Congress, the new US-Peru FTA was implemented on 1 February 2009 after another set of prolonged implementation negotiations. The new trade agenda and subsequent changes in the IP chapter in turn signalled a change of direction of the IP template that the USTR had been gradually developing since the NAFTA negotiations in 1994.

The objective of this book is to demonstrate the importance of domestic politics in understanding the nature and outcome of international negotiations, in particular as they relate to international economic diplomacy. Today, many international FTAs go beyond negotiating market access but constitute frameworks of deep economic integration, which affect numerous public policy sectors, such as education, the environment and public health. Yet, the domestic decision-making process tends to be biased towards the preferences put forward by domestic trade authorities, driven by market access objectives, and fails to appropriately include the diverse political sectors that are affected by the respective agreements. This, naturally, influences the process and outcome of international negotiations and public policy objectives affected by regulatory harmonisation associated with FTAs are often compromised. The US-Peru and US-Colombia FTA negotiations are used as case studies in this book, in particular in relation to regulatory harmonisation in the field of IPRs and the conflict this presented to the public health objectives advocated by the perspective authorities in both Andean countries.

By focusing on the manifestation of the conflict between succumbing to US pressure on increasing IPRs on the one hand, and securing and increasing market access to the US market on the other, this study will demonstrate how structural and institutional characteristics affected the process and outcome of the negotiations in which this conflict manifested. It is worth noting at this point that while the power differences between Colombia, Peru and the US naturally had a large influence on the negotiations, a study of power alone would fail to explain the proceedings and outcome of the negotiations. Only by incorporating the domestic political landscape of the three countries can the negotiation process and outcome be explained and understood.

Broader relevance of this study

This case study does not stand in isolation. Law-making in the field of IPRs as part of US-led FTA negotiations has often failed to respond to public health-related preferences promoted by domestic health authorities in many developing countries and international health advocates. Factors relevant in this regard include the following.

First, the often very hierarchical domestic policy-structure in many developing countries with respect to the negotiation and implementation processes led to a bias against the preferences put forward by public health authorities.

Second, the centrality of government in many countries weakens the negotiation teams. In the Andean case the direct involvement of negotiation principals (such as heads of state) arguably reduced their bargaining power *vis-à-vis* the US team which could always refer to domestic constraints to avoid concessions in certain fields.

Third, the issue-linkage of IPRs to other negotiation subjects in combination with the wider political economy in which FTA processes are embedded often appear to leave negotiators with little choice but to accept a package deal. The intensity of the negotiations, effectuated through both formal and informal channels, further created an impression that the FTA was an 'all or nothing deal'.

Fourth, the nature of the US domestic institutional landscape allows for strong interest group influence in US trade policy formulation. The pharmaceutical industry, as one of such interest groups, was particularly influential during the negotiations because of a range of factors that worked to its advantage including the industry's strong alliance with the Republican Party, which had controlled the US Congress since 1995. Furthermore, the industry's unique lobbying capacity and the services it provided to the USTR had become invaluable to the operation of the agency, providing the pharmaceutical industry with particular leverage over US foreign economic policy.

This study proposes that one way of integrating public interest objectives in international trade negotiations is through transformation at the domestic level, such as through institutional change. To demonstrate this, the case study will show how through a substantial shift in the domestic policy landscape in the US domestic trade preferences were re-shuffled, even if only briefly. This led, among other things, to the integration of certain public health considerations into the traditionally inflexible IPRs template that had been vigorously defended by the US team during the actual FTA negotiations.

Organisation and scope of study

This book is above all a study of law-making. Thus, while it analyses the nature of the IPRs provisions that are central to the IPRs/public health conflict, its principal focus lies in the fields of comparative politics and international relations (IR) with the aim of understanding the processes through which these laws were made. As Schattschneider observed in a ground-breaking study on the influence of pressure groups on the formulation of US tariff legislation between 1929 and 1930:

> In tariff making, perhaps more than in any other kind of legislation, Congress writes bills which no one intended. All policies are deflected and warped in being reduced to statute, but where the difficulties of the

process are great, the original design may be battered beyond recognition and the policy utterly confused. This is especially true in tariff legislation because law making in this field is beset with incomparable embarrassments and perplexities, and the labor in evolving the statute is great to the point of agony. Whatever the ideal systems of protection may be or may have been, and there have been many ideals in this zone of policy, all have suffered a sea change in being made concrete in the law. The distance which separates the ideal from the real is, therefore, a rough measure of the influence of the process of law making on the policy. It follows that the legislation cannot be understood apart from the manner in which it is made.

(Schattschneider 1935: 13)

Chapter 1 provides the analytical framework for the study. It emphasises the study of domestic government as it relates to international negotiations. The importance of understanding government structures, institutions, ideas and principles will be highlighted by showing the ownership and identity of preferences that are put forward on the international level. It is argued that only by accounting for the interaction between domestic and international politics can the process and outcome of international negotiations be understood.

Chapters 2 and 3 are background chapters. Chapter 2 examines how harmonisation in IP legislation has been gradually integrated into the international trade negotiation framework. As such it makes reference to both the integration of IPRs into the WTO framework through the TRIPS Agreement, and the emergence of a range of FTAs that include IP provisions that go beyond the WTO-level of protection. Chapter 3 then provides further information on the nature of some of these so-called 'TRIPS-plus' provisions found in US-FTAs and explains why public health authorities in developing countries have a strong defensive negotiating position towards them. Particular reference is made to the level of protection that was proposed by the US team in the US-Peru and US-Colombia FTAs.

Chapters 4 to 7 form the substantive core of the book, explaining the nature of the domestic political landscape in Colombia, Peru and the US and how they, in turn, affected the process and outcome of the conjoint negotiations. Furthermore, chapter 7 will demonstrate how institutional change caused by the 2006 US Congressional elections triggered a revision of the US sponsored IPRs template that had for more then a decade characterised US-led FTA negotiations.

Chapter 8 will conclude the analysis.

Scope

While some of the negotiation dynamics are applicable to different trade negotiation scenarios, this study will focus on US-negotiated FTAs. Nevertheless, while the IPRs chapters put forward by the US compared to other industrialised nations differ, the larger questions of political economy apply to all asymmetric negotiations in which smaller countries negotiate with larger and more powerful adversaries.

The focus of this book is the conflict between the increased level of IPRs protection put forward through US-FTAs and public health concerns. Given the breadth of public policy sectors that are impacted by the regulatory harmonisation brought about by US FTAs, another sector could have been chosen, such as debates surrounding traditional knowledge and the patenting of plants or the impact of environmental standards. Health is selected as a proxy for public interest concerns because, arguably, it is one of the fields in which regulatory harmonisation through FTAs in the form of IPRs has an immediate welfare effect in developing countries. Furthermore, health has a bearing on all individuals in society and constitutes a fundamental and basic human right.[3]

Methodology, sources and limitations

Most of the empirical data on the conduct of trade negotiations was gathered through interviews with negotiators, their principals and other stakeholder groups.

In Bogotá, interviews were conducted with representatives from the Ministry of Commerce, the Ministry of Social Protection (Health), the Senate, the Ministry of the Environment, the Office of the Mayor of Bogotá, the Copyright Office, academic experts from the Universidad de los Andes and the Universidad Nacional, representatives of the national generic industry, national export promotion groups, the US Embassy, Non-Governmental Organizations (NGOs), church groups, law firms representing either the international pharmaceutical, or the national generic industry in Colombia, and a range of former government representatives that were actively involved in the negotiations.

In Lima, interviews were carried out at the Ministry of Commerce, Tourism and Industry, the Ministry of Health, the Patent and Copyright Division of Peru's conjoint competition and intellectual property authorities (INDECOPI), the Secretariat of the Andean Community of Nations (CAN), academic institutions, the generic industry, the American Chamber of Commerce, law firms representing the international pharmaceutical industry in Lima, NGOs, church groups and former government employees who participated in the negotiations.

In Washington, DC, interviews were held with Democrat and Republican staff of Members of Congress sitting on the key trade policy-making committees, former employees of the USTR involved in the US-Andean negotiations, the US Chamber of Commerce, the Organization of American States (OAS), the Peruvian Embassy, Pharmaceutical Research and Manufacturers of America (PhRMA) and other pharmaceutical lobbying groups representing both national and international research-based and generic industry, non-profit organisations and academic experts.

The study also benefited from 10 interviews conducted in Berne, Switzerland, about exploratory FTA negotiations between the US and Switzerland.

All of the interviews for this study were held on a non-attributable basis due to the political sensitivity of the issues discussed. In order to protect the anonymity of the interviewees few direct quotations are used and any specific evidence that could identify the interviewees is left out. Where relevant, the institutional affiliation of the interviewee will be disclosed in a footnote.

The anonymity of the interviewees was crucial for them to share their true experiences of the negotiation process. Indeed, with the exception of one interview, none of the interviewees refused to respond to a question for confidentiality reasons. Most of the individuals contacted were willing to be interviewed, with only a few not responding and only one refusing to be part of the study. Interviewees were helpful in referring me to colleagues and usually facilitated the respective introduction, which often led to further interviews.[4] Indeed, I found that most interviewees very much enjoyed reflecting on their experiences in the negotiations.

The nature of the interview questions varied, depending on the interviewee. Most negotiators were asked about the negotiations themselves, how the negotiations evolved over time, negotiation strategies, the composition of the negotiation teams, key trade-offs and defining moments of the negotiations. The negotiators from the Ministries of Commerce and negotiating principals were asked how they developed the domestic negotiating mandates and how they decided on preferences and trade-offs. The negotiators from the Ministries of Health were asked about how they were integrated into the process and whether they felt their interests were appropriately reflected in the negotiations. Questions to other policy-makers, such as parliamentarians, were directed towards the domestic institutional framework of the negotiations, including reporting lines and the formulation of the domestic negotiation strategy, domestic political and economic factors, transparency and interest group participation and the particular role of parallel diplomacy throughout the negotiations. Private sector lobbying groups were asked about the nature of their lobbying during the negotiations, and their role in the preparation, negotiation and subsequent domestic ratification of the agreements. Finally, non-profit organisations were asked about their impression of the negotiations, how they felt their constituencies were represented in the negotiations and their views of the legitimacy of the overall negotiation process.[5]

Apart from primary sources, this study also makes use of secondary sources that reported on the negotiations. These include articles on the negotiations published in the leading newspapers and news services in Colombia, Peru and the US. Others include academic pieces written about the negotiations and publications by civil society organisations and interest groups. Finally, publications by governmental institutions in all three countries, such as the US Government Accountability Office (GAO), the US Trade Representative (USTR) and the Colombian Ministry of Commerce are used.

Theoretical framework

Theoretical writings were helpful to identify a useful analytical framework for the negotiations. Essentially, the questions that lie at the heart of this monograph are: how do governments (in this case those of Colombia, Peru and the US) set their preferences in the negotiation of international trade agreements (in this case the FTAs)? How (well) do they represent (which of) them during the actual negotiations? Answering these questions requires elements of a range of often held separate theoretical approaches, a traditional shortcoming identified and addressed by a range of scholars of negotiation. Hanrieder, for example, argues:

> The distinction between international and domestic politics has become deeply embedded conceptually, pedagogically, and institutionally ... Blame is often placed on the lack of purposeful communication between specialists in international politics and specialists in comparative politics. In truth, many of us have imprisoned ourselves in conceptual jails of our own making where we remain incommunicado and deaf to the voices from next door.
>
> (Hanrieder, as quoted by Milner 1998: 759)

A useful approach that attempts to link comparative politics and IR in the study of negotiation is the 'two-level game' approach. Rather than a theory that stands in isolation, it is more of a metaphor that builds on both comparative politics and IR for the study of negotiations. As such it allows for the analysis of domestic political factors as they influence the way negotiations take place on the international level, and vice versa. This includes, for example, the analysis of how domestic political structures, institutions, key stakeholder groups and their preferences, influence the process and outcome of international negotiations. Indeed, some protagonists of the two-level game go as far as to claim that domestic policy may be actively used by parties to (mis)represent domestic constraints so as to strengthen their bargaining power during international deliberations. Similarly, they argue that international negotiations can be used to push through domestic reforms that would otherwise be politically unattainable. As such the two-level game provides a range of useful concepts to gain a better understanding of international negotiations and the complex interplay between domestic and international actors.

Limitations

This book will not use the Colombia and Peru case studies to critique existing schools of thought on the nature of the study of negotiation, but rather emphasise the importance of understanding underlying domestic policy dynamics. As one of the foremost scholars on economic diplomacy, John Odell, puts it:

Debates between partisans may sharpen arguments and focus attention on research needs, but they have their costs. Most important, decades of empirical research have shown conclusively that none of these grand approaches is adequate in itself. I believe the most lasting advances come from research that concentrates on an important empirical phenomenon, shifts attention towards formulating clear casual hypotheses, rejects an overriding commitment to any single 'ism', and combines hypothesis as indicated by the evidence.

(Odell 2000: 17)

Furthermore, in spite of focusing on the conflict that emerged through the integration of TRIPS-plus provisions into FTAs, this study is not a legal study but rather a study of law-making. While some discussion of the extent to which these provisions represent an increase in protection from that contained in the TRIPS Agreement is included, the precise interpretation and possible ways of implementation of new and existing jurisprudence is beyond the scope of this book. In this sense, this book also concentrates on the politics of negotiating the actual FTA and not the following set of negotiations relating to the implementation of negotiated FTAs into national legislation.[6]

Finally, all negotiations entail trade-offs, and all trade-offs, in an ideal scenario, should be based on impact assessments that support the decisions of negotiators on whether or not a trade-off is worth pursuing. This study does not presume to judge whether any of the negotiating teams made the right or wrong decisions regarding one position over another. A cost-benefit analysis of this nature is, given the broad nature of the FTAs, very complex and goes well beyond the scope of this book. As this study is primarily focusing on the nature of decision-making structures, and the process of international negotiations, it will reflect on whether, and by whom, impact assessments were done, rather than which impact assessment is more accurate. In this regard it will not analyse in detail how and to what extent TRIPS-plus provision will affect public health, but how the legitimate concerns of health authorities were reflected in the negotiation process.

1 Economic diplomacy on multiple levels

Introduction

The field of IR theory has primarily involved trying to understand and predict the outcome of inter-state deliberations. The field was dominated by realist or neo-realist theorists who relied on state-centric approaches distinguishing between the domestic, the international and the global or system level.[1] Realists tend to treat the state as one unit of analysis when describing state preferences during negotiations, whereas the relationship between actors is defined by power structures. The liberal approach to international negotiations[2] has moved away from a state-centric focus defined by power politics, towards understanding the interdependence of states while focusing on the international level and ignoring domestic politics as a primary variable in understanding the process and outcome of international negotiation (Milner 1997: ch. 1).[3]

In contrast authors from the field of comparative politics have focused mainly on the domestic sources of international negotiations, like the relationship between institutions and actors.[4] They focus, for example, on how domestic factors such as interest groups, elections, but also government structure and institutions, influence international policy-making. However, the study of comparative politics has to a large extent ignored how international negotiations have influenced domestic politics (Moravczik 1993).

Both IR and comparative politics help analyse influences on international negotiations, although they have certain limits. For example, they are traditionally confined to one level of analysis, while holding the other constant. As a result, their critics argue, they fail to account for the actual complex nature of negotiations where many factors often involving both domestic politics as well as international economic and political structures play a role. Indeed, many scholars of international economic negotiations have found that negotiations have become too complex and involve too many different actors, matters and levels for any theoretical framework to be able to grasp them in their entirety. Instead they have started using different concepts from traditionally separate theories for the analysis of specific case studies (Bayne and Woolcock 2003a).

One such useful point of departure has been provided by Robert Putnam and his concept of a 'two-level game' that aims to bring together the fields of IR, international political economy (IPE) and comparative politics for the study of international negotiation, particularly in the economic field. The metaphor of 'two-level game' seeks to integrate domestic politics (level II) and international negotiations (level I), maintaining that they are heavily inter-linked and should be analysed as such. This chapter draws from the two-level game approach, while also integrating other writings from the field of IR, IPE, comparative politics and some more behavioural negotiation scholars.

The study of economic diplomacy

Introduction to economic diplomacy

The study of negotiation originally followed the realist tradition of identi-fying certain power relationships, in which diplomacy is a means of maxi-mizing one's own relative power. These approaches focus on the state or government as a single unit and negotiations as a form of communication among these units in an otherwise anarchic international environment. Grieco summarises the five propositions of realists as follows:

a   states are the major actors in world affairs;
b   the international environment severely penalises states if they fail to protect their vital interests or if they pursue objectives beyond their means; hence, states are 'sensitive to costs' and behave as unitary-rational agents;
c   international anarchy above all shapes the motives and actions of states;
d   states in anarchy are preoccupied with power and security, are predis-posed towards conflict and competition, and often fail to cooperate even in the face of common interests;
e   international institutions affect the prospects for cooperation only marginally (Grieco 1988).

For traditional realists, power relationships alone determine the outcome of negotiations.

After the end of the Cold War, when border disputes decreased in impor-tance, negotiation analysis moved towards other issue areas, including the increasingly important field of economic diplomacy. This was further high-lighted by a range of newly independent countries in Eastern and Central Europe that wanted to integrate into the international economic system (Bayne and Woolcock 2007).

While some parallels can be drawn from the study of more traditional forms of negotiations, there are certain characteristics of economic diplomacy that distinguish it from other types of negotiations:

First, the study of economic diplomacy is primarily concerned with process, rather than structure. While IPE focuses on the structural factors and how they influence the relationship among states, economic diplomacy looks at the decision-making processes within governments and during international negotiations (Bayne and Woolcock 2003b). While process and structure cannot be entirely separated from each other, an emphasis on process allows an insight into international negotiations that goes beyond the balance of power analysis.

Second, economic diplomacy has gained in significance since the end of the Cold War. While security concerns have re-emerged since 9/11 leading to the US 'war on terror' economic diplomacy remains central to addressing the root causes of terrorism, including poverty and marginalization (Bayne and Woolcock 2003b). Indeed, some authors claim that 9/11 substantially contributed to reaching an agreement at the WTO Ministerial in Doha in 2001 (Odell 2003: 34).

Third, the international legal framework of international economic law is one of the most advanced in terms of enforcement that includes dispute settlement mechanisms and the imposition of sanctions and remedies.

Fourth, there is a bigger need than ever for governments to more effectively enhance economic welfare for its citizens through engaging in the global economy. More than ever national economic success is linked to actions on the international level. Governments have to be increasingly savvy in engaging in economic diplomacy if they want to compete on the international level (Bayne and Woolcock 2003b).

Fifth, governments are under increasing pressure by domestic constituents to be accountable for commitments made on the international level (Bayne and Woolcock 2003b). Few negotiations will affect as diverse a group of stakeholders as economic negotiations, ranging from all levels of government to corporations, interest and consumer groups. Furthermore, increasingly comprehensive trade agreements, by leading to deep regulatory harmonisation, have an impact that reaches far beyond the traditionally 'economic' sectors of countries. Constituents of losing sectors will hold their governments accountable for their actions. Similarly, civil society organisations, likely to be critical of the implication of economic diplomacy on public goods such as the environment or welfare, can function as watchdogs. The interests of these groups are likely to conflict with the interests of those stakeholders that will benefit from increasing international economic activity.

Finally, economic negotiations are ongoing processes. After an agreement, such as an FTA, is signed and ratified, new negotiations on implementation begin.

As a result, today there is a growing literature devoted to the study of economic diplomacy or intergovernmental economic negotiations that has moved far beyond the traditional realist power-based analysis of negotiation.[5] Many of these studies, as with this book, are case specific, ranging from GATT/WTO negotiations to other economic agreements. Furthermore, some scholars have made attempts to draw them together (Odell 2000; Bayne and Woolcock 2003a; Woolcock 2006).

Concepts in economic diplomacy

The actors

Given the comprehensive nature of FTAs, a large number of actors are involved, directly or indirectly, in their negotiation. As will be discussed later, the nature of the institutional and political framework defines who can influence these negotiations.

Woolcock defines the following as the most important actors in economic diplomacy:

- national state actors
    - executive branch
    - legislative branch
    - provincial, state and local government
    - regulatory agencies

- non-state actors
    - business groups
    - trade unions
    - consumer organisations/civil society

- transnational actors
    - global civil society
    - international business
    - international organisations
    - epistemic communities (Woolcock 2003a: 46)

- individuals.

National actors

As economic diplomacy is about negotiations among governments, state actors are at the centre of its analysis with different actors within government having different levels of veto power.

a   The Executive: includes the head of state and their cabinet and all other relevant executive agencies. Ideally all ministries whose constituencies are affected are involved in the negotiations, either through sending staff to participate as part of the negotiation team, or by being consulted throughout the negotiations.[6] In some systems, such as the US, an executive agency, specialising in trade negotiation, will lead the consultative process for all other relevant agencies. In other systems, it is the Ministry of Commerce or the Foreign Ministry that has this role and develops specialised teams that form a central negotiation unit. This process may be defined by statute, whereas in other cases one agency will decide who is consulted, when and how.

b The legislature: relevant bodies will vary from country to country. In most countries, the parliament will provide the final approval of the agreement or its implementing legislation (Milner 1997; Milner and Rosendorff 1997; Woolcock 2003a). The relative importance of the legislature will depend on its credible veto power. This may increase its role in agenda setting, negotiation and ratification of the final agreement. Where party discipline is high, political parties are likely to influence the positions put forward by legislators.

c Local and provincial governments: the importance given to local and provincial governments during negotiations depends on governmental structure. Where regional governments are powerful, their participation is stronger, although generally their interests are represented in parliament. Sometimes, there are conflicting questions of jurisdiction during trade negotiations when regulations that traditionally fall under municipal jurisdictions are affected by the FTA (Woolcock 2003a).

d Regulatory agencies: these include, for example, drug regulatory authorities and patent offices. Such agencies tend to be included either through consultations or direct participation for their technical and legal expertise.

Non-state actors

Non-state actors including businesses, civil society organisations (CSOs) and international organisations are crucial in shaping economic negotiations.

a Business groups: are represented through a range of different organisations. These include confederations of industries, such as the US Chamber of Commerce, that cover a wide spectrum of national industry. Members of these broader groups often have conflicting positions towards the negotiations reducing their effectiveness in lobbying. More effective in lobbying are more harmonious sector-wide trade associations (Woolcock 2003a). The role of sector specific trade associations, such as PhRMA, varies according to country and subject matter, but can contribute to all parts of the negotiation process. Their contribution may range from providing technical and legal expertise in both the preparation and negotiation of the agreement to the lobbying necessary to pass the agreement through the domestic ratification process. Sometimes individual firms lobby for themselves.

b Trade unions: organised labour groups bring together labour unions from different economic sectors. Labour unions tend to be protectionist, fearing that opening the domestic market will lead to domestic job losses through foreign competition. According to Woolcock, the influence of unions is decreasing due to reduced industry membership and the rising importance of less unionised economic sectors, such as services (Woolcock

2003a). Nevertheless, in some countries the influence of unions remains strong, particularly when they have strong ties with political parties.

c   Consumer organisations and national civil society: exist in most countries, however, their respective influence varies, especially if compared to that of industry groups. Particularly in developing countries CSOs are small and poorly funded and often not in a position to lobby as strongly as, for example, those in Europe and the US (Woolcock 2003a). With a handful of exceptions most NGOs from developing countries focus on domestic concerns.[7] In some countries national CSOs are supported by the church, which can raise their political capital. They also draw on the expertise of academics.

Transnational actors

a   Global civil society: as a result of an increasingly global economy, and resulting challenges, civil society groups and networks today often collaborate beyond national borders to form powerful advocacy networks. These movements are motivated by joint principles or values, often related to labour, environment or development (Woolcock 2003a; Braithwaite and Drahos 2000: ch. 20). International civil society groups sometimes support national NGOs in developing countries to gain more leverage with respect to domestic policy formulations and to get their voices heard during the multilateral negotiations. With respect to IPRs civil society today is much more active than during the negotiations leading up to the TRIPS Agreement. The role of NGOs working in this field varies from awareness raising, technical assistance and dialogue facilitation to coordination activities and raising coherence within government delegations at multilateral negotiations (Matthews 2006).

b   International businesses: are without doubt among the most powerful forces in international trade negotiations. Their activities on the international level can take place either through their participation in international trade associations or coalitions that are formed on a sectoral basis, such as the International Federation of Pharmaceutical Manufacturers and Associations (IFPMA). Furthermore, the operations of some MNCs are truly global which also makes them transnational actors (Woolcock 2003a). Their operations include lobbying governments, monitoring, technical assistance, the provision of all kinds of useful information, and participation in the negotiation team, whether through physical presence or in 'side rooms'. The role of international business in influencing global, regional and bilateral economic negotiations, including IPRs negotiations, has been highlighted widely among scholars and cannot be underestimated (Matthews 2002; Braithwaite and Drahos 2000; Sell 2003; Shaffer 2003).

c   IGOs: have different roles during the negotiations. Some such as the World Health Organization (WHO) may provide technical expertise, while others provide a secretariat for international negotiations such as the World Trade Organization (WTO). As IGOs are constrained by the positions of their member states, their advice tends to be administrative and technical and, ideally, unbiased.

d Epistemic communities: Haas defines epistemic communities as networks of experts with a certain (often scientific) expertise and competence that allows them to make authoritative claims that is relevant for policy (Woolcock 2003a: 62; Braithwaite and Drahos 2000: chs 4, 5, 20). As Braithwaite and Drahos emphasise, science is a powerful counterforce against discourses that are simply based on self-interests (Braithwaite and Drahos 2000: 502). A typical example is the group of scientists on the Intergovernmental Panel on Climate Change (IPCC) whose analysis has influenced the course of climate negotiations. With respect to IPRs a range of studies from IPRs-experts, such as those from the UK Commission on IPRs[8] or the Commission on Intellectual Property Rights, Innovation and Public Health (CIPIH)[9] fall into this category. Business-related expert groups such as the International Association for the Protection of Intellectual Property (AIPPI) or legal networks such as the International Federation of Intellectual Property Attorneys (FICPI) also represent such epistemic communities.

Individuals

Individuals can also be important actors in international negotiations, particularly if they have powerful positions, which allow them to influence the preparation, execution and ratification of international deliberations. Indeed, these individuals often see themselves as being capable of pulling strings to their advantage (Woolcock 2003b; Braithwaite and Drahos 2000: chs. 5, 20). Odell defines them as the primary actors and the natural force of negotiations (Odell 2006: 11). A number of scholars have also emphasised the role of strategically placed individuals in influencing the nature and outcome of the TRIPS negotiations (Matthews 2002; Sell 2003; Braithwaite and Drahos 2000). Sometimes negotiations are pushed towards a higher political level specifically to exclude certain individuals. Given the comprehensive nature of trade agreements, even technical negotiators can play an important role.[10]

The win-set

A win-set[11] is defined as the different possible outcomes that would make a party prefer an agreement to no agreement. Win-sets are usually confined by maximum and minimum outcomes (or resistance points) beyond which the negotiating parties would be better off without an agreement (Odell 2000: ch. 2). The sizes of win-sets differ among parties. The keener a party is to make the agreement happen, the larger the win-set. Win-sets are not static and tend to change in the course of the negotiations. This could happen by, for example, adding new issues or incentives to an agreement.

Naturally, parties have an interest during negotiations to undersell their win-set, so that the other party is pushed towards making greater concessions. Thus, the availability of information on the other party's win-set is crucial for each negotiator. Often this is limited by the availability of information on the other country's domestic preferences. Therefore, parties often have to rely on what Raiffa refers to as 'probabilistic information about the other party's reservation prices' (or reservation points) (Raiffa 1987: 56). A good negotiation strategy, therefore, includes not only a clear definition of one's own win-set, but analysis of the other party's win-set.

Zone of Potential Agreement (ZOPA)

The ZOPA is where the win-sets of the negotiating parties overlap. It represents the zone in which an agreement is likely to take place. Within the ZOPA both parties consider themselves to be benefiting from the agreement even though they may benefit unequally. If the two win-sets do not overlap, no agreement is possible (Odell 2000: ch. 2).

Given the strategic misinformation about the other party's win-set, one also needs to distinguish between a 'real ZOPA' and a 'perceived ZOPA' (Raiffa 1987: ch. 4). The real ZOPA tends to be bigger than the perceived ZOPA, as parties often undersell their win-set.

However, the existence of a real ZOPA does not mean that negotiations have to end successfully. Factors that may lead to the failure of an agreement are time, calculation ability, memory, experience of the negotiators, information or simple negotiation expertise. In an overview of a range of possibilities why a negotiation process may be deemed unsuccessful despite an existing ZOPA, Neale and Bazerman (1991) highlight the importance of the decisional bias of the actual negotiators. This may be influenced by different factors, ranging from personal experiences and agendas to incomplete information. The authors demonstrate that while framing the ZOPA is essential if an agreement is to be achieved, a certain negotiator bias is inevitably going to influence the outcome of the negotiations.[12]

BATNA

One of the most important reference points for negotiators and their principals is the point at which a non-agreement becomes more valuable than an

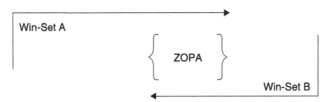

Figure 1.1 ZOPA.

agreement. This point is referred to as Best Alternative To a Negotiated Agreement (BATNA), also known as the reservation point (Clark et al. 2000; Odell 2000: ch. 2). It is the standard against which any proposed agreements should be measured (Fisher and Ury 1982) and essentially defines the size of the win-set. The BATNA is critical because it will determine the way a negotiator acts throughout the negotiations.

Calculating the BATNA is a very challenging task because it requires an estimation of the potential political and economic gains from an agreement and thereafter mirror them to all other possible alternatives. As it defines the win-set, the BATNA is equally affected by issue-linkages (see below) and is, inevitably, not static. Sometimes even outside developments can change a BATNA, such as price variations of key export commodities or the emergence or disappearance of alternatives during the negotiations. Thus the broader context in which a negotiation is placed is of fundamental importance for the calculation of the BATNA (Odell 2002; 2003).

From a strategic standpoint, one way of countering a more powerful negotiating partner is by having a high BATNA. If the agreement is not attractive to the weaker party, its negotiating leverage increases independent of its economic size. Many weaker parties forget that there is always the option of walking away from the negotiation table (Fisher and Ury 1982). Furthermore, being aware of a no-deal option is not only important to strengthen one's own bargaining power but also as a psychological boost for the negotiation team. A principal should always remind themselves and their agents that walking away is a possibility (Lax and Sebenius 2006: ch. 6).

As Cameron and Tomlin point out, the lower the BATNA:

- the more the negotiating party will perceive an agreement primarily in terms of the gains it offers over the alternative to the agreement;
- the more risk averse it will be to achieve those gains, and negotiate respectively;
- the less willing it will be to risk coming to an agreement by withholding concessions;
- the more concessions it will offer in order to obtain agreement; and
- the larger the win-set.

On the contrary, if the negotiating party has the perception that its alternative to the agreement is also fairly high, then:

- the more it will measure a negotiated agreement in terms of the existing alternative – which also sets a higher benchmark to the other party;
- the more willing it will be to risk the agreement by withholding concessions, or offering only very small concessions when it comes to the final trade-offs of the agreement; and
- the smaller the win-set (Cameron and Tomlin 2000; Odell 2000: ch. 3).

The importance of process

Most negotiation analysts emphasise the importance of process. Choices on process (both domestically and at the negotiation table) can make or break deals and relationships. Essentially two negotiation processes are of importance, the first domestic, the second international. Nicholas Bayne, a retired British diplomat, classifies them into the following phases (2003: 67–76):

a   Domestic negotiations

    i   Identifying the lead department.
    ii   Three levels of consultation (implemented by the lead department):

        a.   internal (within the lead department);
        b.   with outside forces (including governmental and non-governmental actors);
        c.   inter-departmental (with the other executive agencies).

    iii Political authority (when the mandate is finalised and approved by the responsible minister or even the head of state).
    iv   Democratic legitimisation (this only takes place in countries where the provision of political authority does not settle the matter. It includes in some cases a parliamentary approval or at least the informing of parliament of the intent to engage in negotiations as well as the publication of expected results. It often also includes a press conference).
    v   International negotiations (the actual negotiations).
    vi   Ratification of the agreement (once the negotiations have been finalised the agreement has to pass parliament for approval/disapproval in most jurisdictions. Good negotiators anticipate the possible objections of this stage while they are still engaging in negotiations, ensuring that the concerns of enough legislators are addressed to secure ratification).

b   International negotiations

    i   Agenda setting (when negotiating parties come together to decide the issues that are to be part of the agreement).
    ii   Mandating (when the parties have received the mandate from the respective agency which will guide the negotiators. Mandates will vary, depending on the decision-making processes in different countries. The tightness of the mandate can have a strong impact on how a party engages in the negotiations).
    iii Negotiating until an agreement is reached (the actual negotiations).
    iv   Adopting the agreement (when a final agreement is reached and ready to be passed on for ratification).
    v   Implementation (the technical implementation of the finalised agreement tends to include follow-up negotiations which may vary in their length and intensity).

Naturally, these processes do not take place in a linear fashion and overlap and influence each other.

Apart from the different stages, Lax and Sebenius (2006: ch. 7) identify two extreme styles of negotiating, the 'Decide, Announce, Defend' (DAD) style, and the Full Consensus (FC) Approach. The DAD allows for quick decision-making by a small group of principals. It tends to provoke substantial criticism and opposition by excluded domestic groups. Depending on the amount of opposition, and their veto power, it is a high-risk strategy by principals. The FC approach on the other hand seeks agreement among all stakeholders. By seeking to satisfy everybody, it is often as equally vulnerable to failure as the DAD approach.

Naturally, most negotiations represent a hybrid between these two extreme forms presented above. Lax and Sebenius provide a useful checklist of negotiation basics for achieving a balanced negotiation process (2006: 113). The following list, based on their concepts, is modified to suit the nature of this study.

a   Auspices: Who hosts a negotiation process is important. It often makes sense to have a neutral third party host the process. Alternatively each negotiating party could host different rounds.
b   Mandate: It is essential to be clear as to the intended output of the negotiations. Participating parties have to be committed to this output. Ambiguity of the mandate (and preferences) within a negotiation team can easily lead to conflict that may terminate the negotiations.
c   Participation: The definition of who puts a negotiation team together and who participates in this team can be a 'make or break' issue. As Lax and Sebenius point out: 'The breadth and basis of participation bears a clear relationship to the underlying vision of the process – that is, a DAD process, an FC process, or some sort of hybrid' (2006: 114).
d   Decision-making rules and procedures: A crucial aspect of the process is how choices are being made within the negotiation team. Will the principal alone have all decision-making power, or will the majority, or even a consensus of the negotiation team, be sufficient? The operating procedures of a negotiation team in this regard are important, such as: what is the decision-making power of the head of the negotiation team, is the team split into subgroups, headed by other sub-principals, do all members have equal access to information on all aspects of the negotiations, how are proposals drafted, put forward, revised and accepted or rejected? The actual language of negotiations also matters.
e   Agenda: Whether an agenda is pre-defined will influence the nature of the deliberations. Similarly, it is important to understand whether the agenda is predefined, or loosely defined, if it is fixed or changeable and if there is a specific time frame to the negotiations. Also important is whether the negotiating items are loose or focused on a pre-existing contract or treaty. Setting the agenda is a powerful tool to manipulate

negotiations and pre-define trade-offs. Often the most complicated or politically sensitive matters are left to the final, or trade-off, phase of the negotiations.

f   External communication: Often conflicting views exist between and within negotiating parties on how much information can be shared with the public. The restrictions on the level of transparency associated with the negotiations will be a function of the agreement among the negotiating parties and any pressure exercised by local constituent groups and the public to have insight into the process.

g   Technical assistance and process support: Especially in more elaborate negotiations secretarial support may be requested. This secretariat can be either more formal and solely responsible for administrative process or actively provide technical assistance in the negotiations. Additionally, negotiation parties may ask for advice from external technical experts to support the negotiation teams during the negotiations.

h   Post-negotiation arrangements: As was discussed above, some negotiations may continue after an agreement has been signed, for example, for the implementation of the agreement.

Issue-linkage

Issue-linkage is a common instrument in the study of negotiations.[13] Linkage itself is not a new phenomenon in international affairs. As Sebenius quotes Francois de Callieres from his work 'On the Manner of Negotiating with Princes', the tactic was already described in 1716:

> An ancient philosopher once said that friendship between men is nothing but a commerce in which each seeks his own interest. The same is even truer of the liaisons and treaties which bind one sovereign to another, for there is no durable treaty which is not founded on reciprocal advantage, and indeed a treaty which does not satisfy this condition is no treaty at all, and is apt to contain the seeds of its own dissolution. Thus, the great secret of negotiation is to bring out prominently the common advantage to both sides and to link these advantages that they may appear equally balanced to both parties.
>
> (Sebenius 1983: 282)

More recently, however, issue-linkage has become a common feature of economic diplomacy. Adding and subtracting issues essentially increases the scope of possible trade-offs and gains that can be made from the final agreement. If the issues or agenda items are considered as variables, issue-linkage essentially takes the form of a 'welfare function' that defines the total outcome of the final deal. Under negotiation are the weights of different variables, although sometimes variables may be added or subtracted during the negotiations (Sebenius 1983). Often the issues are only remotely related.

Today issue-linkage is found in almost every strategy of negotiation. What varies from one negotiation to the next is the particular set of issues that are linked to each other (Odell 2000: ch. 2).

Positions on the effect of issue-linkage differ. Some theorists, such as Roger Fisher, argue that the joining of issues in order to increase bargaining leverage tends to favour those with relatively stronger bargaining power, as they add issues exploiting the dependency of the weaker parties and reduce or destroy ZOPAs (as referenced in Sebenius 1983). Others argue that issue-linkage can, in situations in which direct side payments among countries are not politically feasible, overcome distribution obstacles and create value for all participating parties (Tollison and Willett 1979: ch. 9; Lax and Sebenius 1986). As such they create value to the benefit of all involved rather than claim values in which only one party wins (Bayne 2003: 77).

Through issue-linkage, the negotiating parties are not merely simple competitors bargaining in one issue area (Raiffa 1987). It can have several powerful effects, such as forming coalitions, strengthening bargaining commitments, altering the parties to negotiations, overcoming distributional impediments, increasing ZOPAs or raising the commitment of parties to the agreement (Sebenius 1983).

Probably the largest-scale application of issue-linkage in economic diplomacy took place during the formulation of the WTO, when the previous framework in trade in goods was expanded and coupled with regulatory frameworks in the field of services and IPRs. Bhagwati (2002) argues that some of these linkages, in particular the inclusion of IPRs into the international trading regime, took place even though they actually do not belong to the WTO. The link established to IPRs resulted out of successful lobbying activities by key interest groups in the North that added 'trade-related' in front of this traditionally non-trade-related field.

Ernst Haas (1980: 372) refers to this type of linkage as 'tactical linkage', as it connects issues that are not connected by any intellectual coherence but rather out of increasing bargaining leverage. He claims that the credibility of tactical linkage depends on the 'linkee's' perception that the 'linker' would walk out of negotiations if this issue was removed from the agreement. Typical tactical linkage includes what is often referred to as 'package deals' or 'linkage politics'. It is a means of maximising the gains that parties may get out of the separate issue areas included in the agreement.

However, it should be noted that issue-linkage does not have to be formalised in one treaty text. Sometimes linkages are made informally on issues that have no formalised relation to the actual subject under negotiations. As Bhagwati (2002) points out, in the late 1980s the US developed the 'Structural Impediment Initiative' against Japan, which listed more than 250 domestic policy practices such as saving behaviour or working hours as a basis for denying market access. As we will see in the case studies of this book, informal issue-linkage is a common tool in US foreign economic diplomacy.

Issue-linkages make the calculation of win-sets very difficult as they may imply concessions in one field but negotiation achievements in another. Calculating the trade-offs is politically challenging, especially as it might mean that negotiators lose the support of one group of domestic constituents for another. In this sense issue-linkage can be used in both domestic as well as international negotiations. It can serve to get the opposing party to agree to certain concessions through prospects in another field, while at the same time serve as a 'side payment' to domestic constituencies for their support or opposition. 'Side payments' in the form of side agreements on labour and environmental standards during the North Atlantic Free Trade Agreement (NAFTA) negotiations, for example, were crucial for winning US congressional support for the agreement (Woolcock 2003b).

In this sense issue-linkage can also take place not only among different economic sectors, but also tie political and social factors, such as labour standards, to economic agreements. The legitimacy of institutions such as the WTO to deal with complex issue areas that reach into the normative field has been questioned by critics arguing that this goes beyond the organisation's mandate and professional scope (Bhagwati 2002; Jackson 2002).

Finally, an additional form of strategic issue-linkage is the so called 'carousel retaliation', in which negotiators target particular constituencies at the domestic level of the other negotiating party by offering both positive and negative incentives through, for example, particular tariff increases or reductions, which in turn may influence their lobbying towards their own government and thus change that country's win-set (Woolcock 2003b). An example of this method was highlighted in the *Financial Times*:

> The European Union has fired a warning shot across Washington's bows by publishing a list of US exports on which it plans sanctions, in retaliation against the steel import curbs imposed by President George W. Bush last week. [. . .] The list is designed to 'hit the White House where it hurts' by targeting Dollars 2.2bn (Pounds 1.5bn, Euros 2.5bn) of exports from states critical to Mr Bush's re-election prospects. They include citrus fruit from Florida, steel from the Midwest and textiles from North and South Carolina.
>
> (de Jonquieres 2002)

Power and bargaining leverage

There are many definitions of power, but a typical definition used in the context of negotiation is the capacity to move another party to do something (or not do something) it would not have (or would have) done were it not for the influence of the other (Pfetsch and Landau 2000; Zartman and Rubin 2000). Or, as Meunier puts it, power is equal to obtaining 'the best possible deal in the negotiations – that is, to obtain the most from its opponent while conceding the least, ceteris paribus' (2005: 40). The emphasis here is on relative gains, which typically includes the aim to reduce other parties' trade barriers while not moving on one's own.

Traditionally, negotiation theorists identify two principal measurements of power that affect negotiations. One is military based and the other market based. For economic negotiations the latter is crucial, as is the nature of the other party's market that is attractive for negotiation parties (Clark et al. 2000). Similarly, the dependency of one's own market on the market of the other country is crucial for understanding the power relationship among negotiating parties. Often psychological factors also play a role. Perceived dependency on other countries will have a large impact on the behaviour of negotiators (Pfetsch and Landau 2000). It is thus often the smaller country that ends up being the *demandeur* of the negotiations, aspiring to increased access to the other party's market, either because of the general size of that country's market or because of a specific market-based dependency.

Pfetsch and Landau argue that power asymmetry in terms of the relationship of negotiating parties comes to light in four different ways: (a) the perceived structural relationship among the parties; (b) the actual process of negotiations; (c) third party intervention; and (d) the outcome of the process (Pfetsch and Landau 2000).

Power is central to realist arguments on any kind of relationship between governments. Morgenthau argues that all 'political policy seeks either to keep power, to increase power, or to demonstrate power' (1949: 21). In this sense every realist or neo-realist would argue that power asymmetries end up defining the outcome of negotiations. Consequently, smaller states are better off negotiating in multilateral settings where the possibility of coalitions, and thus their relative power in the negotiations, increases (Clark et al. 2000; Steinberg 1997). These arguments carry a lot of merit. Many developing countries depend on the market of larger developed countries, a dependency that inevitably will influence both the process and outcome of negotiations. Without doubt an economic heavyweight such as the US will have much more leverage in negotiations with smaller economies.

Yet, the question is whether power alone determines the nature and outcomes of negotiations. A range of theorists argue that the nature of institutions and their role in domestic decision-making processes leave real opportunities to influence the results. This is confirmed by a range of case studies, demonstrating that power analysis is not sufficient to explain the distributional outcomes of the negotiation processes (Landau 2000; Cameron and Tomlin 2000; Meunier 2005; Clark et al. 2000; Odell 2000: ch. 6; Odell 1993; Odell and Sell 2006; Odell 2006).

For example, during the NAFTA negotiations, it was really Canada that seemed to have walked away with the biggest negotiation success of the three negotiating parties. This can be explained by two principal reasons: first, Canada already had an FTA with the US at the time, so the BATNA was very high and resulted in Canada making very few concessions; and second, towards the end of the negotiation the US came under increasing pressure to finalise the negotiations in time for the 1992 elections. Canada, aware of this, continued resisting the US demands and managed to achieve a range of its objectives even though compared to the US Canada is a less powerful country, both economically and militarily (Cameron and Tomlin 2000). Other examples include: Panama's relative success in the 1967 to 1977 canal treaty negotiations in limiting US control over the canal until the year 2000 (Pastor 1993); Brazil's achievement resisting US pressure related to changing its domestic patent law (Devereaux et al. 2006: ch. 3); Brazil also succeeded in refusing to give in to US pressure to change its programme to promote a national computer industry that was displacing US firms (Odell 1993); and Ecuador succeeding in its conflict with the EU with respect to the 'banana wars' (McCall Smith 2006). While in all these negotiations power disparities did play a role, other factors such as domestic politics or outside forces, must be acknowledged.

While 'negotiation successes' of developing countries often only impact one subsection of the agreement, they are still successes and indicate a clear domestic preference setting that would influence their negotiation position on a particular matter. In most cases these successes can be attributed to a range of factors, ranging from particular political structures in which these negotiations were embedded, domestic institutions or by making use of outside factors through which the negotiation teams managed to increase their bargaining leverage in one way or another. Pfetsch and Landau (2000) describe, for example, how developing countries have become stronger in 'borrowing power' to confront developed countries in international negotiations. They have done so by formulating alliances and by striving for more equitable negotiation rules. Similarly, Jessica Albin (2001) demonstrates that injecting principles like 'fairness' and 'justice' into negotiations can be a powerful tool during the negotiations.

Odell and Sell (2006) also demonstrate how developing countries have used ethical arguments linking IP negotiations to unnecessary death due to reduced access to medicine. As a result, developing countries succeeded in the adoption of the Doha Declaration on the TRIPS Agreement and Public Health[14] (Doha Declaration) despite resistance from more powerful parties. As noted by these authors, this result demonstrates that power alone is not the single determinant of negotiation outcome but rather a range of factors. Some authors have highlighted how the strategic use of domestic institutions can strengthen bargaining power in international negotiations. The following section will describe one of the most common of these strategies in international economic negotiations.

The Schelling Conjecture and bargaining power

Paradoxically, bargaining power can, in some instances, be derived from a position of negotiation weakness. This was originally described by Thomas Schelling (1960). Negotiators operating under very restrictive conditions (such as very complex domestic legislative processes, domestic checks and balances or existing treaty obligations to other countries) may be in a better position to attain their goals in a negotiation. According to Schelling:

> The power of a negotiator often rests on a manifest inability to make concessions and meet demands . . . When the United States Government negotiates with other governments . . . if the executive branch negotiates under legislative authority, with its position constrained by law, . . . then the executive branch has a firm position that is visible to its negotiating partners.
>
> (as quoted in Putnam 1988: 440)

Domestic constraints may allow weaker countries, other things being equal, to increase their bargaining power. Unfortunately many negotiation teams fail to recognise this as a strategic option, and it is only the more experienced negotiation teams that use domestic constraints to their advantage. In their research on the NAFTA negotiations, Cameron and Tomlin interviewed negotiators from Mexico who claimed that:

> Our greatest strength was also our greatest weakness: we could decide a lot. But we could not say 'Congress won't like this,' or even 'the industry won't accept this'. [On the US side things were different.] There is a separation of powers and strong lobbies that strengthen the executive. They would say 'I can't do that, the Congress will never approve [while in the same time being aware that] . . . all Salinas has to do is pick up the phone and he gets what he wants'. This gave them leverage.
>
> (Cameron and Tomlin 2000: 56)

The Schelling Conjecture also predicts that a party's domestic scenario can be presented as complicated thereby increasing its negotiation leverage (Clark et al. 2000). Fooling the opposing party by claiming domestic complexity can result in pretending that one's win-set is much smaller than it is in reality. This strategy has been frequently used by US diplomats to influence ongoing negotiations, as will be seen in the case study of this study.[15]

Of course, this strategy should not be overdone as negotiations may 'run the risk of establishing an immovable position that goes beyond the ability of the other to concede, and thereby provoke the likelihood of stale-mate or breakdown' as Schelling observes (Putnam 1988: 440; see also Tarar 2001). The distribution of powers between agents and principals has to be credible and ideally of a long-term nature. The negotiators cannot without compelling reasons 'tie their hands' to falsely increased negotiating power. An authoritarian government in a negotiation will find it difficult to convince its opponent that it cannot implement certain domestic changes due to the opposition of domestic institutions (Pahre 1997). Also, evidence shows that the deliberate 'tying of hands' is often difficult to achieve in real life, as principals dislike reducing their decision-making power during negotiations (Evans 1993). Naturally, domestic constraints also differ between parliamentary and presidential systems. Thus, a good negotiator seeks to understand not only his opponent's win-set, but also his decision-making processes as this will allow him to realise when the other party is bluffing with respect to its domestic constraints (Pahre 1997; Odell 2000: ch. 6).

Thus, the institutional setting that countries have set up for negotiating international economic agreements is an essential factor of their negotiation leverage. They matter because they determine the independence of the negotiator in making concessions during the negotiations and thus contribute towards the bargaining power of the negotiator. In order to understand, for example, the relative strength of the EU *vis-à-vis* the US in WTO agricultural negotiations one has to understand the complex institutional shape of the EU's trade policy-making (Clark et al. 2000).[16]

Thus, it can be seen that the value of the two-level approach is that it explains how the factors influencing negotiation leverage and behaviour of the participating parties are the consequence of the interaction of both domestic and international components.

Two-level game

The metaphor[17] of the two-level game was originally introduced by Robert Putman (1988), and subsequently expanded by other authors who applied his writings to a range of case studies.[18] While other authors, such as Rosenau (1969), Haas (1958), Krasner (1977), Pempel (1977) or Katzenstein (1977a, 1976, 1977b) had previously referred to links between domestic politics and international economic policy, Putnam's work was the first to attempt to apply some of this thinking to the study of negotiation and focus explicitly on its nature (Moravczik 1993).[19] He writes:

> The politics of many international negotiations can usefully be conceived as a two-level game. At the national level, domestic groups pursue their interests by pressuring the government to adopt favourable policies, and politicians seek power by constructing coalitions among those groups. At the international level, national governments seek to maximize their own ability to satisfy domestic pressures, while minimizing the adverse consequences of foreign developments. Neither of the two games can be ignored by central decision-makers, so long as their countries remain interdependent, yet sovereign.
>
> (Putnam 1988: 9)

Putnam describes negotiations as a board game. At the international table negotiators face each other, while at the domestic table they face parliamentarians, representatives from executive agencies, interest groups and political advisors. The complexity of the two-level game is that moves on one of the game tables, while acceptable to one party, are objectionable to the other. For the negotiations to succeed negotiators have to ensure that the moves at one table are satisfactory to the other.

For analytical purposes two-level game scholars distinguish between two different levels of analysis: the bargaining that takes place between the actual negotiators, ideally leading to an agreement between the parties involved, is referred to as level I. The domestic discussions that are necessary to develop the initial negotiation position and the win-set, as well as to ratify and implement agreements, are referred to as level II.

Often, level II negotiations are much more complex than level I due to the variety of stakeholders involved. They could include parliamentary debates and elections, but also consultations with all kinds of non-governmental stakeholders and the media. Level II basically includes any decision-making process that has to take place at the domestic level and is needed to endorse the agreement reached at level I (Putnam 1988). Robert Strauss after the Tokyo Round of Trade Negotiations (1973–79) put it this way:

> During my tenure as Special Trade Representative, I spent as much time negotiating with domestic constituents (both industry and labor) and members of the U.S. Congress as I did negotiating with our foreign trading partners.
>
> (as quoted in Putnam 1988: 8)

It is important to note that neither level is static and each is likely to influence the other. One condition for the relationship of the two levels is that any amendment that is made to an agreement on level II has to pass level I before it is signed, as in the end the negotiating parties have to agree to the same agreement. At the same time, each party's win-set, defined by level II negotiations, constitutes the factors that need to be included or excluded in a final agreement (level I) which can thereby receive sufficient domestic support to lead to ratification. The ZOPA is where the level II win-sets of both negotiating parties on level I overlap. Under the usual circumstances we can assume that the larger the win-set, the more likely the negotiating parties will come to an agreement. Putnam, however, also refers to the Schelling Conjecture, arguing that frequently negotiators will overemphasise the complication of its level II constituency, to narrow its win-set in order to push the ZOPA further towards its negotiation objectives.

Indeed, the 'two-level game' allows us to question how domestic factors are being used (and abused) strategically for advancement in international negotiation, as well as how international negotiation processes are being used to push through domestic reforms which, if they had taken place on their own, could not have been defended by the government (Evans 1993). As an example of the latter, Putnam describes how the German Government under Helmut Schmidt in 1980 was able to justify fiscal stimulus amounting to 1 per cent of the Gross Domestic Product (GDP) in light of the government's need to seek a compromise in the Tokyo Round of multilateral trade negotiations that in the absence of the international talks the minority government would never have been able to push through (1988). An example provided by Cameron and Tomlin from the NAFTA negotiations highlights how then President Salinas used the negotiations to push through a traditional land tenure reform that both the bureaucracy and the public would have blocked if they had not perceived them to be crucial for the success of the negotiations (2000). Taken to an extreme, this form of policy-making is criticised by some as 'backdoor lawmaking'. Peter Yu mentions the WIPO internet treaties as an IPRs-related example. In his words the negotiation of the treaties, which go beyond the level of IPRs protection in the US, constitutes:

> a process of outsourcing the legislative process to an international forum of unelected representatives in an effort to create laws that the domestic legislature would not have otherwise enacted. This type of lawmaking is rent seeking at its best. [. . .] harmonization and international legal obligations provided the domestic legislature with politically acceptable justifications to enact laws that it had originally deemed unappealing from the domestic standpoint. What is particularly disturbing is that these pressing international standards were unlikely to have existed in the first place had the initiating country not 'outsourced' the legislative process.
>
> (Yu 2006: 44)

Determining the size of a level II win-set

Putnam identifies three major determinants to the size of the win-set of negotiating parties:

As his first group of determinants he names 'power, preferences, and possible coalitions among the Level II constituents' (1988: 442). This group distinguishes between situations in which the positions of domestic constituents is highly diverse and those in which most stakeholders would be similarly affected. An example of the former situation could be ongoing talks on multilateral trade liberalisation, which usually finds protectionist groups opposing the agreement, whereas export-oriented industry groups may not. However, in countries that are primarily based on export industries, such as Hong Kong, domestic constituents that favour trade liberalisation represent the vast majority. Putnam argues that this is not necessarily an advantage in reaching an agreement as a wider range of constituents, despite being less unified on level II, also provide a wider win-set. A unified constituency may be very clear but also very specific in terms of what they want and consequently have a very narrow win-set. He argues a heterogeneous constituency is more willing to allow for trade-offs as some constituencies will always benefit from the resulting agreement. As long as these constituents can lead to the agreement's ratification, then that is what ultimately counts (Putnam 1988).

The second set of indicators influencing the size of the win-set, as identified by Putnam, is the nature of political institutions. Often the nature of the ratification process (that is, which committees the agreement has to pass, whether a simple or two-thirds majority is needed) is crucial as the more complex the domestic process the smaller the win-set.[20] Putnam finds, as a rule of thumb, that the greater the authority given to the central decision-makers by their constituents, the larger the win-set and the more likely an agreement will result. However, as suggested by the Schelling Conjecture, the more centralised the decision-making process on level II the weaker the bargaining position at level I.

The third set of Putnam's indicators is the strategy of the level I negotiators who will seek to expand their win-set in the interest of increasing the chance of an agreement using a range of tactics, such as, for example, side payments. Side payments are often targeted at marginal supporters or swing constituencies and are aimed at getting their approval to the agreement. Side payments can of course also be used on level II to silence certain opposition groups.

Whose preferences? The 'movers and shakers' behind level II

While Putnam and his colleagues analyse the determinants of the *size* of the domestic win-set, some further analysis is useful for understanding the particular *nature* of a domestic win-set, or in other words, the combination of preferences that are included in a particular win-set. Whose preferences are they? Which actors have enough access to the process of formulating the domestic win-set to ensure that their preferences are included? As one of the central questions of this book is to determine to what extent public health considerations were integrated into the US-Andean FTA negotiations, the setting of domestic preferences is of fundamental importance to this study.

Why preferences matter

The study of preferences is essential as it will define a negotiating party's decision regarding the nature of trade-offs and concessions made during international negotiations. The preferences that make up a win-set are defined by the total amount of preferences of local constituencies, and the respective importance given to each. Many structural determinants that shape domestic preferences exist, ranging from geopolitical concerns to identifying alternative markets to export goods.

The central question is, of course, how do governments identify and determine the preferences they put forward during international negotiations?[21] As Gerhart (2007: 153) points out, within the field of IPRs alone a government, depending on the nature of the constituency it favours, faces difficult decisions about which type of IPRs system it prefers. In other words, preferences within the field of IP alone may be competing with each other.

For realists, according to Milner, heads of state decide about preference setting in a country. Political systems for realists are hierarchical in which some command while others obey. In such a system, setting preferences is easy, as, by definition, the preferences of the one in command will be imposed on the rest of the country. Milner, like many authors, criticises this notion of hierarchy in domestic politics, and argues instead that domestic politics are 'polyarchical', a term originally coined by Robert Dahl (Milner 1997). She argues that states are composed of actors with varying preferences who share, often unequally, the power of decision-making.

Domestic politics, among other the product of the political capital of different groups, determine preferences (Meunier 2005). With respect to IPRs, Gerhart (2007) argues, governments favour the preferences of producers over consumers as their overall aim is wealth creation. He argues that technology-importing countries, for example, will aim to minimise payments for IPRs and thus promote weak IPRs protection in international negotiations whereas technology-exporting countries seek the opposite. This would be true, of course, if IPRs were negotiated in isolation, but when linked to other negotiation issues then the question is which of the many national producer groups the government considers more important. For example, should preferences be given to those industries that are negatively affected by strengthened IPRs, such as the generics industry, or to those industries, such as agricultural exporters, that may benefit through increased market access to the US? On top of that, the government will also have to consider consumer interests in this calculation. Therefore, when the government has to make decisions on which preferences to include in the national win-set, it becomes a broker weighing the interests of different producers and consumers.

For this study three principal factors are considered central for understanding how a domestic win-set is defined and thus how trade-offs between preferences are decided upon: first, the political structure of a country, second, and related, the nature of a country's institutions and third, the ideas and principles that affect the principal decision-makers.

On governance structure and process

To understand government structures requires considering a range of factors, such as whether it has a presidential or parliamentary structure, bicameral or unicameral, party management, whether bureaucracies are appointed or independent and the role of the judiciary (Peters 2005: ch. 5). The nature of the political structure in which institutions function has a large effect on their power as veto-players[22] in the trade policy-making process. The structure of a government or the nature of a political regime defines who are the principals and agents that are in charge of decision-making, their relations and whether they face real opposition. However, as May and Sell (2006: 34) point out, structure may condition agency, but not determine it. As discussed below, agents and institutions can not only be empowered or constrained by structure, but can also induce structural change.

Political regimes

In his book on global political economy, Robert Gilpin (2001) suggests that the role of the state and the structure of the corporate sector and its practices, deserve particular attention when considering the principal difference between national economic systems. States differ in the importance they give to different economic objectives that in one way or another support the welfare of its citizens. A government that pursues a *laissez-faire* philosophy towards economic growth will be more concerned with overall wealth creation, than welfare distribution, assuming that the former leads to the latter. A government that pursues a strong social welfare philosophy will be much more hands on in designing national economic policy and controlling domestic businesses and wealth distribution. Obviously different forms of government engagement are possible and market liberalisation does not necessarily imply that governments do not interfere. Some countries, such as Germany, pursue market capitalism but at the same time continue to maintain a strong government-led social welfare component. Nevertheless, the nature of the national economic structure is essential for understanding the role different agents play in shaping the national economy. This role will subsequently affect how institutions will contribute to international trade negotiations and, above all, in the definition of the domestic win-set. In a corporatist system, for example, organised labour and organised capital will play a fundamental role in shaping the different stages of the negotiation process, whereas in a traditional state centric welfare state, their influence is less prominent (Milner 1997).

Decision-making and the setting of preferences

Of paramount importance in formulating a domestic win-set for international negotiations, are the responsibilities of different institutions in the key decision-making processes which range from agenda setting to ratification and implementation. Which actor has control over which process will fundamentally influence the way preferences are set (Milner 1997).

Whereas in foreign policy negotiations it is primarily the Foreign Ministry that leads international deliberations, in economic diplomacy this is less clearcut. In some countries trade falls under the jurisdiction of the Ministry of Commerce/Trade, while in others Foreign Ministries have a specialised unit that is responsible for international economic affairs (Bayne 2003). However, at a time when trade agreements have become increasingly comprehensive and moved beyond a debate on tariff and tax schedules, inevitably other ministries are affected. Thus, in more decentralised decision-making structures other ministries, such as Finance, Industry/Commerce, Agriculture and even the Ministries of Environment, have a unit that also deals with trade.

With respect to IPRs-related negotiations the cross-sectoral nature of the field further complicates the task. Next to the constituencies of the Ministries of Commerce/Economics and the domestic patent offices, also affected will be the work of the Ministries of Health, Education, Environment, Agriculture, Culture, Justice, Industry, Science and Technology, domestic drug regulatory authorities and competition authorities. Ideally, while all of these institutions should be consulted when the national position on IPRs is developed, the sheer amount of policy coherence necessary to develop a joint negotiation position on IPRs is a challenging task (Abdel Latif 2005).

Indeed, practically speaking, most international negotiations demand a centre of convergence where the different positions come together. The institutional affiliation of this centre is of fundamental importance when preferences are being set. Inevitably, concessions have to be made at the national level to reach a consensus that puts forward a single negotiation position that encompasses a range of preferences. Naturally, a Ministry of Trade will set a different agenda when defending individual preferences in international negotiations as compared to the Ministry of Foreign Affairs or Ministry of Planning. A Ministry of Agriculture would not accept trade-offs that would make domestic agricultural production vulnerable to foreign imports, whereas a Ministry of Trade may well do so, if it can expect gains in other sectors. Thus, whichever institution functions as the central negotiation agency, calculating costs and benefits of the domestic win-set is a complicated and politically challenging task.

An appropriate process of calculating preferences is important not only to achieve the optimal outcome in international negotiations but for domestic political reasons. Eventually, any concessions made have to be passed back to level II for ratification. Questions of political legitimacy may arise if those stakeholder groups that were negatively affected were not sufficiently represented during both the domestic and international negotiation processes. Again, the institutional composition and the process by which domestic preferences were set are likely to affect the level of frustration of affected constituents. The increasing number of constituents that are affected by comprehensive trade deals makes the challenge of stakeholder consultation and representation in negotiations increasingly complex and the setting of appropriate decision-making difficult. The more centralised the process, the easier it is to set preferences during the negotiations, but the harder it is to demonstrate political accountability at home (Bayne and Woolcock 2003b).

Central negotiation authority

Related to decision-making structure is the independence with which the principal negotiation authority in a country, usually the Presidency or Chief Executive's office, can influence and determine the negotiations. This is often referred to as negotiation 'slack'. The more negotiation slack a negotiator has, the more decisions they can take independently. As was mentioned above, negotiation authorities are naturally not neutral units and often come with their own political agenda. The more authority they have in steering the outcome of the negotiations, that is, the more negotiation slack they possess, the more they are able to determine the preferences put forward in the negotiations. Moravcsik (1993: 30) refers to this as the 'Preferences of Statesmen', arguing that a statesman's preferences may reflect (a) his interest in enhancing his domestic position, (b) an attempt to respond optimally to an outside political factor, (c) individual policy preference stemming from political history, or (d) are ideologically based.

Whether the principal/statesman will make use of the power that he has as a result of his relative independence in decision-making with respect to the negotiations, depends on the extent to which his preferences are compatible with those of the median domestic win-set. Many negotiation theorists refer to three possible scenarios, namely, the principal as an agent, as a hawk or as a dove. If he is an agent, his preferences are the same as the ones of his domestic constituents. If he is a hawk then his win-set lies partially outside the domestic win-set and even further away from the win-set of the other negotiating party. And if he is a dove his win-set will be also partially outside the level II win-set and closer towards the win-set of the other party[23] (Moravczik 1993).

Yet, domestic constituents are not at the complete mercy of their principals even in a political structure that allows the Executive to negotiate independently. Level II actors, such as interest groups, NGOs or Parliamentarians have a range of strategies at their disposal that may seek, for example, to influence the other party's level II constituents so that they change their win-set (Krauss 1993). Alternatively, they may seek to influence the Executive of the other party directly for the same effect (Moravczik 1993). As will be seen in the case studies, these and other strategies seeking to influence the setting of preferences domestically, as well as the preferences of the other party's level II, are quite common.

Government structure and negotiating power

There is a further aspect to consider with respect to the nature of decision-making processes, namely, the extent to which it will affect the bargaining power on level I. As we know from the Schelling Conjecture the less centralised a government, the stronger a bargaining leverage it enjoys.

Thus, decentralisation not only seems beneficial to providing a negotiating process that represents a politically legitimate position, assuming that all relevant stakeholders were involved, but also strengthens international bargaining power. It allows a negotiation team to enter the negotiations with a much narrower win-set which is less likely to be opposed by the other negotiating party. As a result, negotiators (or their principals) of centralised, hierarchical and authoritarian states tend to be less responsive to the demands of their level II but more responsive to the demands of the other negotiating party with stronger political institutions, and vice versa (Cameron and Tomlin

2000). Essentially there is a trade-off between increasing the likelihood of coming to an agreement on level I and appropriate stakeholder consultation on level II. The more centralised the decision-making, the more likely an agreement is reached, but the lower the bargaining power on level I and the less accountable the development of a domestic win-set (Woolcock 2003b).

Institutions and their agents

The nature of political institutions is arguably one of the biggest determinants of the way domestic win-sets are designed. They 'shape the process by which preferences are aggregated domestically' according to Milner (1997: 18).

Political institutions

The study of institutions has been undertaken by a range of disciplines, ranging from economics and social sciences to psychology.[24] Even within these disciplines there are differences in the definition of institutions. Scholars of political science have defined institutions using very broad concepts including any rules of the game devised by humans that shape their interaction. This incorporates concepts such as slavery, law, language or traditions. It also includes a narrower interpretation that Shepsle refers to as 'structured' institutions and Peters as institutions that consist of 'formal structures'. These take the form of organisations, such as governmental bodies, regulatory agencies or any other body that takes the shape of an organisation which persists over time (Shepsle 2005; Peters 2005: ch. 1).

For the purpose of this study, a very narrow definition of institutions will be used. The aim is to study, among other things, organization of government, including its different agencies, public administration or simply the state apparatus (Goodin 1996a). For the scope of this study 'institutions' shall refer to political institutions. The concept of agents, as used in this study, refers to individuals that work or are active within, or involved with political institutions, such as Members of Congress, employees of trade associations or NGO representatives (Shepsle 2005).

Milner identifies two principal governmental institutions, namely the Executive and the legislature as relevant for trade negotiations. Milner assumes for theoretical purposes that both the Executive and legislature are rational actors that are above all concerned with re-election. For economic policy-making this means that the Executive has to ensure that the economic policy brings good to the country and its electorate while keeping an eye on benefiting those constituency groups that helped them into, or remain in, office. While the Executive is elected (directly or indirectly) by the general public, interest groups are of fundamental importance to members, whether for campaigning, votes or media attention (Milner 1997: ch. 2; O'Halloran 1994). The legislators, according to Milner, are also concerned with re-election. Milner acknowledges that the legislature is made up of many different units often with different preferences. This applies especially to a bicameral system such as the US, where the House and the Senate have not only different positions on certain issues, but also different responsibilities with respect to legislative duty. Naturally, the Executive and legislature differ substantially in terms of the electorate and constituencies they represent. The central Executive represents the entire country, whereas legislators are elected by local constituents. Gerhart (2007: 159) emphasises how traditionally the legislative branch addresses distributive issues in policy-making in its representation of local constituents.

From a rational choice perspective, decision-makers seek to maximise utility, and they do so within the institutional constraints in which they are placed. While actors have their preferences, institutions provide the rules within which these preferences are expressed. The shape and configuration of institutions subsequently produces a range of consequences, such as vulnerability to interest group pressure,[25] dependency on domestic constituents and the distribution of power among and within the institutional set up. Institutions thus influence the behaviour of the agents who operate within them. Their make-up in conjunction with the politics of its agents will largely determine policy outcome within the jurisdiction of the institution in question (Jones 2001: ch. 1).

Regarding understanding institutions, Shepsle (2005) adds the issue of electorate preferences. He defines the electorate as the collective principal that chooses an institutional politician as its agent. In his view, the electorate is faced with two principal problems, respectively 'adverse selection' and 'moral hazard'. Adverse selection refers to the fact that the electorate cannot know everything about its chosen agent and whether he will succeed in representing its preferences. Moral hazard refers to hidden action by the agents, often driven by their own agenda.[26] This primarily refers to initiatives taken by the agent that cannot be observed, such as secret committee or lobbyist meetings that raise questions of accountability. Other 'unexplained' behaviour may be influenced by the personal agenda of the agent.

Advancing a personal agenda may be a strong motive for certain political decisions. As O'Halloran points out, this form of dysfunctional principal-agency relationship, referred to by some as 'runaway bureaucracy', occurs when oversight is ineffective (O'Halloran 1994: ch. 3). Indeed, the assumption that each agent acts purely based on their institutionally provided duties fails to explain the behaviour of many politicians. As Goodin says: 'What matters is not what people are supposed to do, but what they actually do' (1996a: 13). Furthermore, he emphasises that it is an undeniable fact that people are socially embedded and bring with them certain commitments (whether to people, ideas or causes) which in turn will affect their behaviour, whether agent or principal.

Woolcock argues that, in respect to economic diplomacy, the rational choice models fail to take account of path dependencies or policy emulation. Referring to the relationship between bilateral, regional and multilateral negotiations, he argues that they often influence one another and cannot be observed in isolation. Referring to Baldwin's 'Domino Model', Woolcock argues that the deeper economic integration of some countries creates pressure on decision-makers in other countries to also seek similar integration. Especially among neighbours this has a strong domino effect (Woolcock 2006: 9; Shadlen 2008). For example, negotiators from the CAFTA countries felt a certain peer pressure to join CAFTA, because their neighbours and in some cases economic competitors had already joined.[27] It was their view that this lowered their BATNA and subsequently weakened their bargaining power during the process. Inevitably this had a psychological effect on the negotiation principals.

A concept that has been useful in trying to explain why rational choice is not satisfactory for explaining the behaviour of agents is the concept of 'bounded rationality'.[28] According to Bryan Jones, rational choice is a powerful tool in understanding why decision-makers prefer one preference over another, yet it fails to account for the human behavioural factors in influencing the choices that they make. Especially in situations of change or the availability of new information the reactions of decision-makers will differ (Jones 2001: ch. 7, Woolcock 2003b). Furthermore, as Odell (2006) argues, it is practically impossible to compute optimised decisions. Negotiators lack full information about the other parties' full preferences and reservation points, let alone the domestic politics that may influence those. As a result negotiators have to make rough judgements, which are inevitably subjective and open to bias thereby making them and their principals open to persuasion and increasing the power of interest groups, and other influencing forces.

Non-governmental actors and institutions

Particular importance has to be placed on the role of domestic interest groups, which seek to influence trade negotiations. These range from consumer organisations, and organised labour to business trade associations. Arguably, the most influential ones with respect to trade negotiations are those representing the private sector, given the amount of financial resources available to them and their vested interest in economic negotiations.

The well-being of national industry is of fundamental importance to governments. Thus, supporting domestic business, particularly in capitalist economies, is overall considered to be an important part of successful domestic political leadership, and one that most policy-makers will seek. In turn, losing business confidence, or even worse, fleeing investment, will have an immediate effect on the career of policy-makers (Milner 1997). It is therefore no surprise that governments tend to be biased towards representing producers, rather than consumers, at the international level (Gerhart 2007).

Interest groups are concerned with the distributive outcome of international trade negotiations. Unions, for example, concern themselves with the impact that the agreement has on their constituents, whereas trade associations focus on the income the trade agreement will generate for its members. The activity of these groups is focused on specific issue-areas, and the definition of their preferences tends to be narrowed down to the respective policies. The nature of the influence is often determined by the size of the interest group and the stakes it represents. According to Neil Komesar:

> The character of institutional participation is determined by the interaction between the benefits of that participation and the costs of that participation . . . Interest groups with small numbers but high per capita stakes have significant advantages in political action over interest groups with large numbers and smaller per capita stakes.
>
> (as quoted in Shaffer 2003: 16)

Small interest groups also tend to be more harmonious in the preferences they put forward, unlike larger groups that, although powerful in size, often experience internal conflict regarding proposed policy changes.

Milner identifies two principal roles that interest groups play with respect to international negotiations. First, they work as pressure groups, and through campaign contributions, through mobilising voters and through creating momentum, they directly influence the preferences of both, Executive and legislature. Second, more informally, they work as informants, monitoring policies and providing negotiators' updates on new developments, strategic information, or technical detail (1997: ch. 2).

Public choice theorists, in particular, claim that it is predominantly political support, money and power that influence decision-making (Shaffer 2003: ch. 2). As such, policy-makers are vulnerable to the work of interest groups for a range of reasons. First, going against important interest groups can have an impact on their re-election success. Especially in countries where political campaigns depend on interest group support, the loss of this support can threaten a policy-maker's political career. Thus, policy-makers will seek the informal 'ratification' of interest groups on issues they negotiate on the international level.

Epstein and O'Halloran, however, claim that the power of interest groups to influence policy-making is overrated as today so many influence groups exist that cancel one another out. Furthermore, they claim that the increasing fractionalisation of interest groups has limited their influence (1995).

Institutions, agents and principals

A central problem of the study of institutions in political science is the relationship between principal and agent. The question of delegation, whereby principals delegate certain powers to agents, is central in this relationship. The 'rules of the game', that is how the conditions under which this delegation takes place and how it is monitored, is defined by institutional design (Goodin 1996a). As shown above, powerful non-governmental actors can also be principals in the sense that their preferences will shape the domestic win-set. Indeed, there can be many principals, varying from the electorate to other constituents, such as domestic businesses. The principals of Legislators and the Executive may differ. Naturally, this will affect the preferences put forward when developing a trade mandate (Lohmann and O'Halloran 1994).

Furthermore, some agents function as principals and agents at the same time. A US Member of Congress, for example, will have to take the role of an agent for their principals (constituents) whereas they will need to function themselves as a principal when dealing with the USTR. In this sense constituents delegate their role as a principal to their Member of Congress. However, as the behaviour of the Member of Congress will affect their chances of re-election, their constituents will also remain principals. This forces the Member of Congress to remain sensitive to constituents' needs.

Things become more complicated, however, when a Member of Congress has more than one principal, which is often the case. One could imagine a scenario in which constituents have one position on reducing tariff barriers on cotton, the Member's political Party (another principal) has another, and they are also being pressed by interest groups to take a third (and different) position. It is in such scenarios that the nature of an institution plays a fundamental role, such as through the definition of election cycles. With respect to the US system, for example, a Senator will be less dependent on representing individual constituents, as their constituents are much larger and less homogenous than his counterpart in the House of Representatives. Furthermore, their election cycle is one of six years. So even if they decide to move against the wishes of their electorate in favour of party or interest group pressure, by the time the next elections are scheduled they may have been able to reduce the frustration of those constituents through his other votes. Members of the House, however, face re-election every two years and can subsequently take less risk with respect to upsetting their electorate. Thus the shape of institutions influences the nature of delegation between principals and agents, especially in scenarios in which we have many agents and many principals.

Lohman and O'Halloran (1994) analyse the extent to which institutional changes affects the principal-agent relationship of the US legislature and Executive. They find delegation from legislature to Executive takes place most frequently when government is not divided. However, under divided government the President is more constrained than under a unified government. Naturally, this is related to preferences. Taking partisanship as a proxy for preferences, O'Halloran (1994: ch. 3) finds that the greater the differences in preferences between agent and principal, the less likely the principal will delegate power to the agent.

Ideas and principles

Some economic negotiation literature has included the study of the role of ideas and principles as drivers of policy-making. Ideas and principles are particularly important for the study of negotiation as they contribute to explaining why decision-makers place one preference above another, when the study of government structure and institutions is insufficient (Woolcock 2003b).

For Judith Goldstein (1993: ch. 1) ideas and beliefs have a dual role in policy-making.[29] First, she argues, they essentially serve as road maps and provide guidance to political leaders and other actors on how to maximise their interests, whether they are material or ideological. As such, she argues, ideas help policy-makers steer through conditions of uncertainty. Goldstein also argues that ideas and beliefs are among the most powerful determinants of policy, and once set, have long-term ramifications. Once norms and rules are based on ideas, they also influence the environment for future policy-makers and their choices, and influence the development and evolution of institutions.

Ideas and principles in the form of ideology will shape economic negotiations. Woolcock points out how in the late 1940s nation-states believed in the importance of state intervention for the promotion of economic development. By the end of the Cold War, however, state planning lost out to capitalism as an alternative model and since then the liberal paradigm has been the principal ideological paradigm steering international economic negotiations (Woolcock 2003b). What is under discussion today in international economic negotiations is not whether to liberalise markets but first and foremost the speed with which countries open their market and to whom (Landau 2000).

In a historical analysis of IPRs, May and Sell trace the ideas and social norms that led to the development and evolution of IP regimes. They emphasise that laws and their development are a reflection of social norms and do not emerge out of a vacuum. Essentially, the fact that ideas and knowledge can be subject to a property regime stems from a view that is part of a larger neo-liberal agenda of global governance (May and Sell 2006: ch. 2). The principle that 'intellectual property rights are private rights' thus (successfully) contested with other principles, such as those put forward by the New International Economic Order (NIEO) protagonists, who believe technological information and knowledge should be freely available to all based on a principle of 'common heritage' (Braithwaite and Drahos 2000: ch. 21).

Drahos and Braithwaite emphasise the importance of principles in their study on global business regulations. They argue that principles stand behind rules, influencing their application as well as leading to the creation of new rules. Principles, unlike the rules that derive from them, are much less specific and can conflict with one another. This 'contest of principles' in turn will affect the preferences of the respective decision-makers (Braithwaite and Drahos 2000: chs 4, 5). As such the principles that drive the principals and agents who are responsible for the design of international regimes, such as the TRIPS Agreement, or bilateral FTAs, will have a tremendous impact on the content of the Agreement. Susan Sell's analysis of the TRIPS Agreement essentially demonstrates how a small group of US private sector employees were the principal driver of the integration of IPRs into the 'single under-taking' and to a large extent were responsible for the final wording of the Agreement. Their principles were crucial for the nature of the final agreement (May and Sell 2006; Sell 2003).

The quantity of different principles that address trade negotiations beyond a traditional neo-liberal trade agenda has increased dramatically over the last decade. This becomes more and more evident in international economic nego-tiations. Perhaps the breakdown of the Cancun WTO Ministerial Conference in 2003 is the most powerful example of how concerns driven by environ-mental or social factors could trigger the collapse of negotiations. Other examples include the impact of farmers' protests against agricultural liberali-sation negotiations that place traditional farming practices and communities above economic efficiency; or the success of the principle-based access to medicines campaigns that lobbied in favour of including public health safe-guards into the WTO, leading to the Doha Declaration (Odell and Sell 2006).

So while trade negotiations are run as if they were solely based on economic interests, other values continue to play a role. This is highlighted by the increasingly comprehensive nature of trade agreements, which include not only chapters on services, investment and IPRs but also labour and environ-mental standards. Most trade negotiations deal with non-trade issues that are integrated into the agreements as if they were trade-related. This poses a range of jurisdictional challenges as trade policy-making bodies decide over issues that influence other policy sectors simply by linking regulatory standards to trade frameworks.

Finally, it is important to note that ideas and principles do not by them-selves explain outcomes. It is their incorporation into institutional processes, which essentially define whether ideas and principles are 'implemented' or not. As Goldstein put it:

> [f]or ideas to become politically salient they need to have sponsors, and those sponsors must either hold political power or influence those who do.
> (Goldstein 1993: 15)

May and Sell (2006) take this matter one step further. Referencing Michael Gorges, they also argue that while ideas by themselves and the institutions in which they are embedded are important, what is crucial to understand is why some ideas take certain institutional formats at a particular time.

Of ideas and principles and political institutions

One of the most obvious forms of the affiliation of principles to certain insti-tutions is through a country's executive bodies. Individual agencies, based on their responsibilities, will have different policy objectives, which they follow in their day-to-day activities. Each institution reflects different positions on which values should be promoted (Sell 2005). A Ministry of Environment will thus have different views on the use of pesticides compared to a Ministry of Agriculture. Different actors will associate themselves with different principles, which will naturally affect their preferences setting (Braithwaite and Drahos 2000: ch. 4). Naturally, most policy issues affect more than one political sector, and thus provoke reactions from multiple ministries. The ministry with jurisdiction over the matter will then make a decision that ideally aims for 'policy coherence' among the different agencies.

Intellectual property, as mentioned above, affects an unusually high amount of sectors, many of which may conflict with each other. One of the principal conflicts is the one that is addressed in this study, namely the conflict between IPRs and their impact on medicine prices, which in turn affects public health. Subsequently, when negotiating international trade agreements that also include IPRs provisions, health authorities are unlikely to argue for compromises that would lead to higher IPRs standards. For them, any negative impact on public health is unacceptable. Ministries of trade, however, tend to be more willing to make concessions as long as the agreement secures market access for critical export groups.

Principles and political parties

Principles and ideas are embedded in the political agenda of political parties (Peters 2005: ch. 7). Naturally, the principles and ideas represented by the majority political party in government will both dominate political agenda-setting on the domestic level and affect international negotiations. This increases the importance of party politics when it comes to negotiating international agreements. A liberal government will not pursue the curbing of emissions in international climate negotiations as aggressively as a government that includes a green party.

Things get even more complicated when government is politically divided. In those scenarios a clash of interests can result in political stagnation on important decisions. As mentioned above, Epstein and O'Halloran find that the US Congress has given less trade negotiation authority to the Executive under a divided government compared to a united government (1996). Another interesting study by Helen Milner and Peter Rosendorff (1997) analyses the role that elections and divided governments have on the nature of trade negotiations. If the position of the legislature is clear, the authors argue, the ratification of international agreements should be straightforward, given that the negotiators were aware of level II preferences at the time of the negotiations. Domestic positions, however, are less clear in a situation in which the legislative branch is split, for example through coalition governments, or if congress is controlled by one party and the administration by another.

Similarly, if elections are imminent, negotiators are often not willing to take the risk of a failed ratification if they are unable to predict the position of level II preferences post-elections. One such example is the NAFTA negotiations, where side letters had to be renegotiated when Democrat President Bill Clinton took over from Republican President George Bush (Milner and Rosendorff 1997). Tsebelis also highlights that if a change in the identity or political position of a critical veto player takes place, this will be reflected in policy-making (1995). As we will see later in this book, political change as a result of the 2006 congressional election also resulted in significant changes to trade policy in the US in general, and the Andean FTAs in particular.

Ideas and principles and the power of global civil society

Among the most powerful influences on the way both international and national negotiations are conducted are the ideas and principles put forward by global civil society networks. With the increasing engagement of civil society in trade policy-making the liberal market driven value system is today challenged by the inclusion of principles of environmental and labour protection, development concerns and, of course, public health. Policy concerns that are seen as not being sufficiently reflected by democratic governments are taken up by CSOs and directed at the respective decision-making processes. Furthermore, CSOs monitor accountability and transparency of domestic and international negotiations (Woolcock 2003a).

In the field of IPRs the international public health movement has significantly increased the political stake of the issues, eventually leading to the Doha Declaration (Matthews 2006; Odell 2003: 29; Odell and Sell 2006). The principle that the protection of public health can override the principles of IPRs is a powerful message that affected the process of negotiations. In these case studies it is demonstrated how this principle resulted in inclusion of Colombian and Peruvian health authorities in national FTA negotiation teams. While, as discussed above, ideas and principles in isolation are often powerless, as soon as they are 'institutionalised' they gain teeth.

The 'institutionalisation' of ideas and principles that can influence the way that negotiations take place, both on level I and on level II, is often the result of the hard work of CSOs or other interest groups. Their work is not confined to national borders as they associate themselves with groups that work on the same principles abroad. The international HIV/AIDS movement, for example, started as a result of US HIV/AIDS groups identifying themselves with the plight of HIV/AIDS patients abroad (Gerhart 2007). Through their work they raise the stakes of certain public interest principles to such levels that policy-makers, fearing electoral repercussions, represented their preferences.

Conclusion

In addition to providing an introduction to a range of concepts that are important for the study of economic negotiations, this chapter has established that power alone does not suffice to explain the process and outcome of international deliberations. It has been argued that the interaction between the domestic and the international level of all negotiating parties has to be understood in order to account for the process and outcome of international negotiations.

As the case study of this book focuses on the integration of public health objectives into the negotiations and outcome of the US-Peru and US-Colombia FTAs, particular emphasis has been made on the setting of preferences and the development of the domestic win-set. It has been argued that this is to a large extent determined by three sets of factors: the political structure of the nego-tiating parties, the nature of their institutions and agency, and the ideas and principles that influence domestic decision-makers and negotiators. It was argued that all of these factors matter and none of them unitarily will define the level II preferences that will dominate level I negotiations. As May and Sell (2006: 33, 34), referring to the work of Margaret Archer, argue, neither structure nor agency can determine social outcome alone.

Before applying this framework to the case studies of this study the following two chapters will provide some further background material. The next chapter will describe how IPRs were integrated into trade agreements and place the case studies in their historical context, while chapter 3 will take a closer look at the individual IPRs provisions that lead to the concern of Colombia and Peru's public health authorities in the first place.

2 Integrating IPRs into the international trading system

Introduction

The last 25 years have witnessed a new trend: the incorporation of IP legislation into the broader international trading system. While discussions surrounding the relationship between trade and IPRs go back to the 19th century the last few decades have seen the integration of much broader IPR chapters into FTAs than ever before. The process has involved multilateral as well as plurilateral and bilateral fora. Although not evolving in parallel fashion, multilateral and plurilateral trade negotiations have mutually reinforced each other in advancing a global agenda of liberalising trade featuring broad IPR provisions. By doing so they have not only set the agenda of an ever-increasing level of IPRs protection but have also seen to its global expansion. This following chapter outlines this development.

Early developments

Discussions surrounding IPRs reach back to the late 15th century, much before those related to the WTO or the Paris and Berne Conventions.[1] As May and Sell argue, the history surrounding IPRs has been one of contestation 'between monopoly power or private rights (limiting public access) and the public-regarding intent to free the flow of information (at the cost of the rights of the individual creator)' (2006: 25, 26). The authors argue that three social forces, namely technological, legal/political and philosophical jointly led to the development of property rights over information and knowledge and defined the scope of such rights.

The first institutional (legal) form of a patent system emerged in the 15th century in Venice. As the authors note, even then a balancing act between monopolies and public access had to be achieved. In the preamble of this law it was stated that the system would induce more people to invent devices for the greater common good (Hestermeyer 2007). Some of those early patents were deliberately passed into the public domain, including the manufacture of 'glasses for the eyes, for reading' (May and Sell 2006: 60). The Statute of 1474 was a clear instrument for the protection of IPRs for the benefit of the right holder, and also introduced concepts of 'novelty', 'usefulness' and 'obligation' to work the patent that in varying degrees today can still be found in patent legislations.

Legislation passed in the 17th and early 18th century in England, outlining a method of granting patents (limited in time and scope) and later on copyrights, was identified as the beginning of modern IP law (May and Sell 2006: 79/80; Machlup and Penrose 1950: 2). Similar systems and practices of granting patents started to evolve in a number of European countries, many of which were driven by the desire of rulers to support their national economies through the acquisition of new technologies. In such a system it was not the inventor who was protected but those who first brought it to the attention to the courts often through importation. Copyright was used by the printing industry to control competition (May and Sell 2006: 97). In the US, on the other hand, the individual creator was placed at the centre of IP law. Unlike in Europe where the 'first to file' was granted a patent, in the US it went to the 'first to invent'.[2] Patents were only for those inventions that were not previously known or used prior to their filing (Hestermeyer 2007). With this distinction and the fact that foreign inventors initially were ineligible to apply (and post-1836 subject to higher patent application fees), the US aimed to benefit national inventors, rather than foreign 'introducers' of the technology (May and Sell 2006).

The treatment of foreign nationals in domestic patent legislation was only one of the differences of the early patent systems. Others included the interpretation of novelty, length of patent protection, whether patents needed to be 'worked' domestically, and exceptions to patentability (Dutfield and Suthersanen 2008).

IPRs remained a purely national matter until the end of the 19th century. It was a system that was increasingly under strain as international commerce grew more dependent on domestically invented goods. For example, the foreign copying of books was a problem for British authors and publishers due to the thriving industry in the US reproducing the works of British authors such as Charles Dickens. Thus, the regulation for international control of the book trade was called for (Sell 2003). Similarly, inventors were increasingly concerned about the protection of their products abroad. At an international inventions exhibition in Vienna in the 1870s, exhibitors, particularly those from Germany and the US, were concerned about their products being stolen. A temporary law adopted by the Austro-Hungarian empire was set up to ensure that foreigners would continue to exhibit at foreign shows.

Several countries, some already with domestic patent protection, proposed the idea of an international agreement to protect patents. The idea was further developed and subsequently became the Paris Convention for the Protection of Industrial Property in 1883.[3] It was strongly supported by the lobbying of a range of private sector actors (Sell 2003; May and Sell 2006: 119). A similar Convention, completed in 1886 in Berne covered Literary and Artistic Work.[4]

While not all variables among national patent law were harmonised through the Conventions, they affirmed some of the fundamental principles of modern IP law, such as national treatment (that is, disallowing discrimination against foreigners and their inventions in national IP legislation) (Dutfield and Suthersanen 2008).

Integrating IPRs into international trade

Early conflicts

In the early debates in the 19th century between the 'free trade community' and those favouring strong IP protection, free trade liberals criticised the idea of monopolies on patented/copyrighted goods as an inhibitor of free trade and limitation of commercial practice. Indeed, many free traders argued that inventions were a result of technological change instead of the outcome of one individual's work. In their groundbreaking work on patent controversies in the 19th century Machlup and Penrose (1950) outline the different schools of thought in the mid-19th century that fiercely disagreed about the extent to which the patent system satisfies the competing interests of inventors (who have the right to a patent) and society as a whole (which has a right to the invention). As they point out, even *The Economist* back then was highly critical of the concept of a patent system:

> Before . . . [the inventors] can . . . establish a right of property in their inventions, they ought to give up all the knowledge and assistance they have derived from the knowledge and inventions of others. That is impossible, and the impossibility shows that their minds and their inventions are, in fact, parts of the great mental whole of society, and that they have no right of property in their inventions, except that they can keep them to themselves if they please and own all the material objects in which they may realize their mental conception.
> (*The Economist*, 28 December 1850, as quoted in Machlup and Penrose 1950: 15)

Members from trade associations and chambers of commerce, particularly from Germany and Holland, submitted reports, pamphlets, books and journals recommending the reform or abolishment of the patent system (eventually the patent system was repealed in Holland in 1869). IP supporters in turn argued that inventors had a natural (property) right over their invention, and that the copying of exported products abroad needed to be addressed through patent protection beyond national borders, something that would benefit society as a whole (Machlup and Penrose 1950). After substantial back and forth, the free trade movement began to decline and a more protectionist perspective emerged. Corresponding to this more protectionist phase, free traders had to come to terms with an international agreement on IPRs in spite of its restriction of trade (May and Sell 2006; May 2007a; Hestermeyer 2007). What made the concept more tolerable was the fact that with an international regime it would be applicable to all (May 2007a).

Neverthless, what was needed was greater coordination of cross-border recognition. Before the Paris and Berne Conventions, cross-border recognition was based on a complex web of bilateral commercial treaties featuring some form of copyright or patent protection. The key drivers behind this more coherent system of patents were the US and Germany, both driven by powerful domestic lobbies, such as in the field of chemistry (May and Sell 2006). Regarding international copyright protection, the US, which did not participate in the negotiations of the Berne Convention, integrated copyright provisions in a Friendship and Cooperation Treaty (FCN) with China. The US eventually followed this approach with at least another 15 countries from 1891 to 1904. By the mid-20th century, bilateral and regional trade agreements increasingly incorporated IPR provisions and became a dominant feature of US foreign economic diplomacy (Okediji 2004).

However, beginning in the 1970s and reaching a peak in the 1980s, concerns similar to those that led to the Paris and Berne Conventions re-emerged. It was argued that the current level of protection did not adequately protect the technology-intensive industries of developed countries. US firms witnessed their own competitiveness, particularly in high technology commodities, decreasing *vis-à-vis* an increasing level of global engagement by Japan, as well as some large, primarily Asian, developing countries. Criticism of these countries emerged quickly as companies saw their products reengineered and sold on foreign markets. It was felt that IP protection provided by the Paris and Berne Conventions was not adequate to deal with this threat because of: (1) a continuing lack of harmonised IPRs standards; and (2) a lack of enforcement mechanisms for IPRs. Despite the existence of nominal enforcement mechanisms,[5] dispute resolution was, in a practical sense, very difficult (UNCTAD-ICTSD 2005; Helfer 2004; Drahos and Braithwaite 2002; Ryan 1998).

Disappointment with the international system was particularly acute after the Diplomatic Conference for the Revision of the Paris Convention for the Protection of Intellectual Property (1980–84), held under the auspices of the World Intellectual Property Organization (WIPO) which administers the Conventions. During the conference, IPR supporters were forced to defend the existing standards of the Paris Convention, rather than strengthening their protection (Drahos and Braithwaite 2002; Helfer 2004; Sell 1998).[6]

The increasingly rigorous inclusion of IPRs in international economic agreements was a direct response to this disillusionment. Trade agreements often included either dispute settlement mechanisms or allowed for other trade-related punitive measures (such as the withdrawal of trade preferences). It was felt by many developed countries that this approach was an effective means for strengthening enforcement of IPRs. Among the first agreements that integrated all key forms of IPRs in a broad economic framework and linked it to market access were the so-called 'Economic Recovery Agreements' or 'Trade Promotion Agreements'. The first example is the Caribbean Basin Economic Recovery Act of 1983 (CBERA).[7] The CBERA was the first of three Acts (1983, 1990 and 2000) that together formed the Caribbean Basin Initiative (CBI) that provided duty-free customs entry for a broad range of products into the US market. The International Intellectual Property Alliance (IIAP) heralded the CBERA arguing:

> The 1983 enactment of the CBERA was a pivotal moment in time regarding the use of U.S. trade policy to promote exports of products and services protected by copyright, patents, trademarks, and other intellectual property laws. For the first time, Congress explicitly linked trade benefits to intellectual property protection by beneficiary countries. Under CBERA program, countries can only receive trade preferences if they satisfy statutory criteria which include intellectual property rights (IPR) standards.
>
> (IIPA 2003)

The CBERA stated clearly that in case of a violation against the IPRs of a US citizen, the US President may suspend any preferential treatment expressed in the treaty for the country in question (IIPA 2005, 2007).

With the full integration of IPRs into economic agreements, the pressure to implement and enforce intellectual property standards changed. Unlike the prior system under the Paris and Berne Conventions, IPRs protection within economic agreements allowed for cross-retaliation in other economic sectors. This mechanism represented a much stronger political tool than what was traditionally available under the multilateral IP regimes (Drahos 2001a).

The integration of IPRs in international economic agreements was also reflected by domestic policy developments in the US. The domestic economic outlook at the time grew more complex as US firms were faced with increasing competition in their domestic markets as well as abroad. In order to improve international competitiveness the US government sought to improve its balance of trade situation. With the 1974 Trade Act the US Congress refurbished its domestic trade policy formulation process and created the office of the United States Trade Representative (USTR), which would report directly to the White House. The newly developed Trade Promotion Authority (TPA) provided the President with the authority to engage directly in international commercial affairs, including trade issues, such as foreign domestic acts, policies and practices that violate US businesses foreign commercial activities (Mundo 1999).[8]

The particular relevance of intellectual property for the US domestic industry was reflected in the 1988 US Omnibus Trade and Competitive Act. The specific goal of the Act was to further expand the 1974 Trade Act and support US industry to become more competitive at home and abroad. Specific attention was placed on encouraging the development and protection of new technologies. One of the Act's most notable features included the implementation of the 'Special 301', which targets violations of US IPRs on an annual basis abroad (Mundo 1999).[9] This unilateral tool provided the legal basis for imposing tariffs on the import of products from countries that did not sufficiently protect US IPRs abroad.

While these specific tools proved useful for the relevant parties involved, it was felt at the time, particularly by the US government and certain domestic industrial groups, that significant reliance on unilateral or bilateral mechanisms of IPRs enforcement would compromise the development and expansion of a truly enforceable international IPRs protection regime. This concern grew to such an extent that in 1988 the USTR specifically asked the US International Trade Commission (ITC) to quantify financial losses to US foreign commercial activities as a result of unauthorised appropriation of IPRs. The ITC estimated that in 1986 alone, US industries faced worldwide trade losses ranging from US$43 billion to US$61 billion and that principal US industries lost $23.8 billion in revenue due to the lack of IPRs enforcement worldwide. Particular losses were attributed to a specific group of countries, namely Brazil, India, Mexico, Nigeria, the Republic of Korea, China, Hong Kong and Taiwan. The report also carried out a sector specific study, finding that the industries most affected were chemicals and pharmaceuticals, computer software and entertainment (audio and video) (Tully 2003; Abbott 1989).[10]

Given the scale of perceived counterfeiting abroad, case-by-case policy-making via unilateral punitive measures was not considered to be cost effective. A multilateral solution was thought essential.

The integration of IPRs in the multilateral trading system

In order to address the problem of alleged counterfeit products on a multilateral level, two principal options were available: either the strengthening of existing multilateral IPRs regimes or the creation of a new forum.

(1) Reviving the role of existing international organisations dealing with IP meant a reform of WIPO. WIPO, a UN specialised agency that hosts most international treaties related to IPRs was, and remains today, the principal international agency dealing with IPRs. However, it does not possess an adequate enforcement mechanism and is thus ill-equipped to monitor and police acts of counterfeiting. One option could have been establishing such an enforcement infrastructure.

(2) As disillusionment with WIPO was high, the potential for using the parallel negotiations on the expansion of the multilateral trading system constituted a welcome opportunity for the strengthening and expansion of the IPRs system on the multilateral level. Traditionally the multilateral trading system and the multilateral fora for IPRs protection (for example Paris Convention) had been kept separate. Yet, integrating IPRs into the dispute settlement of the General Agreement on Tariffs and Trade (GATT) was seen as a possibility in order to renovate what was perceived as an inefficient model. Further, integrating

IPRs into what was to become the WTO would link IPRs negotiations to all other negotiation items that were to be part of the WTO system (Dutfield 2003). The US was one of the principal proponents of this second option.[11]

By the end of the Tokyo Round of GATT negotiations (1979), frustration had grown high with multilateral trade negotiations. Least developed countries (LDCs) were disappointed with the inadequacies of 'Special and Differential Treatment' (S&D) in relation to their major trade interests (agriculture and textiles), while developed countries felt that developing countries were free-riding in economic sectors that did not deal exclusively with trade in goods and that were not properly addressed through the GATT. These sectors included services, trade-related investment measures and IPRs[12] (Primo Braga 1989).

Against this backdrop, the US called for a ministerial meeting on trade in 1982 to pave the way for a new round of negotiations on GATT reform, including the discussion of the new themes. At a time of world recession, however, many countries, including several industrialised countries, were not in favour of an expansion of the GATT system but preferred to first address the existing inadequacies of the GATT-based system. Nevertheless, what was included in the 1982 Ministerial Declaration was a section that clearly called for the examination of:

> . . . the question of counterfeit goods with a view to determining the appropriateness of joint action in the GATT framework on the trade aspects of commercial counterfeiting and, if such joint action is found to be appropriate, the modalities for such action, having full regard to the competence of other international organizations.
>
> (as quoted in Primo Braga 1989: 246/247)

When the Uruguay Round of negotiations was finally launched in Punta del Este on 20 September 1986, trade-related aspects of IPRs officially became a subject of negotiation. Its mandate was defined as the following:

> In order to reduce the distortions and impediments to international trade, and taking into account the need to promote effective and adequate protection of intellectual property rights and to ensure that measures and procedures to enforce intellectual property rights do not themselves become barriers to legitimate trade, the negotiations shall aim to clarify GATT provisions and elaborate as appropriate new rules and disciplines.
>
> Negotiations shall aim to develop a multilateral framework of principles, rules and disciplines dealing with international trade in counterfeit goods, taking into account work already undertaken in the GATT.
>
> These negotiations shall be without prejudice to other complementary initiatives that may be taken in the World Intellectual Property Organization and elsewhere to deal with these matters.
>
> (Ministerial Declaration Punta del Este, 20 September 1986)[13]

The creation of a new negotiation forum, embedded in the larger negotiations on multilateral trade and primarily driven by a handful of technology exporting countries under the leadership of the US, did not take place in a political vacuum. Indeed, developing countries also sought contemporary reform of the international economic system, in particular through the NIEO as a counter-movement to GATT-related multilateral trade reform. The NIEO intended to reflect a more just and equitable model of international economic governance that included social concerns into an international trade framework. One of its primary objectives was to establish a system for technology transfer, thus allowing greater access to technology developed in the North by countries in the South. This included attempts to limit the scope of IPRs in developing countries (UNCTAD-ICTSD 2005).

The formation of TRIPS

The final round of trade negotiations that ultimately led to the formation of the WTO was launched at a meeting of 74 nations in 1986 in Punta del Este, Uruguay. The Uruguay Round was mandated to reduce tariffs, eliminate certain non-tariff barriers and subsidies, move forward on agricultural negotiations and to expand the coverage of GATT principles to trade in services, investment and IPRs. The round came to a final Agreement, signed in April 1994 in Marrakech, Morocco, which included a resolution on IPRs,[14] also referred to as Agreement on Trade-Related Aspects of Intellectual Property Rights (TRIPS) (Mundo 1999).[15]

Until the very end of the Uruguay Round, discussions continued on whether IPRs were sufficiently trade-related to become part of what was to be the WTO. Many developing countries opposed the inclusion of a substantive agreement on IPRs that would be part of a package that included other trade issues, such as agriculture and services, often referred to as the 'single undertaking' (UNCTAD-ICTSD 2005).

Particular concern with respect to IPRs was related to those industrial sectors that had been traditionally exempt from patent protection prior to the formation of the WTO. For example, at the time of the commencement of the negotiations on the TRIPS Agreement, more than 50 countries did not grant patents to pharmaceutical products. In 1988, WIPO identified 37 countries that excluded pharmaceuticals from patenting, eight that excluded pharmaceutical processes and 12 that excluded chemical products. These included also the developed countries Finland, Greece, Iceland, Monaco, Portugal and Spain (Watal 2000). The Paris Convention had left members considerable freedom in the design of patent regimes. Members were free to determine their own patentability criteria and to exclude from patentability entire areas of technology including certain products or processes. They could also define their own grounds for the granting of a compulsory license (Roffe *et al.* 2005).[16] Consequently, the integration of IPRs into the GATT system not only provided for an enforcement mechanism, but also expanded the level and subject matter of protection.

The TRIPS Agreement grants its Members certain flexibilities with respect to their domestic IPRs policies and laws.[17] As identified by Roffe *et al.* (2007) and Correa (2006) these include the following:

- the freedom to define the criteria of patentability;
- the authorisation to exclude certain non-mandatory subject matter from patentability;[18]
- the choice of whether to protect 'new uses' of existing products or inventions;
- the possibility of establishing limited exceptions, under certain conditions, by national laws to the exclusive rights conferred by a patent, such as research, experimental use or early working (Bolar) exceptions;[19]
- the authorisation to control IPRs abuses through competition laws and policies;[20]
- the determination of the substantive grounds for the issuance of compulsory licences;[21]
- the determination of an IPRs exhaustion regime that best suits domestic conditions;[22]
- the definition of the nature of protection of pharmaceutical test data submitted to regulatory authorities for marketing approval purposes;[23]
- the authorisation to LDC Members to benefit from special transition periods for the implementation of the TRIPS minimum standards (1 January 2006 in general; 1 January 2016 in the area of pharmaceutical products) (Roffe *et al.* 2005, 2007; Correa 2006).[24]

From this perspective, the TRIPS Agreement signalled a significant change in the formulation of international IPRs policy. First, it provided for minimum standards in IPRs protection for all WTO Members in designated fields of technology. Second, it mandated Member States to allow for IPRs protection without discriminating against the place of invention. Third, it provided Member States with a certain, albeit limited, degree of flexibility to adapt national IPRs policy to domestic industrial needs (UNCTAD-ICTSD 2005: ch.25; Roffe *et al.* 2005).

The actual impact of TRIPS on developing countries is still widely debated. Proponents of TRIPS argued that stronger IPRs would lead to increased foreign direct investment and technology transfer, a benefit for technology-importing countries.[25] However, some economic scholars assert that the impact of patent protection varies depending on a country's level of development (Ostergard Jr 2007). Keith Maskus suggests that middle-income and large developing countries can benefit from IPRs, but not the very poorest. He also suggested that other factors influence FDI, such as market liberalisation, deregulation, competition regimes, technology development policies and low levels of corruption (Maskus 2004; Gervais 2007: ch. 1). Others suggest that technology transfer is sector specific and thus will not have the broad impact initially predicted (Mansfield 1994). Furthermore, a study by Correa pointed out that although the TRIPS Agreement entails provisions that are directed towards encouraging greater technology transfer,[26] the Agreement is unlikely to provide a stimulus for technology transfer on its own (Correa 2005). A World Bank study further suggested an expected net rent transfer of substantial magnitude from technology importers, such as developing countries, to technology exporters (World Bank 2002: ch. 5; UNCTAD-ICTSD 2003). During the last decade analytical literature has been developed on the economic and welfare impact of TRIPS on developing countries,[27] but more empirical work is needed to better understand the long-term consequences of the Agreement on poorer countries (Ostergard Jr 2007). The need for further research in the field has also been highlighted by the Report of the UK Commission on IPRs, that discusses in detail the role of IPRs for economic development (2002: ch. 2).

Countries' rationale for signing on to TRIPS

Given the scepticism expressed by developing countries with respect to integrating IPRs into the GATT system, one may wonder why they ultimately acceded to TRIPS. To answer this question one has to consider that TRIPS was just one of the three pillars of the WTO Agreements. The other two included provisions for sectors crucial to developing countries such as textiles and agriculture. This meant that developing countries were forced to make concessions on services and TRIPS. In exchange they gained preferences in traditional sectors by ridding themselves of the Multi Fibre Agreement (MFA) and thereby achieve better deals in agriculture and textiles (Bhagwati 1991; Stewart 1999; Ryan 1998). This tactical 'issue-linkage' connected negotiation items that were previously unrelated to one another through one overreaching negotiation, leaving countries with little choice but to sign on to the agreement.

This negotiation scenario was confirmed by trade negotiators of the time, stating that 'TRIPS was part of a package in which we got agriculture' (Drahos and Braithwaite 2002: 11). The desperate need of developing countries to gain better access to the agricultural and textile markets of developed countries was a strong incentive to agree to the Single Undertaking that included the agreement on IPRs. They believed that the net benefit arising out of the creation of the WTO and its promises in terms of market access would outweigh the poorly defined trade-offs resulting from TRIPS (UNCTAD-ICTSD 2003; Dutfield 2003). The fact that both the EC and the US withdrew from GATT 1947 after joining the WTO, thus terminating their MFN guarantee to countries that did not sign on to the WTO, further limited the choice for developing countries (Steinberg 2002).

Furthermore, with the notable exception of countries such as India, Argentina and Brazil, there was limited coordinated engagement among developing countries during the IPRs negotiations. From 1987 to 1990, 97 documents were submitted to move the negotiations forward in the TRIPS negotiation group. Of those, only 19 were authored by representatives from developing countries, even though some developing countries were vociferous to the very end in their objections to the integration of IPRs (Drahos and Braithwaite 2002). There are several reasons for this, including:

1   overall, negotiating teams from developing countries lack resources, especially relative to the resources and technical expertise available in developed countries;
2   the negotiations surrounding IPRs included concepts that were alien to many developing countries, and which were therefore ill-equipped to engage more pro-actively in the often very technical debate;
3   the absence of sufficient NGOs and academics to support developing country governments in IPRs-related negotiations. Indeed, it is likely that many countries were not aware of the potential impact of IPRs (Stewart 1999; Drahos and Braithwaite 2002; Matthews 2007).

Additional external factors provided further incentives for developing countries to join the WTO. Among them was the hope of preventing the continuation of unilateral trade measures and related trade barriers and sanctions (El-Said 2005; Drahos 2001a; Ryan 1998). Indeed, during the crucial negotiation years from 1989 to 1993, a range of developing countries were placed on the Special 301 'priority foreign country' and 'priority watch list'[28] by the USTR. The hope that a multilateral system would end these provocative and punitive actions was great, and influenced the outcome of the negotiations. In this sense the adoption of the TRIPS Agreement represented for many a victory of multilateralism through the hope of a new institutional trading system that would privilege international solutions and see an end to unilateral trade measures (Roffe *et al.* 2005).

Nevertheless, the final outcome of the TRIPS Agreement did not fully satisfy all constituencies in developed countries. Many industries that had lobbied substantially throughout the negotiation process,[29] most notably the pharmaceutical, film, sound recordings and software industries, did not achieve the level of protection to which they had originally aspired. The following are three examples of this disappointment during and after the final negotiations.

1   During the Dunkel Draft[30] negotiations of 1992, the US Pharmaceutical Manufacturers Association (PMA) considered the ten-year transition period remaining for LDCs to implement TRIPS unacceptable. Unease was also expressed about an extension of the five-year transition period for developing countries by an additional five years for product patents in areas of technology that were traditionally not subject to domestic patent protection. Similar concern was articulated by the PMA with respect to the absence of pipeline protection[31] in the draft (and eventually the final text) of the Agreement (Stewart 1999: 510; Dutfield 2003).
2   The Motion Picture Export Association of America and the Recording Industry Association of America were dissatisfied with the level of

protection provided by the Draft on copyright, particularly with respect to the lack of provisions on national treatment and loopholes regarding certain rental provisions (Stewart 1999 510).

3   A criticism was expressed with respect to Art. 39.3 of the Agreement which refers to the protection against unfair commercial use of undisclosed test or other data submitted for gaining marketing approval for pharmaceutical and agrochemical products including new chemical entities (NCEs). The US, in particular, hoped for more specific language with respect to the nature and length of protection and less specific language with respect to the definition of NCE serving as the basis for the protection of data and attempted to exclude the 'new' criterion from NCE in Art. 39.3 (Stewart 1999).[32]

The final outcome of TRIPS frustrated both the critics and proponents of incorporating IPRs into trade mechanisms. The critics, who were primarily from developing nations, believed that while TRIPS would result in a substantial wealth transfer from developing to developed countries, it would also protect them from further increases in IPRs protection via unilateral trade measures. IPRs proponents, on the other hand, saw in precisely those parallel unilateral fora an alternative means for further promoting the increase of international IP protection, in particular for those sectors and issues where multilateralism did not live up to their expectations. It is in this role that bilateral and regional trade agreements re-emerged as a key policy tool for the formulation of international IPR-policy.

The re-emergence of US plurilateral trade negotiations

Early developments

As was mentioned above, bilateral and plurilateral trade agreements are not a new phenomenon, but rather a common feature of US foreign policy dating back to the pre-World War period. Shortly after independence the US commenced negotiating economic treaties that were referred to as Friendship, Commerce and Navigation treaties (FCNs) that became the country's principal mechanism for securing economic commitments abroad. Some FCNs included IPRs provisions, such as the 1903 treaty between the US and China that included mechanisms for protecting some aspects of copyright, patents and trademarks between the two countries (Okediji 2004). Later, in the 1970s and 1980s, FCNs were replaced by Bilateral Investment Treaties (BITs), which were much broader in scope and also incorporated links to IPRs.[33]

Further integration of IPRs into trade-related bilateral/plurilateral agreements was made through preferential trade agreement schemes in the 1980s and 1990s, such as the CBI described above. The domestic developments in the US reinforced this trend, particularly with respect to the 1988 Omnibus Trade Act. However, even though unilateralism had proved to be particularly successful, the US still decided to pursue the multilateral strategy, that is the formation of the WTO (Helfer 2004). Bilateralism, although successful, was time and cost-intensive, while potentially of limited value in isolation. In regard to IPRs the immediate need was the establishment of a global system of minimum protection. Once IP standards were globally harmonised, bilateral engagements in specific cases could be used to reach the desired (higher) level of protection.

Although multilateral negotiations were never intended to stand alone, the US actively pursued and perfected the art of formulating strategic bilateral or regional trade policy while multilateral negotiations were ongoing. The principal reason for this coordinated approach was two-fold. First, the very slow evolution of multilateral negotiations on specific issues was the cause of much frustration within the US and thus alternative routes were pursued; second, advances on bilateral or plurilateral fronts with respect to stagnant trade issues could potentially influence their development at the multilateral level.

An example of the interdependence between the different fora occurred in 1982, when after the failure of launching a new round of multilateral trade negotiations, US policy shifted back towards bilateral negotiations (US House of Representatives 1989). In 1983 the US, under President Reagan, agreed to FTA negotiations with Israel, which had initially proposed negotiations in 1981. The agreement was finalised in 1985 and was the first ever truly reciprocal bilateral FTA negotiated by the US (USITC 2003).

The emergence of a new generation of US-FTAs

Just over a month after the US-Israel FTA was signed in 1985, Canadian Prime Minister Brian Mulroney formally requested the opening of negotiations between the US and Canada on a joint FTA. It was signed in 1988 and entered into force in 1989 (USITC 2003). The Canada-US FTA (CUFTA) was important in several ways for the future of US IPRs policy-making through FTAs. Even though IPRs were not included in the agreement, they were discussed informally and extensively between the negotiating parties. Canada, unlike its southern neighbour, had a much less stringent patent system at the time. This had provoked much concern within the US. In 1985 the Conservatives under Mulroney were elected into power and political pressure grew further. At what became known as 'Shamrock Summit' between Prime Minister Mulroney, a strong proponent of an FTA with the US, and President Reagan, one of the top items on the agenda was Canada's drug legislation. Eventually, and though there was no formal IPRs chapter in the agreement, an exchange was made. In return for the US signing CUFTA, Mulroney would introduce Bill C-22 that would lead to the amendment of the Canadian Patent Act to cover pharmaceutical products. This gesture took place November 1986 less than two years before CUFTA was signed (Clarkson 2002).

So while CUFTA did not officially include a reference to IPRs, it marked the beginning of a new generation of US-led FTAs that would link the signing of FTAs with pressure for an extensive overhaul of the domestic IPRs system of the respective trading partner. More importantly, CUFTA offered an important starting point for opening up trade negotiations with Mexico, which eventually resulted in the launch of NAFTA negotiations (Morici 1991; Hockin 2003).

In June 1990 the US and Mexican Heads of State announced their interest in negotiating a comprehensive FTA. This was followed by Canada expressing an interest in joining the negotiations, which were formally opened in 1991. The agreement was completed in 1992 in the midst of the Uruguay Round, but only approved by the US Congress and Senate in 1993, six months before the WTO was signed (USITC 2003).

The ongoing impact of NAFTA and the multilateral trade negotiations on one another was substantial (Hockin 2003; Cameron and Tomlin 2000).[34] The parameters of the trilateral negotiations were formed, in part, by the failure to reach multilateral consensus on agricultural subsidies and trade barriers. While Canada, Mexico and the US agreed to leave the more controversial aspects of the negotiations for the multilateral discussions, NAFTA often served as an alternative negotiation forum (Hockin 2003). The interrelationship between the two fora was so strong that the negotiation draft for the Uruguay Round served as a foundation for NAFTA. The US used the bilateral negotiations precisely to venture into negotiation areas where existing rules were deemed inadequate (Landau 2000). With respect to IPRs the NAFTA negotiators clearly benefited from the parallel negotiations of the Uruguay Round. The relevant section in the agreement was both comprehensive and complete, based primarily on US negotiation objectives. Apart from requiring the participating parties to apply the TRIPS standards, it enlarged the subject matter of protection to unprecedented forms and levels (USITC 2003). Particularly with respect to the protection of clinical test data, NAFTA exceeded TRIPS. The scope of protection in NAFTA, with its limited negotiating parties, reflects precisely those issues that were important to the US in the multilateral negotiations, but were not integrated into the final version of TRIPS.[35]

As discussed above, the IPRs provisions within NAFTA also had a significant influence on the course of the multilateral negotiations. The draft of the final text of the Uruguay Round was initiated by negotiators less than a month after NAFTA was approved by the US Congress. The success of finalising NAFTA and the final wording of the IPRs provisions at the regional level functioned as a strong incentive for Canada and Mexico to support the US in replicating the same agreements in the final outcome of the Uruguay Round. This, however, was only partially achieved.

Furthermore, including Mexico in NAFTA marked the first time that the US had engaged in a comprehensive trade deal with a developing country (Smith 1993). This resulted in substantial debate fuelled by the fear of job losses in Canada and the US due to cheap labour coming from Mexico. Further concerns related to the low environmental standards in Mexico. These and other factors caused significant opposition to NAFTA within the US (Lustig *et al.* 1992) and continue to fuel criticism of ongoing US engagement in FTAs with developing countries.

In bringing together countries of varying economic strength and in its ambition to tackle issues for which multilateral agreements were difficult, NAFTA outlined a course for the future, in which bilateralism and regionalism re-emerged as popular instruments for the formulation of foreign economic policy that included IPRs. While NAFTA negotiations were still ongoing, exploratory talks were being held between the US and Chile for the initiation of a similar trade agreement (Roffe 2004).

FTAs as a mean of US foreign IPRs policy-making

According to the WTO website on regional trade agreements, the number of enforced agreements surpassed 270 in February 2010, with nearly another 200 at the notification stage.[36] The majority of regional trade agreements currently active were negotiated post-1995. However, not all of these agreements are considered comprehensive FTAs as many of them do not include, for example, chapters on IPRs.[37] However, most of the new generation of comprehensive FTAs that were negotiated by the US, including the more recent FTAs with Colombia and Peru, include IPRs. An overview of all the US negotiated FTAs since CUFTA is given in Appendix I of this book.

The structure of IPRs chapters in recent US-FTAs

While each US FTA is different, the IPRs chapter tends to be similarly structured. As described by Roffe *et al.* (2007) three principal characteristics can be found:

a   Similar to the TRIPS agreement, the IPRs chapters in FTAs are based on a minimum standard system of IPRs. Thus, Member States can agree to provisions for protection that are higher than the FTA level of protection, but not lower.
b   FTAs often call for the ratification of certain WIPO treaties, such as UPOV 1991[38] or the WIPO Performances and Phonograms Treaty.[39]
c   FTAs tend to expand the substantive nature and scope of IPRs protection found in TRIPS, referred to as TRIPS-plus provisions. One example of this is the provision of exclusive rights in pharmaceutical test data submitted to regulatory authorities in the course of marketing approval procedures.

FTAs and the MFN principle

IPRs chapters of FTAs are based on the MFN principle of the GATT as a result of Art. 4 of the TRIPS Agreement:

> With regard to the protection of intellectual property, any advantage, favour, privilege or immunity granted by a Member to the nationals of

any other country shall be accorded immediately and unconditionally to the nationals of all other Members.

The application of this principle in the TRIPS Agreement was an innovation in the multilateral context, it has no precedent therefore, and knowledge of its long-term effects is limited (UNCTAD-ICTSD 2005).

The inclusion in the TRIPS Agreement of a MFN clause without exception for future regional and bilateral agreements thereby generates an expansive effect of new IP commitments in FTAs. It obliges parties to FTAs to extend any increased level of IPRs protection that are contained in regional or bilateral agreements to all WTO Member States without receiving any compensation. This in turn substantially raises the importance of bilateral fora for international IPRs policy-making (Roffe *et al*. 2007).

Forum shifting and the coordination challenge[40]

Forum shifting as a useful tool of IPRs policy-making

Apart from the political and economic interests of both developed and developing countries, the nature of FTAs in relation to IPRs raises structural concerns, which demand further attention. Identifying and changing fora in order to advance a political interest has been referred to as 'forum shifting',[41] 'regime shifting'[42] or 'forum management'.[43] It allows actors to move the negotiations from one forum to another, based on where political movement is most feasible and where particular norms and principles might be more easily elaborated (Steinberg 2002). The method has been proven to be very effective in international IPRs policy-making (Helfer 2004; Okediji 2004; Abdel Latif 2005; Sell 2005; Drahos 2004; Dutfield 2006; Dutfield and Suthersanen 2008: ch. 2). An example of this is the way that developed countries, led by the US, have skilfully moved global IPRs policy-making from WIPO to the GATT on the grounds that WIPO was not properly equipped to enforce global IPRs standards.

The shift from multilateralism back to plurilateral negotiations, signals another example of forum shifting. In addition to power shifts within the multilateral level, however, this shift raises some additional concerns. By definition, bilateral and regional agreements reduce the number of negotiating parties at the table. This in turn prevents the development of potential alliances among developing countries during the negotiations. Some authors have observed that in cases of negotiations among very disparate partners, asymmetric concessions typically work in the favour of the larger parties (Whalley and Hamilton 1996; Abbott 2003). Often it is smaller economies that tend to approach larger ones in this process. Usually in this situation, larger countries make few concessions, and smaller countries are likely to make many. The larger country, in exchange, provides more stable and continued market access for the smaller economy. Overall this results in the larger countries enjoying higher negotiating leverage in comparison to the smaller economies, often requiring a certain premium or other specific guarantee that is of interest to the larger negotiating party. Usually, smaller economies are willing to pay this price. While these power disparities, mentioned in the previous chapter, and further noted in the case studies, are not the sole drivers of negotiation process and outcome, they certainly constitute a substantial disadvantage for smaller countries as they decide to 'shift forum' from multilateral to bilateral settings.

An increasingly complex institutional environment

Complexities arising from the proliferation of fora for negotiations on IPRs have led to further structural challenges in IPRs policy-making. One of them relates to the difficulty to achieve policy coherence among the different fora. Such concerns are found at both the national and international level. The last 10 years have witnessed the expansion of available fora and processes for the creation of IPRs policy. Examples include not only the WTO, WIPO and the bilateral and regional agreements discussed above, but also other international bodies, such as the Convention on Biological Diversity (CBD), the UN Economic, Scientific and Cultural Organization (UNESCO), the Food and Agriculture Organization (FAO), the World Health Organization (WHO) and, more recently, Interpol (IP Watch 2005). This diversity of fora demands substantial coordination skills on the part of under-resourced developing countries in order to maintain IPRs policy-coherence. Frequently, small countries find themselves overburdened in navigating the different arenas for IPRs policy discussion. Frequently negotiators from the same country who are responsible for different fora fail to communicate with each other to ensure that the positions they represent in one forum do not come into conflict with their positions in another (Abdel Latif 2005; Roffe et al. 2007).

This international problem is compounded by difficulties in national coordination. As was mentioned in the previous chapter, different ministries often maintain jurisdiction over different aspects of international diplomacy. In IP this is also the case given the many different intergovernmental fora where IPRs are being negotiated. While it is often the Ministry of Health that coordinates the country's activities within the WHO, it is the Ministry of Commerce or Foreign Affairs that governs engagement with the WTO and within bilateral or regional agreements, and the Ministry of Science and technology or national IPRs offices that determine national policy for WIPO. Few developing countries, with the notable exception of India and Brazil, have established units of policy coherence that attempt to streamline national policy-making in this respect (Abdel Latif 2005; Roffe *et al.* 2007). While these challenges are not unique to developing countries, as a rule developed countries have systems in place that ensure the careful coordination of activities with respect to the ratification and implementation of new laws. Frederick Abbott in this regard emphasises:

Differences in the capacity of the United States and many developing countries to create and manage legal IP infrastructure may lead to a disparity in the way FTA rules are implemented. The United States already has in place a sophisticated system of checks and balances to offset the general intellectual property and regulatory standards which are reflected in the FTAs. Historically, the internal law of the United States has reflected a careful balance between the interests of intellectual property rights holders and the general public. While over the past two decades the balance may have shifted in favour of IPRs holders, nonetheless, U.S. law continues to reflect a balance.

Developing countries may not have such checks and balances in place and may be limited in the technical capacity to implement such checks and balances effectively. Unless developing countries are effectively enabled to legislate appropriate checks and balances, they may find themselves with substantially stricter intellectual property systems than the United States.

(Abbott 2006: 1).

Conclusion

This chapter has outlined how IPRs have successfully been integrated into multilateral, regional and bilateral trade fora even though originally the free trade movement in the 19th century was opposed to the concept of IPRs. Since then the two movements have become increasingly integrated until a multilateral trade negotiation framework became the key platform to create and enforce an international minimum standard in all fields of IP. Bilateralism, particularly since the 1980s, has carried out a complementary function and has come to serve as a means for US foreign economic policy to put forward provisions which either have failed to be integrated in intellectual property frameworks on the multilateral level or have emerged since the TRIPS negotiations have been finalised. The combination of multi-fora IPRs policymaking, bearing in mind the MFN principle as put forward in Art. 4 of TRIPS, has led to new forms and increased levels of IPRs protection, with potentially large negative implications for developing countries.

One of the fields where the welfare effects of TRIPS-plus provisions in developing countries are likely to have an immediate impact is that of public health. The next chapter will look at this in detail.

3 Negotiating IPRs

A defensive position of developing countries and the new challenges posed by FTAs

Introduction

The previous chapter described the introduction of IPRs into international trade negotiations. As was pointed out, developing countries were resistant to the integration of IPRs into the international trading system. Since then countries that have negotiated bilateral trade agreements with the US, the EU and other industrialised countries have been confronted with the integration of further IPRs into these agreements. These standards go beyond the level of protection provided by TRIPS. Much of the scepticism that was expressed at the time of the TRIPS negotiations is relevant today in light of the additional scope and forms of IPRs that are put forward in bilateral and regional FTAs.

However, some differences between IPRs-related FTA negotiations today and the TRIPS negotiations in the past can be found. First, today's awareness of the potential implications of increased IPRs protection is much higher, particularly with respect to their likely impact on drug prices and subsequently public health. Second, health authorities are more aware of this impact and are eager to be integrated in IPRs negotiations. Third, these public health concerns have been taken up by civil society networks that have raised their political stake.

This chapter will explain the overall defensive negotiation position of developing country governments that engage in FTA negotiations with the US. It outlines why developing countries had traditionally very little to gain by harmonising IPRs standards and how this situation has been exacerbated through FTAs and the new levels of protection that are brought with them. Particular emphasis will be placed on explaining the resistance of public health authorities and advocates[1] in developing countries to a range of specific patent provisions that are included in the traditional US FTA IPRs negotiation template.

The North-South divide of international IPRs negotiations

In chapter 2 it was explained how most developing countries were hesitant to integrate IPRs into the international trading regime, above all because many of them were, and still are, technology net importing countries. That does not mean to say that there was not then, and there is not now, any innovative capacity in developing countries. However, the IPRs standards integrated in trade-related agreements and other negotiation fora were primarily tailored towards the needs of the technology intensive industries in developed countries (Dutfield 2008). Creativity that can be found in the vast majority of developing countries, often in the form of traditional practices developed and passed on over many generations, whether in agricultural or medicinal practices or incremental innovation through manufacturing or service industries has, at best, only marginally benefited from the format of IPRs that is being negotiated in international fora.

Naturally, the division between technology importing and exporting countries is blurry. Large developing countries, such as India, South Africa and Brazil are increasingly investing into Research and Development (R&D) of industries that benefit from IP protection, which also leads to increasing domestic interest in IPRs.[2] Nevertheless, as we will see in the next section, these activities are still relatively small and particular to specific industries in comparison to the technology-intensive resources in the North that cross a range of industrial sectors. In this sense the adoption of increased IP protection is likely to be of only little benefit to the majority of developing countries. It brings with it not only higher prices for products that would otherwise be sold as generic but also constitute a challenge to domestic manufacturing industries that have emerged in the absence of IP legislation.

Global distribution of IPRs

Looking at the statistics on the international distribution of patents, the vast majority of patent filings stem from inventors in developed countries registered in their patent offices. The OECD publishes annually a set of statistics on triadic patent families[3] that allows a comparison of the distribution of patents across the globe.

Figure 3.1 indicates that the distribution of patents is highly skewed. While we can see some larger developing countries such as Korea contributing to the number of global triadic patent families, it is mainly the EU, Japan and the US that dominate global patenting. Statistics reflecting the share of individual countries in the overall number of PCT patents, confirms this trend (see Fig. 3.2).

The precise impact of this highly skewed distribution of patent filing on developing countries is difficult to measure. An obvious one is the sheer increase in revenue flows in the form of cross-border licensing fees from license holder to licensee.

According to the World Bank Development Indicators (2005) the following broad data on revenue flows based on royalty payments can be observed. In 2003 low and middle-income countries paid a total of US$12.5 billion in royalties for licences from abroad while they only received US$1.6 billion

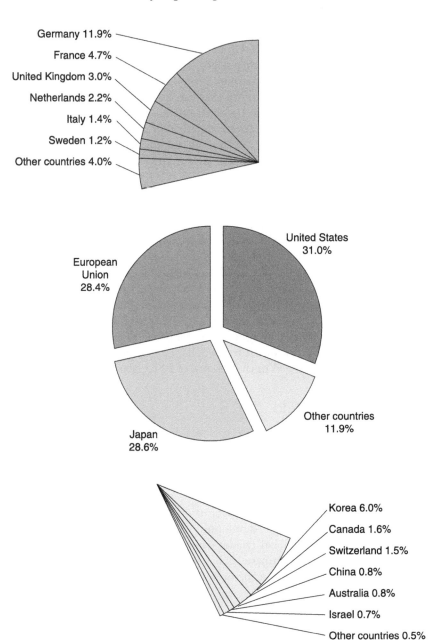

Figure 3.1 Share of countries in total triadic patent families (2005).
Source: OECD 2007: 11.

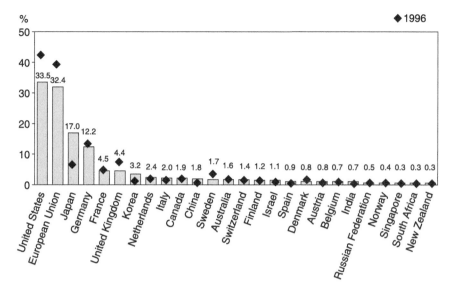

Figure 3.2 Share of countries in patent filed under the PCT procedure.
Source: OECD 2007: 16.

in licensing fees. US$111 million of that amount went to low-income countries, which in turn spent US$1.47 billion on royalties in the same year. In high-income countries, on the other hand, the discrepancy between receipt and payment of licensing fees is much more balanced. In 2003 the group as a whole received US$90 billion in licensing fees from abroad and spent a total of US$87 billion on paying royalties. This balance between payment and receipt at least on a macro-level reflects the balance that the IPRs system is designed to achieve, that is, to provide incentives to R&D and access to knowledge and inventions (World Bank 2005).

More recent data from individual countries suggests that in developing countries the gap between royalty payment and income remains large, even among large developing countries. India received approximately US$147.82 million in royalty revenues in 2008 but spent US$1.58 billion. Brazil spent about US$2.7 billion and received about US$465.44 million. Even China spent US$10.32 billion and raised only US$570.54 million. On the other hand, in key exporting countries these figures continued to be more balanced. Japan received US$25.7 billion and paid about US$18.31 billion in licensing fees, whereas Germany received about US$8.8 billion and paid approximately US$11.96 billion. The one remarkable exception to this is the US where royalty payments received were approximately US$91.1 billion but its expenditure was only US$26.61 billion (World Bank 2009).

The uneven distribution of IPRs naturally has a range of other effects. These include, for example, the impact of IPRs on technology transfer or the capacity to build stronger innovative capacity in developing countries.[4] The aspect that is critical for this study, however, is the role of IPRs in raising the prices of technology-intensive consumer goods in developing countries, and thus limiting respective access. Where the goods in question are of substantial welfare enhancing value, above all in the field of public health, this has lead to substantial concern.[5]

The debate between patent protection and the protection of public health

Historically, the relationship between patents and medicines has been controversial. The protection of medicines through patents and the use of compulsory licensing as a remedy to deal with possible abuses in the exercise of exclusive rights have been at the centre of the evolution of the national and international patent legal regimes. As mentioned in chapter 2, the Paris Convention of 1883 left countries with the freedom to decide which industrial sectors were appropriate for the granting of exclusive production and marketing rights. As a result, in many countries pharmaceuticals were excluded from patentability. The adoption of the TRIPS Agreement significantly transformed this picture. It introduced the concept of non-discrimination in all fields of technology for patent applications but also incorporated a set of procedural rules for the issuance of compulsory licenses (Roffe *et al.* 2005).

Some of the IPRs/public health discussion took place before the TRIPS Agreement was finalised, but it was during its negotiations and in its implementation phases that the intensity of the debate increased. This was also stepped up in light of the rising HIV/AIDS pandemic (CIPR 2002). During the debate it was acknowledged that patent protection was essential as an incentive for further investment in R&D. The question was how to balance this incentive with the desperate need for access to essential medicines in developing countries that also had to comply with TRIPS.

According to the WHO, in 2006 the prices of first-line antiretroviral drugs (ARV) were driven down by a range of initiatives from approximately US$10,000 per patient per year, to between US$160 and 500 (WHO 2006). According to MSF (see figure 3.3) in 2008 the prices were down to US$87. This was achieved either as a result of the expiry of patents, drug production in countries such as India where pharmaceutical product patents did not apply until 2005, discounted offers from the research-based industries or threats of compulsory licences and subsequent price negotiations, such as in the case of Brazil.

As of 1 January 2005 all countries apart from LDCs were obliged by TRIPS to introduce patents on pharmaceuticals which resulted in the loss of substantial supply chains of affordable ARVs, above all from India. This is particularly poignant as with the introduction of patented second-line ARVs, essential for patients that have grown immune to first-line ARVs, prices

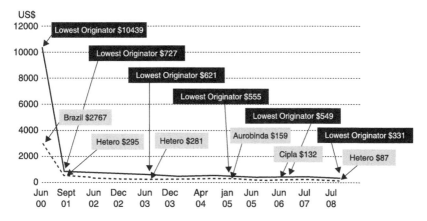

Figure 3.3 Prices of first-line ARVs, 2000–08.

Source: MSF, *Untangling the Web of Antiretroviral Price Reductions* (11th edn 2008).

increased from between 6 to 12 times. Given the lack of freely available generic competition due to the new legal framework, the most important source of pressure to reduce prices was absent, which made price reductions similar to those in first-line ARVs unlikely (WHO 2006).

The Doha Declaration recognised the complicated relationship between IPRs and public health. Therefore, it clarified that:

> . . . the Agreement can and should be interpreted and implemented in a manner supportive of WTO Members' right to protect public health and, in particular, to promote access to medicines for all.

As a result, the Declaration encouraged members to make use of measures, such as compulsory licensing and parallel import which can limit the monopoly rights granted by IPRs, in the interest of public health (Gervais 2003: 46–7).

The outstanding issue in the Doha Declaration of how countries with insufficient manufacturing capacity would be able to make use of compulsory licensing was temporarily overcome by the compromise reached on 30 August 2003 in the form of an interim waiver to the TRIPS Agreement. The waiver facilitates under certain circumstances the production and export of generic versions even if the product is still under patent protection (Gervais 2003: 48–9).[6] In December 2005 Member States agreed to integrate this decision into the TRIPS Agreement on a permanent basis. This decision will come into force when two-thirds of the Member States have ratified this amendment (WHO 2006). The complexity of the process of applying for a compulsory licence is illustrated by the case of Rwanda, the only country so far to make use of the waiver. Rwanda registered its intent to import 260,000 packs of the

HIV/AIDS drug TriAvir from the Canadian generic industry Apotex with the WTO in July 2007 (IP Watch 2007). Canada equally notified the WTO of its intent to export a generic version of TriAvir to Rwanda in October that year. The entire process from the decision to issue a compulsory licence to its actual implementation in both countries took more than four years (Bridges Weekly 2007a).

Nevertheless, the Doha Declaration and the 30 August Mechanism meant a major success for the public health community, not least because they were an acknowledgement that the protection of public health should not be put at risk through the setting of IPRs standards at an international level. While solutions to the IPRs/public health conflict were being pursued at the multilateral level, however, bilateralism emerged as an increasingly important means of introducing new IPRs standards into a range of US-FTA[7] partner countries. As is shown below, these FTAs did not reflect the ongoing parallel multilateral developments, such as the Doha Declaration, but instead put forward even higher levels and newer forms of IPRs protection, referred to as TRIPS-plus provisions.

The following section will outline the most important of these changes and their potential impact on developing countries from a public health perspective. Before going into detail on a selected group of TRIPS-plus provisions and why health authorities in developing countries are against them, the section will outline the offensive negotiation interests of the pharmaceutical industry, one of the strongest proponents of the provisions.

Overview of the TRIPS-plus provisions in US-FTAs since NAFTA

An industry in crisis and a push for increased levels of IPRs protection

IPRs provisions, as they are found in US FTAs since NAFTA, increase the level of protection beyond the standards put forward in TRIPS. The US and other technology-exporting countries have a clear overall interest in seeking further protection. Another aspect, particularly related to the pharmaceutical industry, explains a further motivation for seeking an extension of scope and length of protection.[8]

Despite the robust financial image of the pharmaceutical industry, in the mid-1990s the industry was finding it difficult to introduce truly innovative products. The dramatic increase in investment into R&D did not produce a proportionate increase in new drugs or, more precisely, NCEs. Rather, the opposite occurred and the number of new drugs approved for market use declined from 53 NCEs during 1996 to about 20 NCEs in 2000 (IMS 2003). Similarly, as suggested by a survey in *The Economist* (2005), while global pharmaceutical R&D almost doubled in the previous decade (from about US$30 billion in 1993 to almost US$60 billion in 2005), the number of NCE-based drugs had shrunk by more than 35 per cent, from about 40 NCEs in the 1990s to about 20–25 NCEs in the early years of the new millennium (von Braun and Pugatch 2005).

At the same time, research-based pharmaceutical companies had started appropriating greater resources into the launch of improved versions of original drugs, so-called 'me-too' drugs. This made sense as with relatively little investment into R&D and little 'scientific' risks, revenue streams of patent monopolies could potentially be extended. According to Angell (2004), of the 415 new drugs approved from 1998 to 2002, 133 were NCEs while the others were variations of older drugs. Additionally, of the 133 NCEs, 58 were actually priority review drugs.[9] This made a total of 12 new innovative drugs per year-only 14 per cent of the actual products on the market. In addition, the rate of new products entering the market had actually been declining, for example, in 2000 and 2001 only seven innovative drugs entered the market (Angell 2004). This pattern of successive patents on the same basic molecule, known as 'ever-greening', serves to maintain monopoly rights beyond the time frame of protection for the original chemical entity and is a practice that is becoming increasingly common. Given the industry's dependence on blockbuster drugs (those that have a potential market of more than US$1 billion a year) and bearing in mind the increasing difficulty of bringing innovative drugs into the market there was an incentive to maintain monopoly rights as long as possible. It was thus no surprise that the pharmaceutical industry claimed that without strong IPRs protection, including the protection of 'me-too' drugs, no money would flow into new R&D.[10] While few people doubt that IPRs protection is needed for safeguarding future research, it should not be oversimplified by stating that without increasing protection the 'goose that lays the golden eggs' will be killed, as is often stated by industry representatives (Abbott 2005a; Von Braun and Pugatch 2005).

As will be shown in chapters 6 and 7, the US government has traditionally been a strong ally of the industry's push for increasing protection of its products at home and abroad. It has strongly defended the industry's push to 'export' US standards of IPRs protection into different negotiation fora, including processes of patent law standardisation, harmonisation and enforcement in multilateral and bilateral fora.

Key issues and salient TRIPS-plus provisions for developing countries

While this section will highlight the most salient TRIPS-plus provisions[11] as they relate to public health in developing countries, it should be noted that the very length and complexity of the IP chapters of US-FTAs is remarkable. Given that they build on the already existing framework of the TRIPS Agreement, the fact that they are equal and longer in length demonstrates the sheer quantity of changes put forward.

Measuring the impact of TRIPS-plus provisions is a complicated task. As economists are still in disagreement over the precise impact of the TRIPS Agreement on developing countries, understanding the specific impact of TRIPS-plus provisions further complicates such assessments bearing in mind the relative youth of TRIPS-plus provisions. As pointed out in a literature survey by Keith Maskus, one thing most economists agree on is that TRIPS-plus provisions further delay the entry of generic competition into the domestic market, which will keep prices high and medicines out of reach of the poor (Maskus 2006).

The WHO jointly with PAHO produced a modelling scenario that helped to calculate the expected cost implications for drug expenditure due to TRIPS-plus provisions. It was developed by Joan Rovira (2005), has been applied in different scenarios, including Colombia (2005, 2006, 2009)[12] and Peru (2009),[13] Guatemala (2005), Costa Rica (2005, 2008), Bolivia (2006), Dominican Republic (2008) and Thailand (2010)[14] and has been further developed through the support of the World Bank Institute and ICTSD.[15] Other country studies include Peru (INDECOPI, 2005 and 2006) and Australia (Drahos *et al*. 2004).

Next to higher drug prices, other secondary effects are likely to occur from TRIPS-plus provisions. These include issues of rent transfers from one ministry to the other, deadweight losses due to higher drug prices, enforcement costs, incentives to prescribe unnecessary medicines due to higher prices and even corruption effects (Baker 2006). Last, but not least, the introduction of TRIPS-plus provisions in countries that possess pharmaceutical manufacturing capacity are expected to have considerable effect on the domestic generic industry in developing countries (Fink and Reichenmiller 2005). Many of these industries are thus among the strongest opponents of the FTAs.

Defining novelty: protection of chemical entities/new use patents

Article 27.1 of the TRIPS Agreement defines that patents:

> . . . shall be available for any inventions, whether products or processes, in all fields of technology, provided that they are new, involve an inventive step and are capable of industrial application.

The Agreement allows Member States to define the patentability criteria according to national policy objectives.

A critical question in relation to pharmaceutical (and other) products relates to whether a new medicinal application of existing medicines meets the patentability criteria and justifies the grant of a new patent. This process, referred to as 'new' or 'second (medicinal) use' or 'application' patents (or new patents for chemical entities that have been previously protected for other reasons) would apply to chemical entities which have been patented previously, but are discovered to have some additional benefit through a previously unclaimed application. Azidothymidine (AZT), for example, was originally patented as a cancer drug and then re-patented as an ARV (Weissman 2006). The possibility of protecting these new uses differs in different national jurisdictions.[16]

Treatment under TRIPS

'New' or 'second' use (or advantage or improvement) patents are not required under TRIPS. Subsequently, Member States are free through their interpretation of novelty and the inventive step criteria to decide on whether to grant such patents or not.

Treatment under US law

According to 35 U.S.C §101:

> Whoever invents or discovers any new and useful process, machine, manufacture, or composition of matter, *or any new and useful improvement thereof*, may obtain a patent therefore, subject to the conditions and requirements of this title.

Improvements to already patentable subject matter are themselves patentable provided that the usual criteria for patentability are satisfied (Dutfield and Suthersanen 2008: ch. 5). According to the UNCTAD-ICTSD Resources Book:

> ... the patenting of use inventions, where admitted, depends on whether the purpose of the use is novel and non-obvious. Method inventions may be judged independently of the purpose. Even if intended for a novel purpose, the key consideration in determining the patentability of a method invention is whether it could be anticipated by other methods. In the United States, patents on uses are confined to a particular 'method-of-use', which does not encompass protection of the product as such.
>
> (UNCTAD-ICTSD 2005: 356)

Furthermore, as stated by Merges and Duffy:

> Under § 100 (b), new use patents are *process* patents. [. . .] the discoverer of a new use or a new property cannot obtain a patent on the old substances, only on the use. The *structure* of the composition being previously known, the new use cannot justify a patent on the composition itself. [. . .] Yet, even though discoverers of new uses can obtain process patents, they face two practical problems: (1) Where a patent on the composition remains in force, it will block the practice of the new use unless a license can be

obtained from the holder of the composition patent. (2) The process patent may be difficult to enforce.

(Merges and Duffy 2002: 392–3)[17]

TRIPS-*plus condition*

Some US-FTAs require that the signatory country provide patent protection for new uses. Not specified is whether these include only the 'new use' or whether they extend to the actual product.[18] 'New uses' are also protected through data exclusivity provisions, such as in the case of the US-FTA with Jordan, that provides for three years of data protection for 'new uses' of pharmaceutical products.[19]

Potential consequences

The application of 'second' or 'new use' patents is likely to extend the monopoly of a patented product. Such 'ever-greening' can be abused for anti-competitive practices (Musungu and Oh 2006: 66). The discovery of additional use is likely to be based on less investment into additional R&D and yet may allow for similar patent protection. This creates an incentive for companies to delay the announcement of the discovery of a potential second use of a product until the very end of a patent period, in order to prolong the overall monopoly as long as possible. Finally, some products have many uses, such as Aspirin, which is more than 100 years old and surprises with new medicinal applications (Childs 1999; Dutfield and Suthersanen 2008: ch. 5). While they may not have been patented, the mere fact that new applications are not necessarily based on new sizeable investment into the product raises questions about the justification of further protection. Given the role new use protection may play in delaying the entry of domestic or foreign competition, developing countries have strongly argued against their inclusion in FTAs.

Utility *vs* industrial application

Regarding Art. 27.1 of TRIPS, the importance of a balanced definition of 'industrial application' for the success of a country's industrial policy has been widely discussed among innovation scholars (CIPR 2002: ch. 6). As Rebecca Eisenberg writes, the industrial application criteria (or utility requirement in the US) should be seen as 'a timing device, helping to identify when an invention is ripe for patent protection' (as quoted in FTC 2003: 199).

Treatment under TRIPS

According to UNCTAD-ICTSD, 'industrial application' can be interpreted in both a narrow or broad sense, either requiring a product to be usable by industry or simply to provide a basic degree of utility that does not require specification. Accordingly:

> Members considerably differ in their treatment of industrial applicability. Under U.S. law, the concept applied is 'utility'. Hence, certain developments that do not lead to an industrial product may be patented in the USA: an invention only needs to be operable and capable of satisfying some function of benefit to humanity (i.e. be useful). This concept is broader than the industrial applicability required in Europe and other countries. The U.S. rule permits the patentability of purely experimental inventions that cannot be made or used in an industry, or that do not produce a so-called technical effect, as illustrated by the large number of patents granted in the United States on methods of doing business, and by the patenting of research tools, such as expression sequence tags (ESTs) and single nucleotide polymorphisms (SNPs).
>
> (UNCTAD-ICTSD 2005: 361)[20]

Treatment under US law

35 U.S.C. §101 also sets the basis for usefulness/utility:

> Whoever invents or discovers any new and *useful process*, machine, manufacture, or composition of matter, or any new and *useful improvement* thereof, may obtain a patent therefor, subject to the conditions and requirements of this title.
>
> [emphasis added]

While the vast majority of patent applications at the USPTO do not encounter problems in satisfying the utility requirements, there have been controversies, especially in the protection of research tools. Given the brevity of the only elaboration on the usefulness requirement in US patent law,[21] the matter has been left to interpretation by the courts (Merges and Duffy 2002: 211; Chisum *et al.* 2004: 735). As Chisum *et al.* note, satisfying the utility requirement does not tend to be an obstacle for mechanical or electrical inventions, but rather in the biological or chemical fields. Unlike in the mechanical fields, it is difficult to demonstrate utility through drawings or diagrams. More importantly, chemical and biological inventions are often not 'end results' as such but rather contain a factor of evolving utility. One invention often builds on another. While some may be useful for basic research others may have more specific and applied utility with immediate results (2004: 735–6).

Deciding on utility in some technological fields where the boundaries between basic and applied research has become increasingly blurred, the USPTO in 2001 published the Utility Examination Guidelines.[22] The specific aim of the guidelines is to guide patent examiners as to whether patent applications satisfy the utility criteria. It is emphasised that a patent has to be more than just 'useful' but also have a *well established utility*. In addition, the claim has to disclose a *specific and substantive purpose* that should be *credible*. While these guidelines do not have the power to set the law, the Federal Circuit may use them to clarify the state of the law.[23] The guidelines emphasise that very basic utilities, such as basic research tools do not satisfy the utility requirement if they are not specific in their purpose or substantial enough. Nevertheless, if a certain research tool does have specific application and can demonstrate well-established utility then it can be subject to patent protection independent of whether it has industrial application. Whether it will be is a question of whether the research is substantial enough and whether it is presented with an appropriate level of experimental evidence (Thambisetty 2008; Chisum *et al.* 2004: 751–3).[24]

TRIPS-plus condition

US-FTAs tend to deny other signatory parties the flexibility to define which level of 'industrial application' they chose as a patentability criterion. The other parties are obliged to adopt the US definition of the 'industrial application', that is, having to either prove 'utility' or be 'useful'.[25]

Potential consequences

The impact of this may be considerable, as inventions can be patented at much earlier stages in the development process, which could influence the strengthening of domestic R&D capacity.[26] This may allow for the protection of health-related research tools, unless negotiating parties develop specific research exceptions that would prevent such protection. While in the FTAs it does not explicitly state that parties are not allowed to include such exceptions, the 'utility' criteria could be used to challenge them in the FTA internal dispute settlement body.

Furthermore, as the UK Commission on IPRs points out, given the less competitive technological base in many developing countries, a higher standard of patentability criteria (and narrower patent scope) would be more appropriate, as it facilitates the emergence of domestic (often incremental) technologies. It encourages the investment of domestic resources into R&D and in general may lead to a faster learning process in comparison to one that blocks follow on innovation (CIPR 2002: ch. 6). In this sense the Commission recommends:

> [t]he underlying principle should be to aim for strict standards of patentability and narrow scope of allowed claims, with the objective of:
>
> a   limiting the scope of subject matter that can be patented
> b   applying standards such that only patents which meet strict requirements for patentability are granted and that the breadth of each patent is commensurate with the inventive contribution and the disclosure made

    c   facilitating competition by restricting the ability of the paten-
         tees to prohibit others from building on or designing around
         patented inventions
    d   providing extensive safeguards to ensure that patent rights are
         not exploited inappropriately (p.21).

To allow WTO Member States to adapt patentability criteria to their respective industrial policies, the TRIPS Agreement did not define them. Thus, the
export of the US interpretation of the industrial applicability requirement
through FTAs denies the other signatory parties this important flexibility.

Patent term extension

Patent term extensions are provisions that require the extension of the patent
term if the *de facto* monopoly of the patent holders is reduced as a result of
delays caused by domestic patent or other regulatory authorities.

Treatment under TRIPS

The TRIPS Agreement does not require the extension beyond the 20-year
period that is granted in cases of delay for the granting of a patent, or the
provision of marketing authority.

Treatment under US law

The US Patent Act (35 U.S.C. § 154) allows for a patent term extension due
to delays of the USPTO, defined as anything beyond three years after filing
the patent. However, there are exceptions under which the delay may not be
compensated, for example if the patent is under appeal or subject to national
security (Abbott 2006).

    35 U.S.C. §156 provides for patent term extension with respect to delays
in the granting of marketing approval of drugs by the FDA. It is a complex
provision that is subjected to a large amount of conditions and exceptions.
The process is split into two phases, parts of which may be compensated
(up to five years). Furthermore, the total effective patent term may not exceed
14 years after the patent has been approved, that is, 20 years minus the
different regulatory approval phases plus any granted compensation (Chisum
et al. 2004: 1264–79; Abbott 2006).

TRIPS-plus condition

Patent term extension clauses can be found in most of the new generation of
US-FTAs due to 'unreasonable delays' in the patent granting process.[27] However,
the chapters differ in the definition of unreasonable delay, which is measured
from the date of filing (three to five years) and date of request for the examination

of the application (two to four years). In some cases, countries even have to compensate a delay caused by an examination delay in another country.[28] Furthermore, some FTAs also oblige parties to provide for patent extension in cases in which the marketing approval, such as the one for pharmaceutical products, has been delayed.[29] Similarly, this can also be based on the marketing approval delay in other countries[30] (Weissman 2006; Roffe *et al.* 2005; Abbott 2006).

Potential consequences

Similar to other TRIPS-plus provisions, patent term extensions are likely to delay the entry of generic competition in the market of a country. Given the administrative burden of patent filing in countries with small and under-resourced patent offices the delay in patent examination or marketing approval is not rare (Correa 2006). Even at the USPTO it takes an average of 2 to 3 years to grant a patent and more than four years in the biotechnological field (Rogan 2002; Fernandez 2003). Given the substantial price difference between patented and generic drugs this could lead to a severe delay in accessing affordable drugs. Most affected will be the consumers that pay out of pocket for medicines or the national health authorities that have to pay the monopoly prices for a longer period out of their limited budgets. While neither of the two groups will have any influence in speeding up the patent filing process, they bear the consequences of the delays caused by an often under-resourced patent administration (Weissman 2006; Correa 2006).

Data exclusivity

Data exclusivity is perhaps the most politically sensitive example of the changing international topography of IPRs through US-FTAs, and relates particularly to the pharmaceutical and agrochemical market. With respect to pharmaceuticals, it is aimed at protecting and safeguarding the information contained in data submitted by pharmaceutical companies to regulatory authorities for the purpose of obtaining marketing approval.[31] Proponents suggest that data exclusivity is a form of protection of trade secrets[32] and, as such, should be treated separately from patents. They also contend that, in theory, data exclusivity constitutes weaker market restriction than patents on the same product as it does not legally prevent other companies from generating their own registration data. However, in practice, the financial resources and extended time required for gathering and generating pharmaceutical registration data for a new drug create a *de facto* barrier that is generally too high for generics-based companies to overcome.

Treatment under TRIPS

Article 39.3 of TRIPS makes reference to the protection against 'unfair commercial use' of 'undisclosed test or other data' required as a condition of approving the marketing of pharmaceutical and agrochemical products the 'origination of which involved considerable effort'. However, while the paragraph does refer to products, which utilise new chemical entities, it is vague in specifying what constitutes 'undisclosed information', 'considerable effort' and how the 'protection against unfair commercial use' should take place in practice. One of the reasons for this vagueness is because no agreement could be reached by Member States during the TRIPS negotiations (UNCTAD-ICTSD 2005: ch. 28; Correa 2004c; Reichman 2004).

Treatment under US law

Current data exclusivity provisions in the US originate from the 1984 Drug Price Competition and Patent Term Origination Act (the Hatch-Waxman Act).[33] This Act amended the Federal Food, Drug, and Cosmetic Act[34] by providing a process by which pharmaceutical manufacturers could file Abbreviated New Drug Applications (ANDAs). This meant that they did not have to carry out the safety and efficacy tests required for FDA marketing approval provided they could prove bioequivalence to the original product. The Act provides for a five-year period of data exclusivity for new drugs (containing a new active ingredient) plus the approximately two years necessary for obtaining FDA approval, which *de facto* adds up to seven years (Engelberg 1999: 406). The Act also provides for a three-year data exclusivity period for new indications or uses of already approved medicines so long as new clinical investigation was needed for the approval of the new use (FDA 2006).

TRIPS-plus condition[35]

All US-FTAs since NAFTA include provisions on data exclusivity, albeit with variations in content and language. The usual time frame for the protection provided is five years with respect to test data submitted for marketing approval of pharmaceuticals, and 10 years with respect to agrochemical products. It applies to both patented and non-patented products.

Variations exist in the information that is subject to protection. While in some FTAs reference is made to 'undisclosed information/data'[36] others refer to 'information/data'[37] only – substantially broadening the amount of information that is subject to protection (Correa 2004c).

Other variations exist with respect to the subject for which the data is submitted. In most cases this has to be an NCE.[38] In some countries an NCE is defined as a chemical entity that has not been approved in the territory of the party,[39] whereas in other countries an NCE is defined as a chemical entity that was not previously approved, independent of the territory.[40]

Another variation exists with respect to the extent that the exclusive protection reaches into the territories of other parties. Regulatory authorities may decide to base their decision on the decision made by another regulatory authority. In some FTAs this is possible as long as the originator of the data gives their consent, otherwise it has to be newly submitted, examined and registered for a period of five years for pharmaceuticals and ten years for agrochemical products independent of the protection term in the originator country.[41] In this case, however, one option is to rely on the data itself submitted to the foreign regulatory agency. Only automatic recognition is prohibited, but domestic generic industries, for example, can rely on the 'foreign' data for applying for their own marketing approval at home.

Other FTAs, however, do not allow for this option.[42] In these cases the agreement works either by not allowing domestic regulatory authorities to rely on the decisions made by regulatory authorities abroad, or by relying on the data submitted to the foreign authorities in other territories – for a period of five years. Effectively this may extend the protection of data for an additional five years, as the rights holder can first submit his data in country A, and after five years in country B. In country B the data will be protected from the time when it is protected in country A, even though the data has not been submitted in country B. Once submitted to country B another five years of protection apply (Abbott 2004; Correa 2004c; Roffe *et al.* 2005; Correa 2006; Musungu and Oh 2006).

Finally, some FTAs allow for an extension of the term of data protection in the case of a 'new use' (three years for pharmaceuticals and ten years for agrochemical products).[43] In such cases the 'new use' protection can be extended in practice if the owner of the data chooses to first introduce the 'new use' only in country A before submitting it in country B. The time period he has to do so is three years for pharmaceuticals and ten years for agrochemicals.

Possible consequences

The possible consequences of data exclusivity apply when the protection period extends beyond that of a patent for the same product. Given the shorter period of data exclusivity in comparison to that of a patent, there should be no significant effect on the entry of generics into the market. However, in practice, data exclusivity can delay the entry of generics and keep the prices artificially high (Weissman 2006: 25).

For example, a situation could occur in which there is no patent in a country, or the patent is about to expire. In this case, even without patent protection, the monopoly status would be upheld through data exclusivity. The same applies in a situation in which the patent has expired and is in the public domain, but the product has never been introduced in the territory of a country. Given that an NCE is defined as a chemical, which has never been introduced in a given country, data protection would apply. Indeed, the particular definition of NCEs as well as the fact that data protection can reach beyond national borders for five years before it has to be registered in a given country allows for the ever-greening of monopoly rights. A patent holder can, where relevant TRIPS-plus provisions permit, maintain a monopoly through data exclusivity far beyond the patent term through the combination of registration in different countries at different times and the re-registration of new uses. Furthermore, data exclusivity can often be seen as an 'easy' option for keeping monopoly status in countries where the patent registration infra-structure is weak.

All of these situations can postpone the entry of generic competition keeping prices artificially high. In addition, there is a danger that data exclu-sivity prevents the use of certain TRIPS flexibilities, such as compulsory licences. In such cases the patent right may be waived through non-voluntary licensing, yet if the test data is still protected no generic industry will be able to enter the market (Weissman 2006: 26; Correa 2004c).

In Peru a study was undertaken to understand the impact a fully fledged data exclusivity regime on the country's health budget and Peruvian house-holds. It predicted that in the first year of data exclusivity the impact on welfare would be US$34.4 million, US$28.9 million of which would be covered by the consumers themselves. The study also predicted that this number was likely to increase each year due to the introduction of new products, so that by year 13 alone the annual impact on Peruvian welfare would be US$170 million, US$110 million would have to be covered by consumers. Given the current size of the Peruvian pharmaceutical market (US$650 million) (60 per cent of which is accounted for by the value of the patented drugs, which in terms of numbers only constitutes 3 per cent of the drugs on the market), these costs generated by data exclusivity alone are considerable (Pichihua Serna 2006).

Finally, independent of the actual costs that are likely to occur from data exclusivity, serious ethical concerns should be voiced. The repetition of clinical testing for the sake of market exclusivity constitutes a breach of the ethical guidelines established for clinical testing, which ought to aim for the maximum possible reduction in animal or human risk-taking as emphasised by the Helsinki Declaration of the World Medical Association[44] (Correa 2006, 2004c).

Linkage

Another important patent provision expected to have an impact on access to medicines is the link established by most recent US-FTAs between the regu-latory approval procedure and the patent right covering the respective product.

Treatment under TRIPS

There are no obligations under TRIPS to link the patenting process with the drug regulatory approval process.

Treatment under US law

In the US a patent holder lists his pharmaceutical patent in the so-called 'Orange Book'. If a generic producer applies for marketing approval with the

US FDA they have to certify whether a patent is granted on the product in question and, if so, whether it seeks to market the drug before the patent expires. In this case the generic producer is obliged to challenge the validity of the patent and state that it is their intention to produce the product in question as soon as the FDA approves it. The patent holder is then notified of the generic producers' intent and has a limited period of time to challenge the generic in court. Regardless of whether the patent is valid the generic application process is put on hold for 30 months. If the generic producer wins they gain 180 days of exclusive marketing right.[45] The intention of this mechanism is to set incentives for generic companies to seek early entry in the market and to challenge invalid patents. Nevertheless, the system has been subject to substantial abuse by patent holders in the past (Abbott 2006).

TRIPS-plus condition

In many US-FTAs[46] provisions exist, with varying strengths, that oblige domestic regulatory authorities to make the marketing approval dependent on the consent of the patent holders, thereby linking the two separate processes of regulatory approval and patent granting. As a result the *de facto* term of the test data, protection is extended to the length of the patent as the patent holder can always block the process by making use of the domestic drug regulatory process (Weissman 2006).

Potential consequences

'Linkage' creates an additional administrative burden in developing countries. Linkage, which even in the US is a large hurdle, will place a considerable burden on domestic judges and regulatory administrations. Many developing countries may not be able to accommodate a system that emphasises domestic courts (Abbott 2006). On top of that it can shift the *de facto* patent enforcement responsibility from the patent office to the regulatory authorities, which are not qualified to make those kinds of decisions (Correa 2006). Generic companies are less likely to enter the market if they fear a lengthy and expensive court battle. Thus linkage may create a formidable barrier that prevents generic entry into the market despite patents that may be invalid.

Furthermore, an additional question is whether in cases of compulsory licensing the patent holder can, through the linkage provision, block the marketing approval even if the patent office has granted a waiver towards their patent rights. Compulsory licences only apply to patents, they do not automatically facilitate market entry through drug regulatory authorities.

Finally it should be noted that the system of linkage put forward in some US-FTAs goes beyond the equivalent standards in US law. There the FDA only has to *inform* patent owners if a third party applies for marketing authority for the same product (if registered in the 'Orange Book') but there is no obligation to seek the patent holder's consent before granting marketing authority.

If the patent owner feels its product has been infringed then it is their responsibility to act on it, rather than the responsibility of the drug regulatory authority or generic manufacturer to seek the patent holder's consent. The FDA does not require express consent by the patent holder as is the case under a fully fledged linkage system (Correa 2006).

A reduction of health-related policy space

All the TRIPS-plus provisions mentioned above, in one way or another, delay the entry of generic competition into the domestic market and keep drug prices artificially high. On top of that, TRIPS-plus conditions have a much more systemic impact beyond the individual provisions that merits attention. As was mentioned in chapter 2, the TRIPS Agreement left considerable flexibility for Member States to adopt the minimum standards put forward. As Musungu and Oh demonstrate, many Member States have made use of this practice (2006). As mentioned above, the TRIPS Agreement emphasised the need to operate in a way that was:

> . . . conducive to social and economic welfare, and to the balance of rights and obligations . . .

This spirit was confirmed by the Doha Declaration, providing that:

> . . . each provision of the TRIPS Agreement shall be read in the light of the object and purpose of the Agreement as expressed, in particular, in its objectives and principles.

The Doha Declaration also emphasised the particular need to not put trade objectives above health objectives, by stating that the TRIPS Agreement

> . . . can and should be interpreted and implemented in a manner supportive of WTO Members' right to protect public health and, in particular, to promote access to medicines for all.

TRIPS-plus provisions deny those FTA partners a range of these specifically established policy spaces by adopting the US approach[47] to IP protection and its institutional set up. Bearing in mind the long, but ongoing, development of US law and policy in the field of patents it is unlikely that this approach is equally suited to the needs of developing countries. US IP laws have been developed for the US domestic institutional landscape and have been fine-tuned over many years. Many developing countries will not have the checks and balances in place, whether through the courts or other mechanisms, which exist in the US and which help to maintain a certain balance in the working of the IPRs system. The interpretation of a certain provision may be very different when implemented outside of the US institutional landscape. As a result, next to the direct influence that the actual wording of the US-FTAs has on providing affordable access to medicines in FTA partners, it also constitutes a substantial intervention into the overall design of domestic health and industrial policy and is likely to significantly overburden domestic institutions in developing countries.

Table 3.1 outlines some of the policy spaces that recent US FTAs have reduced.

Table 3.1 Health-related policy spaces available under the TRIPS Agreement and their reflection in US-FTAs since NAFTA[48]

TRIPS *provided policy-space*	FTAs
Freedom to define patentability criteria, such as 'novelty' or 'inventive step' and 'industrial application'	Limited in most FTAs; that is, industrial application has been defined as a specific, substantial and credible utility
Authorisation to exclude certain subject matters from patentability	Limited in most FTAs – such as 'best efforts clauses' or direct obligations to make available patents to plants or animals
Choice to protect 'new use' patents	Limited in some FTAs – patents available to 'new uses' or 'methods'
The determination of the substantive grounds for the issuance of a compulsory licence	Limited in some FTAs to certain grounds (only in cases of national emergencies, anti-trust remedies, and public non-commercial use)
	Limited through links made with test data protection
The determination of an IPRs exhaustion regime that best suits domestic conditions	Limited in some FTAs by the obligation to request authorisation of the title-holder
The possibility of defining the nature of protection of pharmaceutical and agrochemical test data submitted for regulatory authorities for marketing approval	Limited countries are obliged to provide for test data protection
The authorisation to control IPRs abuses through competition laws	Available

Source: Based on Vivas-Eugui and von Braun (2007).

Parallel understandings and side letters on certain public health measures[49]

The concerns with respect to TRIPS-plus provisions and their impact on public health were prominent during most FTA negotiations. The majority of governments that negotiated with the US expressed their particularly defensive interest when it came to public health issues and sought to protect themselves by preserving those safeguards and flexibilities that were offered by the TRIPS Agreement and the Doha Declaration (Fink and Reichenmiller 2005).

Even some US policy-makers emphasised the importance of the issue, including some Members of Congress who expressed their concern to the USTR:

> . . . contrary to the Doha Declaration the U.S. Trade negotiators have repeatedly used trade agreements to restrict the ability of developing nations to acquire medicines at affordable prices.
>
> (Waxman 2005)

As a result, US negotiators agreed to certain 'side letters' or 'parallel understandings' which confirmed that the standards put forward through FTAs should not affect the parties' ability to protect public health. Nevertheless, with the exception of the US-FTA with Chile (and the later revised agreements with Peru, Colombia and Panama as described in chapter 7) no reference was made to the Doha Declaration in any of the FTAs (Correa 2004c; Roffe 2004). None of the side letters softens the new IPRs obligations put forward which questions their usefulness. The fact that the side letters do not create exceptions to the provisions included in the FTAs is furthermore confirmed by the USTR itself (GAO 2007a). Thus, the actual content and legal value of those side documents remains controversial.

Conclusion

This chapter demonstrates why developing countries traditionally had defensive negotiation positions in the field of IPRs. Particular emphasis has been placed on the impact that TRIPS-plus provisions have on drug prices in developing countries where national health budgets are constrained and many consumers pay for medicines out of their own pocket. The price differences between patented drugs and their generic equivalent is that large that any extension of the monopoly, whether through patents or data exclusivity, is heavily contested by public health advocates. Furthermore, the 'export' of US level of IP protection into an institutional environment without the equivalent checks and balances may lead to an even stricter implementation of IPRs protection than can be found in the US.

It is therefore no surprise that health authorities in developing countries have very defensive negotiation objectives towards a range of IPRs provisions that form part of the traditional US IP template. The following chapters demonstrate the domestic settings of Peru, Colombia and the US within which such concerns could inform and influence the negotiation process.

4 The domestic source of Peru's and Colombia's engagement in the FTA negotiations

Introduction

The negotiation of the US-Andean FTAs, originally including Bolivia (as an observer), Colombia, Ecuador, Peru and the US, started on 18 May 2004 in Cartagena de las Indias, Colombia. Bolivia and Ecuador withdrew during the course of the negotiations. The negotiations with Peru and Colombia were finalised on 7 December 2005 and 17 February 2006 respectively, in Washington, DC. Further amendments to the FTA were subsequently approved in Peru and Colombia on 27 June 2007 and 30 October 2007 respectively.

As was stated in a newspaper article in the influential *El Tiempo* in Colombia, a day ahead of the commencement of the negotiations:

> [t]his is one of the few topics where we can find consensus in the country: the negotiations, which Colombia will begin tomorrow in Cartagena, are the most important in the country's history: the free trade negotiation with the US. [. . .] In addition to an exchange of industrial and agricultural products, it includes norms on investment, services, public procurement, dispute settlement, intellectual property, subsidies, antidumping and compensatory measures and competition policy, as well as labour and environmental standards. Thus, defendants and critics alike agree that this FTA will determine the economic and social future of the country over the next 50 years.
>
> (*El Tiempo* 2004; translated by author)

This chapter aims to analyse the nature of the domestic political and institutional landscape that shaped the policy preferences put forward by the Peruvian and Colombian governments during the FTA negotiations, in particular as they relate to the IPRs negotiations. The following chapter will then explain how this in turn affected the actual negotiations.

Background

Domestic policy-making structure

Power in Peru and Colombia, as in many Latin American regimes, rests in a strong (presidential) Executive.

Colombia is a presidential republic in which the President, elected for a four-year term, is the head of state and government. Despite its violent history, its political system, one of the oldest of the continent, is characterised by strong institutions. Thanks to a constitutional amendment lobbied for by President Uribe in 2005, a second term is possible, something he took advantage of, subsequently being re-elected.[1] Colombia has a bicameral system with a senate and a house of representatives. Furthermore, Colombia has an independent judiciary with a powerful constitutional court whose jurisdiction includes the constitutionality of laws or treaties.

For most of its history Colombia has had a centralised political structure with most power in the Executive. In an effort to decentralise power and provide further checks and balances, a constitutional overhaul in 1991 gave more responsibility to the country's 32 regional governments. Other changes included the independence of the Judiciary which further increased the amount of veto players in the country.

While such measures laid the groundwork for a firm and decentralised government with reliable checks and balances, critics have accused President Uribe during his time in office (2002–10) of having negated this through the appointment of political allies as heads of institutions which could have threatened his policies (Velásquez 2006; ILD 2009).

He was further accused of micro-management and being in permanent campaign mode. He was blamed for weakening national executive, legislative and judicial institutions by further strengthening presidential power in Colombia (Colombia Hoy 2006). This in combination with his overwhelming support in office, fluctuating from 60 to 75 per cent, meant that during his eight-year administration he tightly controlled Colombia's domestic and foreign policy.

Peru, like Colombia, is a presidential system, in which the President is Chief Executive and head of state. He is elected for a five-year term along with the entire Legislature. Similar to Colombia, central policy-making has historically rested in the Executive, which has often been driven by the personal agendas of the respective heads. As has been argued by Morón *et al.* (2006) Peruvians have often placed their faith in strong individuals rather than institutions, partially due to repeated swings between democracy and dictatorship. The country's leaders have often focused on short-term interests rather then the building of institutions that could mediate conflict, respond to external shocks and deliver to the needs of the larger population. The national Constitution in turn, even though it has been subject to regular revision, continues to concentrate power in the Executive and provides few checks and balances on policy-making (Morón *et al.* 2006).

Peru's drive towards strong individuals can be explained by the country's conflicted history of changing political regimes, a fragmented political party system and changing electoral systems (Morón *et al.* 2006). Many of the country's political parties have been constructed around individuals rather than based on an ideological basis. President Toledo founded his own party, Peru Posible, with a vision towards running a presidential campaign. With respect to trade, only the left party (Partido Nacionalista) had a fairly uniform position on the FTA negotiations. APRA[2], the most established political party in Peru, only more recently developed a clear position on trade, embracing the opening up of Peru's economy. During the course of the FTA negotiations, other parties usually expressed criticism in relation to specific concerns highlighted by the general public. These mostly related to biodiversity, or health or agricultural issues.

Nevertheless, Peru's Constitution provides for some checks and balances, above all when a government is run with minority support in Congress. Other veto players include organised interest groups and public institutions such as the Judiciary. However, according to Morón *et al.* (2006), over the last 25 years none of these veto players have provided strong opposition, mostly due to persistently weak political parties and civil society groups failing to design consistent work programmes or policy agendas.

Economic integration and the pursuit of a neo-liberal agenda

Beginning in the mid-1980s, most Latin American countries turned away from a state-driven economy to one of greater economic liberalisation. The trend, accelerated by the debt crisis in the 1980s, led to increasing privatisation, market deregulation and above all trade liberalisation. According to Acre this development has been largely driven by a fraction of political elites. Accordingly:

> Political leaders and technocratic elites are widely perceived as market vanguards crafting reforms in a highly autonomous and insulated policy-making environment with limited input or interaction with social forces.
>
> (Acre 2005: 1)

In Peru, mirroring the swings between political systems, the country has historically moved between market-oriented economic policies and those that have favoured state intervention (Morón *et al.* 2006). Trade liberalisation was aggressively introduced by Fujimori in the early 1990s, jointly with a broad array of neo-liberal policies. When limited Congressional support undermined some of his reforms, in a self-administered coup ('autogolpe'), he implemented rigorous market reforms through a range of Presidential decrees (Acre 2005). While Peru's economic policy has remained export-oriented with a view towards regulating previously highly dispersed tariffs and eliminating non-tariff bariers, Morón *et al.* (2005) argue that it was by no means a clearly defined and reliable economic policy. Some have eyed the FTA with the US as a first step to correct this.[3]

Utilising the ideas of economic reform proposed by President Lleras' economic secretary, Rodrigo Botero in the early 1960s, President Gaviria opened up Colombia's economy in the early 1990s. Similar to Peru, the economic policy developed by President Gaviria was largely derived from the thinking of a small group of economic technocrats associated mostly with the Universidad de los Andes and the Banco de la Republica referred to as the Club Suizo. It developed into one of the largest trade liberalisation policies in Latin America while ensuring that possible opposition groups, for example those industrial groups fearing foreign competition, would not resist such a move. As trade liberalisation became part of a broader economic modernisation process that included reform crucial for Colombia's export sector, many of the so-called *gremios* remained reluctantly supportive. Within a few years, however, Gaviria lost some of the previous supporters, particularly those representing agricultural industries (Edwards 2001).

Backed by domestic economic and policy reform the continent saw greater hemispheric integration over the last two decades, including the negotiation of regional agreements such as NAFTA, the G3 (Venezuela, Mexico, Colombia), Mercosur (Brazil, Argentina, Uruguay, Paraguay) and the Andean Community of Nations (CAN – today including Bolivia, Colombia, Ecuador, and Peru) and a range of free trade negotiations with the US including the failed attempt for a Free Trade Area of the Americas (FTAA).

FTAA talks began in 1994 and aimed to include all 34 American nations into one FTA with the aim of finalising it in 2005. Soon, however, a range of issues, including IPRs and service negotiations, became a stumbling block. Two major factions headed by Brazil and Argentina on one side and the US on the other, led to an eventual stagnation of the talks.[4] After the 2003 WTO Ministerial in Cancun and the FTAA Ministerial in Miami it became evident that negotiations were not going to succeed as originally anticipated. At the same time a set of smaller plurilateral negotiations were initiated to continue with the overall regional integration. During the FTAA Ministerial in 2003 the US announced its intention to negotiate an FTA with the ATPDEA Member States, namely Bolivia, Colombia, Ecuador and Peru (Alvarez Zarate 2004). In his notification to Congress[5] in November 2003, USTR Zoellick expressed his intention of entering into FTA negotiation with the four countries, highlighting not only the benefits of advanced market access to the Andean markets, or the promotion of the US agenda in increasing IP protection, but also his belief that the Andean negotiation would revive the FTAA negotiations.

This move followed a trend in the region in which other Latin American nations, including Chile[6] and the Central American[7] countries, were seeking bilateral trade agreements with the US. Since then many other commercial agreements, notably for Peru, today one of the most open economies on the continent (de la Flor 2010), but also Colombia followed. Peru's US FTA implementation package included a large range of political reforms attractive for further economic liberalisation (Perales 2010). Peru's subsequent commercial agreements have included pacts with Canada, Singapore and China as well as the European Union. Under negotiations are agreements with the P4 countries (Brunei, Chile, New Zealand, Singapore) as part of the Trans-Pacific Partnership (TPP) negotiations, that also include Australia, Malaysia, the US and Vietnam.[8] Furthermore, Peru is negotiating with South Korea and APEC, EFTA and Thailand (Diaz 2010).

Motivations for entering into a FTA

The US is the most important commercial partner of both Peru and Colombia. At the time of the negotiations, more than 50 per cent of Colombia's exports (US$7.3 billion in revenues) were sent to the US (Alcaldía Mayor de Bogotá 2004a). The US also accounts for about 25 per cent of FDI into Colombia. In Peru, approximately 26 per cent of the country's exports are sold on the US market. Since its entry into the ATPDEA (see below) in 1993, its exports to the US had been growing by an average rate of 15 per cent annually, reaching US$3.4 billion in 2005 (Mincetur 2005). This includes equally products that are not covered by the ATPDEA, however, indicating that not all of the increase is due to preferential market scheme (Morón et al. 2005). For the US, the Andean region represented a market of about US$8.5 billion for US exports in 2004, less than 1 per cent of total US exports (USTR 2005b; Semana 2004).

A 2004 study by the National Planning Department in Colombia estimated that 183,000 jobs would be generated as a result of the FTA. Domestic production was expected to increase by 0.5 per cent and import and export would rise by 12 per cent and 6.5 per cent respectively. The Department warned the government, however, to take into account the potential costs of the compromises and measure them against the possible benefits (El Tiempo 2004).

Finally, regional competition was an additional incentive for negotiating the FTA, given that Chile, the Central American countries and Mexico had already signed an FTA with the US. Alongside the general benefits of preferential market access the FTA was also expected to serve as protection against the rising competition from South Asia, particularly in the textiles, manufacturing and agro industries (El Peruano 2005d; Shadlen 2008).

ATPDEA

Most of the preferential market access under negotiation through the FTA was already available to Colombia and Peru before the negotiations, through the so-called Andean Trade Promotion and Drug Eradication Act (ATPDEA). The scheme offered Peru, Colombia, Bolivia and Ecuador preferential market access with the aim of providing alternative employment and income sources for the

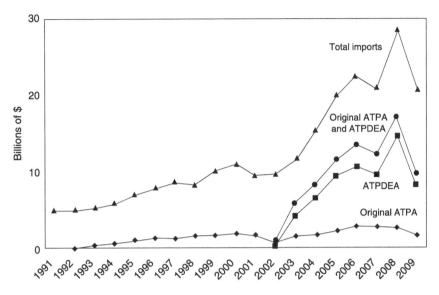

Figure 4.1 US imports under the ATPA and ATPDEA (including oil and copper), 1991–2009.

Source: USITC (2010: 2–2).

cultivation of illegal substances and an overall compensation for drug eradication. This Act, originally referred to as the Andean Trade Preference Act (ATPA), first came into force in 1991 and was limited to a given number of years after which it had to be renegotiated. A crucial renegotiation took place in 2002 when it was further extended until 2006 increasing its coverage from 5.524 to 6.300 tariff lines. Now called ATPDEA it included new key products such as certain textiles, petroleum and derivates and watches (USITC 2010; Pulecio 2005). According to US estimates the combined share of ATPDEA country exports to the US market fluctuated in a range from 0.8 to 1.1 per cent of total US imports. Excluding oil and copper, volume-wise it increased from US$1.4 billion in 2000 to US$2.6 billion in 2004 (Campondónico 2006).

Over the course of the existence of the Act many industries had grown dependent on it and would have collapsed if the preferences were not continued. Indeed, 60 per cent of Peru's exports benefited directly or indirectly from the ATPDEA. A loss of the preferences was calculated in Peru to lead to a decrease of US$700 million in textile exports, and US$300 million in agricultural exports alone (Mincetur 2005). Nevertheless, and as pointed out by Ken Shadlen (2008), often only a handful of key export categories dominate the large share of export under such preference schemes. A table put together by the USITC monitoring export trends under ATPA/ATPDEA confirms this:

Table 4.2 Leading U.S. imports for consumption under ATPA (2002–2004)

Leading U.S. imports for consumption under ATPA, by HTS provisions, 2002–2004

HTS provision	Description	2002[1]	2003[1]	2004[1]	Change, 2003–2004	Leading ATPA source
		------------- 1,000 dollars -------------				Percent
2709.00.10[2]	Petroleum oils and oils from bituminous minerals, crude, testing under 25 degrees A.P.I.	119,804	1,434,729	2,891,605	101.5	Ecuador
2709.00.20[2]	Petroleum oils and oils from bituminous minerals, crude, testing 25 degrees A.P.I. or more.	66,571	1,556,843	1,742,257	11.9	Colombia
7403.11.00	Cathodes and sections of cathodes, of refined copper	248,663	447,368	422,392	-5.6	Peru
2710.19.05[2]	Distillate and residual fuel oil (including blends) derived from petroleum or oils from bituminous minerals, testing under 25 degrees A.P.I.	7,263	236,458	378,163	59.9	Colombia
6110.20.20[2]	Sweaters, pullovers, sweatshirts, waistcoats, and similar articles, knitted or crocheted, of cotton, n.e.s.o.i.	0	202,262	297,903	47.3	Peru
2710.11.25[2]	Naphthas, not motor fuel/blending stock, from petroleum oils/oils from bituminous minerals, minimum 70 percent by weight of such products	9,722	174,970	253,009	44.6	Colombia
0603.10.60	Roses, fresh cut	69,765	204,473	238,799	16.8	Colombia
0603.10.80	Cut flowers and flower buds suitable for bouquets, n.e.s.o.i.	43,302	124,475	181,902	46.1	Colombia
6105.10.00[2]	Men's or boys' shirts, knitted or crocheted, of cotton	0	115,382	153,443	33.0	Peru
6109.10.00[2]	T-shirts, singlets, tank tops, and similar garments, knitted or crocheted, of cotton	0	84,559	128,319	51.8	Peru
0603.10.70	Chrysanthemums, standard carnations, anthuriums and orchids	46,539	98,709	98,123	-0.6	Colombia

HTS	Description				Country
6203.42.40[2]	Men's or boys' trousers, breeches, and shorts, not knitted or crocheted, of cotton, not containing 15 percent or more down	0	50,922	96,972	90.4	Colombia
0709.20.90	Asparagus, fresh or chilled, n.e.s.o.i.	31,589	60,498	79,478	31.4	Peru
7113.19.50	Gold jewelry and parts thereof, except necklaces and clasps	36,704	59,108	76,376	29.2	Bolivia
6204.62.40[2]	Women's or girls' trousers, breeches, and shorts, not knitted or crocheted, of cotton, n.e.s.o.i.	0	37,888	63,767	68.3	Colombia
2402.20.80	Cigarettes containing tobacco but not clove, paper-wrapped	20,524	55,271	57,946	4.8	Colombia
6106.10.00[2]	Women's or girls' blouses and shirts, knitted or crocheted, of cotton	0	29,743	44,605	50.0	Peru
7113.19.29	Gold necklaces and neck chains, other than rope or mixed link	21,828	42,039	40,765	-3.0	Peru
0603.10.30	Miniature (spray) carnations, fresh cut	13,239	23,213	32,035	38.0	Colombia
1604.14.30[2]	Tunas and skipjack, not in oil, in airtight containers, n.e.s.o.i.	0	25,474	31,466	23.5	Ecuador
	Subtotal	735,514	5,064,384	7,309,324	44.3	
	All other	265,302	771,648	1,049,934	36.1	
	Total	1,000,816	5,836,032	8,359,258	43.2	

[1] ATPA includes imports under ATPDEA.

[2] Item is newly eligible under ATPDEA.

Note. – The abbreviation, n.e.s.o.i., stands for 'not elsewhere specified or otherwise included'.

Sources: Compiled from official statistics of the U.S. Department of Commerce; USITC (2005: 2–16).

Next to the already covered products the FTA did not bring much additional market access but instead was to make these preferences permanent (Rojas 2005). Thus, with respect to market access, the FTA is a continuation of the ATPDEA, locking in the existing preferential treatment for a range of products on a permanent basis, while also adding a handful of new ones. On the contrary, given that the ATPDEA was a unilateral market access scheme, the majority of tariff reductions covered in the FTA were to benefit US exports. With respect to Peru the USITC stated:

> As most of the effects of tariff elimination on goods are driven by Peru's removal of tariffs facing U.S. exports, . . . U.S. imports from Peru may be higher by approximately $ 439 million, U.S. exports to Peru higher by $1.1 billion, and U.S. GDP higher by more than $ 2.1 billion. Only three U.S. sectors – metals [. . .], crops [. . .], and paddy rice – are estimated to experience a decline in output, revenue, or employment of more than 0.10 percent.
>
> (as quoted in Levy 2009: 19)

Thus, expected job creation through improved export and investment in Peru and Colombia has to be counter-measured against the job losses incurred as a result of increased US competition in the local market. Critics in Peru estimated that of the 85,500 jobs created by the FTA over a 15-year time span, 67,400 jobs are likely to be lost because of increased US imports. The net gain is estimated as a total of 18,100 jobs in a population of over 12 million people (Campodónico 2006).

Campodónico's statement, however, is based on the assumption that the ATPDEA preferences would remain in place even if FTA negotiations would not succeed, which both Presidents deemed unlikely. It was argued that the renegotiations of the ATPDEA had been subject to increasing conditionality in the past, raising concerns over its future (Uribe 2004; Pulecio 2005). During the negotiations Colombian and Peruvian policy-makers were repeatedly told by US officials that the ATPDEA was coming to an end and that the FTA negotiations would start 'from zero'. Should the negotiations fail the governments would be without ATPDEA and without the FTA (Acosta Medina 2006: 106, 217). The looming threat of the end of preferential market access and the hope to lock them in once and for all was thus at the heart of the FTA negotiations, bearing in mind that many key export industries had become dependent on the preferential market access enjoyed over the previous years (de la Flor 2010).[9]

Thus, the negotiators for both Colombia and Peru negotiated the FTA with the constant threat looming of the end of the ATPDEA. The expiry date was first announced as December 2005, then extended to December 2006 (El Peruano 2005b). Extensions thereafter were July 2007, February 2008, the end of 2008, 2009 and 2010 respectively and most recently until February 2011 after which it has not been renewed until the time of writing this book

(Reuters 2008; Andina 2009; Bridges Weekly 2011). As extensions were increasingly short-term and interventionist through their conditional nature (Levy 2009) the repeated reminder of the end of the preference scheme and the related threat of non-renewal served as a powerful bargaining tool and was actively used when negotiations were not advancing (Alcaldía Mayor de Bogotá 2004a).

Preference schemes similar to the ATPDEA have been described as 'political trade dependence', exposing governments to the political pressure of its benefactor. As these are unilateral schemes, countries have no dispute mechanisms at hand based on which they can challenge their implementation. Instead they are subjected to repeated pressure from the market access providing party (Shadlen 2008).

Best Alternative to Negotiated Agreement (BATNA)

As was explained in chapter 1 of this book, understanding the BATNA is crucial for understanding the overall domestic win-set of a negotiating party. In the case of Colombia and Peru there were a range of communalities on what would have happened if the FTA talks had failed.

The negotiation principals of both countries repeatedly stated that 'no agreement' was not an option for them. According to the Minister of Commerce in Peru:

> I would like to ask the backbiters of the FTA, especially those that criticise the agreement demagogically and from an ideological perspective: What is the alternative to the FTA? Up to now, nobody has answered me. You know why they have not answered? Because the cost of not signing the FTA is immense, and it is a cost we cannot afford and they know it.
>
> (El Peruano 2005f; translated by author)

The Presidency and other senior members of the Executive in Colombia followed an equal trend, strongly arguing that there was no alternative to the FTA. Indeed, the agreement was often referred to by the Minister of Commerce as a 'development plan' for Colombia for the next 50 years. Anyone who was critical of the negotiations was presented as someone who was 'against progress' (Acosta Medina 2006).

Yet, many disagreed with this assessment. Economist Alan Fairlie, of the Catholic University in Peru, for example, argued much in favour of regional integration with Mercosur, reopening FTAA talks, a strengthening of the Andean Community and even then a still outstanding FTA with the EU rather than the US (Fairlie 2005b). While he agrees that the end of the ATPDEA preferences could have cost Peru dearly, he argues that these costs need to be balanced out with the costs of signing an FTA with a precise cost-benefit analysis (Fairlie 2005c).

With respect to market access, a number of alternatives presented themselves. The first and foremost would have been to push for extending ATPDEA preference instead of signing on to a fully fledged FTA that demands a deep process of economic integration. An extension of the ATPDEA would mean a continuation of the trade preferences without having to submit to the different forms of structural reform needed for signing an FTA. Given the importance of the regions' drug policies for the US the permanent expiry of the scheme is unlikely (Cabrera 2006). Yet, responding to international pressure, Colombian negotiation principals were convinced that the preferences were about to expire. This position severely lowered their BATNA in the negotiations (Acosta Medina 2006: 329).

A second alternative at the time was offered by ongoing multilateral negotiations in the WTO. The commitments made by developed countries in Hong Kong in December 2005, to terminate agricultural subsidies by 2013, for example, was expected in the long-term to reduce the relative value of the FTA as by 2013 every WTO member would enjoy the same preferences (El Peruano 2005h). On the other hand, this would also pose an increasing threat as China, one of the biggest competitors to many Latin American countries, would equally enjoy preferential market access (Shadlen 2008). However, at the time of the negotiations WTO deliberations in the Doha Round experienced tremendous difficulty not leaving much hope for a multilateral solution (Levy 2009).

A third option was of course further economic regional integration through a strengthening of CAN, a stronger relationship with Mercosur or even a new attempt at the FTAA (Fairly 2005b). In such agreements negotiations would have continued to focus on market access and would not have included the same level of regulatory integration that was required by the US. Even an FTA with the EU would have required less economic policy reform. While none of these agreements are mutually exclusive, having established stronger trade links with other partners before negotiating with the US would have inevitably strengthened the Andean countries' bargaining power during the negotiations.

Nevertheless, with the status quo of the failed FTAA negotiations and the need to maintain existing market access to the US market the temptation of an FTA was large. This was further exacerbated by the domino effect generated with other countries in the region that had already secured their preferential market access to the US market. For Peru in particular the fact that its neighbour and competitor, Colombia, was trying to enter into FTA negotiations with the US raised the possible cost of not participating in the negotiations, generating fears of exclusion (Shadlen 2008). Without doubt such fears influenced the negotiation principals.

Nevertheless, while searching for alternative market access is crucial for defining the national win-set, an additional aspect has to be borne in mind. This relates to the nature of FTAs negotiated with the US. As has been mentioned above, US FTAs seek deep regulatory harmonisation including the field of investment policy, environmental and labour standards and IPRs. Harmonisation of this magnitude will redefine the policy space governments have available for designing, among other, national development policy. While the WTO also demands a certain amount of economic integration from its members, the level of harmonisation, as can well be observed in the case of IPRs, is lower than what has been demanded by the US FTAs. According to Shadlen:

> . . . the additional constraints imposed by regional-bilateral agreements are most threatening to the remaining vestiges of industrial policy in developing countries. Countries whose integration into the global economy is guided by their obligations as members of the WTO retain the rights and opportunities to use policy instruments that are designed to create new productive capacities, alter comparative advantages, and, hopefully, achieve upward mobility in the international economic order. In contrast, regional-bilateral accords encourage specialization and pursuit of competitiveness via exploitation of existing comparative advantages. Thus, the price to be paid for increased market access under regionalism-bilateralism is that countries must relinquish many of the very tools that historically have been used to capture the developmental benefits of integration in the international economy
>
> (Shadlen 2005: 752)

Finally, of course, the social costs resulting from regulatory harmonisation for certain public policies such as health provision also have to be included in the BATNA. Increased or locked in market access may become of much less importance when all the related costs are included in the calculation of what constitutes a win-set. More simply put by Tello, without integrating the FTA into a broader national development policy rather than neo-liberal rethoric, it is unlikely that it will bring the anticipated socio-economic success (2005).

Therefore, in order to fully calculate a BATNA an appropriate impact assessment across all sectors that calculated costs and benefits in the short, medium and long term would have been necessary. As we will see below, with the exception of certain academic exercises, real impact assessment, above all one that was transparent, integrated relevant stakeholder groups and provided in-depth cross-sectoral analysis was limited. Instead, statements that there was no real BATNA putting immense pressure on the Andean negotiators and substantially increasing US bargaining leverage dominated political rhetoric.

Status quo of regional IP protection

A number of international treaties defined Peru's and Colombia's level of IP protection at the onset of the FTA negotiations.

First, with the formation of the WTO all Member States were obliged to introduce a minimum standard of IPRs protection. Many Latin American countries at that time did not have a patent system, in particular for pharmaceutical products. However, Art. 65 of TRIPS gave all developing countries until 2000 to implement the new obligations in the field of IPRs and until 2005 for the introduction of pharmaceutical patents. Most Latin American countries did not make use of this transitional period and introduced a full patent system including pharmaceutical products from the mid to late 1990s. The reason behind this varies between the countries, but in many cases US industry or bilateral pressure motivated the premature changes (Correa 2007). In the case of Peru and Colombia the original ATPA negotiations in 1994 were one of the motivations behind their decision to becoming TRIPS compliant ahead of time.

Second, the G3 treaty was signed between Colombia, Mexico and Venezuela in 1994. It includes a detailed IPRs chapter that is formulated on the basis of NAFTA (Vivas-Eugui 2003). It also contains a five-year minimum protection for clinical test data for pharmaceutical and agrochemical products.[10] However, the provisions did not lead to Colombia or Venezuela implementing data exclusivity provisions at that time, while Mexico did so as a result of its obligations under NAFTA. Venezuela chose to resign from G3 in 2006 (Bloomberg 2006).

Third, CAN's common regime on IPRs is one of the most developed supranational features of the Community. The regime supersedes national law, which was tested, for example, when the Andean Tribunal upheld the illegality of a 'second use patent'[11] registered by Pfizer in Peru's IPRs and competition authority, INDECOPI. Thus, in case of conflict, the IP Common Legal Framework[12] prevails. National legislation from FTAs by any member in the region is considered national law and subsequently superseded by CAN.

An earlier version of CAN's joint IP regime included TRIPS-plus provisions, such as CAN Decision 344 (1994),[13] paragraphs 78 and 79 that stipulated five years of data exclusivity. However, CAN Decision 344 was revised in 2000 in the process of becoming TRIPS compliant. The subsequent Decision 486[14] on industrial property reworded the existing section on data protection and adopted, in Art. 266, the language put forward by TRIPS Art. 39.3. The decision to lower the data protection standards reflected the ongoing debate at that time between the national and the international pharmaceutical industry.[15] However, a paragraph not longer than a sentence was added to the end of Art. 266 at the last minute of the negotiations:

> Member Countries may take steps to guarantee the protection provided for under this article.

This sentence provided a window of opportunity for data exclusivity laws to be developed in the years to come. Just two years later Colombia was the first of the Member States to attempt to make use of this provision through Decree 2085.

Decree 2085[16] is one of the first introductions of TRIPS-plus provisions in the region as a result of bilateral trade negotiations with the US. In the run up to ATPDEA renewal negotiations in 2002 the Colombian government was placed under increasing pressure to introduce data protection into national law. The renewal of trade preferences and the domestic introduction of data protection were directly linked during the negotiations (Uribe 2005; Moreno-Piraquive 2004: 134). The pressure was intensified through the strategic listing of Colombia on the US Special 301 'Priority Watch List' demanding that Colombia developed a data protection framework.[17] Colombia introduced Decree 2085 in September of the same year (Alcaldía Mayor de Bogotá 2004a). Under the Decree, undisclosed information on clinical tests submitted for the marketing approval of pharmaceuticals is protected for three years when issued in 2002, four years in 2003, and five years in 2004 and thereafter. The Decree was challenged at the Andean Tribunal of Justice but after substantial back and forth eventually permitted through CAN Resolution 632 of 2006 (MinComercio 2007).

Notably, the discussions surrounding Decree 2085 triggered the emergence of a fierce IP/health debate in Colombia, which had been mostly absent during the TRIPS negotiations. For the first time national health NGOs and other players including domestic health authorities linked IPRs to access to medicines, raising awareness on the matter among the wider public and confronting the government about it. The debate was further fuelled by related international debates going on at the time such as those relating to the Doha Declaration as well as the highly publicised court cases against the South African government (Rodriguez-Franco 2008).

Unlike Colombia, Peru's level of patent protection was that of CAN 486, and did not include provisions on data protection. This was of particular concern to the US. In a report summarising the visit of a US Congressional delegation to the Andean region, the US Ambassador to Peru, Struble, is quoted as saying:

> . . . an FTA with Peru would help promote protection for intellectual property rights, which remains a serious problem in the country. In 2004, IPR losses totalled almost $200 million [. . .]. He noted that an FTA will combat optical disk piracy and ensure data and patent protections for medicines.
>
> (Committee on House Ways and Means 2005)

Domestic political structure, institutions and the preparations for negotiations

Separation of powers in international economic diplomacy

Colombia

The overall responsibility for the direction and execution of foreign relations, including economic diplomacy, in Colombia is held by the Executive. According to the Constitution:

> Article 189. It is the responsibility of the President of the Republic, as the chief of state, head of the government, and supreme administrative authority to do the following: [. . .]
>
> 2. Manage international relations; appoint the members of the diplomatic and consular corps; receive the corresponding foreign officials; and negotiate international treaties or agreements with other states and international bodies to be submitted for the approval of the Congress.

As it was further confirmed by a range of Constitutional Court sentences, the expression of interest of negotiating a treaty is at the virtue of the President as the Head of State and director of foreign relations. Furthermore, sentence C-344 of 1995 confirmed:

> It is the President of the Republic, as Head of State who is responsible for the conduct of international politics and the management of foreign affairs. In accordance with Article 189, paragraph 2, of the Constitution, it is his competence to celebrate international treaties or conventions with other states and entities of international law, which shall be subject to subsequent approval of Congress and constitutional review by this Court before its completion. [. . .] The President should enjoy full autonomy in deciding when to enter negotiations on a particular topic of international interest to Colombia, when it is opportune to conclude a treaty or convention, and what will be its terms, without having to have the prior consent, authorization or mandate of another branch of government. In this regard, it would be unconstitutional as a rule of law if Congress intended to interfere within the realms of competence of the Head of State himself, giving orders to celebrate a treaty or to prevent him from doing so, or granting authorization not required for such purposes [translated by author].
>
> (Garcia Orijuela 2005: 150)

The Executive's authority with respect to the FTA has been further confirmed by Decree 2314[18] that was put into effect at the end July 2004, more than two months after the negotiations had started. This Decree reconfirmed the absolute control of the Executive over international negotiations, placing the Ministry of Commerce, Industry and Tourism in charge of the coordination of the negotiation team and its Minister in charge of appointing the head negotiator. It further highlights the Council of Minister's involvement in the development of the negotiation strategy with a commitment of keeping the Council as well as the 'Superior Council of Foreign Commerce'[19] regularly informed about the state of the negotiations. Finally, the Decree states that only those who hold public office can be part of the negotiation team.

Furthermore, Art. 224 of the Constitution gives additional powers to the Executive with respect to economic treaties, stating that:

Article 224. [. . .] However, the President of the Republic may give temporary effect to provisional treaties of an economic or commercial nature negotiated through international organizations. In such a case, as soon as a treaty enters into force provisionally, it must be sent to the Congress for approval. If the Congress does not approve the treaty, its application will be suspended.

The role of the Colombian Congress is limited to the approval or rejection of treaties in order to make them valid. The Colombian Constitution states:

Article 224. In order to be valid, treaties must be approved by the Congress [. . .].

Article 225. The Advisory Committee on Foreign Relations, whose membership will be determined by law, is a consultative body of the President of the Republic.

Article 150. It is the responsibility of Congress to enact laws. Through them its exercises the following functions:

Article 16. Approving or disapproving treaties which the government makes with other states or international organizations [. . .].

The Colombian Congress becomes primarily involved at the ratification stage of international treaties. Unlike in the case of law-making, where the role of Congress includes the interpretation, amendment and appeal of laws,[20] its role with respect to international treaties is limited. Here Congress is only allowed to approve or reject the treaty and cannot amend individual sections of it (Tangarife Torres 2004: 314). Law 5a of 1992 provides Congress with some further limited rights in this regard; for example, Congress may vote to only partially approve a treaty, formulate reservation towards individual provisions of a treaty and make interpretative declarations without rejecting the treaty as a whole. It may not, however, make amendments as this would intervene into the President's jurisdiction of being in charge of international relations (Garcias Orijuela 2005). To what extent these powers would apply to international economic treaties, such as the FTA, is debatable. The Ministry of Commerce rejected the option for partial approval arguing that the nature of trade negotiations where 'nothing is agreed until everything is agreed' does not allow for a partial ratification, which could result in the reopening of the negotiations. This in turn would invade into the jurisdiction of the Presidency (MinComercio 2007).

The lack of involvement of Congress in earlier stages of the negotiation process of international agreements was criticised by several members of the Senate given the importance of the negotiations. They requested a process of detailed notification to Congress including about the intentions of the negotiations, and both expectations and threats for the country 90 days before negotiations would commence, which was turned down (Moreno Piraquive 2004).

According to interviewed Senators, the Colombian Congress had traditionally held very little involvement in any part of international diplomacy, with the exception of the Panama Canal treaty negotiations.[21] Already during the negotiations of the FTAA the lack of involvement and awareness of other public entities was criticised by a group of Senators that called for the establishment of a Commission that would provide a forum of exchange between different government agencies, the private sectors and civil society. A range of fora were organised and studies commissioned, looking closer at the topics of agriculture, industry, IPRs and services with respect to FTAA negotiations (Moreno Piraquive 2004).

This marginalised role of the Colombian Congress as well as the disappointing participation of other public and private bodies in the negotiations resulted according to some critics in insufficient political debate surrounding the negotiations (Alvarez Zarate 2004). While Members of Congress were regularly informed by the Ministry of Commerce about the negotiations, Congress' real power as veto player during the FTA negotiations remained limited, also bearing in mind Uribe's overwhelming support in Congress, which was as high as 82 per cent at some stages throughout his Presidency. Yet, as will be pointed out in the next chapter, some Colombian Congressional Representatives did participate in the 'Cuarto de al Lado'.[22]

Another important veto player in the Colombian system is the Constitutional Court. Once a treaty and related implementing legislation has been ratified by Congress, its constitutionality has to be tested. According to the Constitution:

> Article 241. The safeguarding of the integrity and supremacy of the Constitutional Court according to the strict and precise terms of this article. For this purpose, it will fulfill the following functions: [. . .]
>
> 10. Decide in definitive manner on the constitutionality of international treaties and the laws approving them. For this purpose, the government will submit them to the Court within the six days subsequent to their sanction by law. Any citizen may intervene to defend or challenge their constitutionality. Should the Court declare them constitutional, the government may engage in a diplomatic exchange of notes; in the contrary case the laws will not be ratified. When one or several provisions of a multilateral treaty are declared invalid by the Constitutional Court, the President of the Republic alone may ratify it, under reserve of the offending provision.

Unlike Congress, Colombia's Constitutional Court analyses the enforceability of the treaty by analysing each article of the agreement. Similar to Congress, however, the role of the Court remains one that is reduced to the very end of the negotiation process, namely at the ratification stage. It has no input at the onset or during the negotiations.

Colombia's judiciary is remarkably strong compared to other countries in the region. With the constitutional reform in 1991 an explicit attempt has been made to strengthen the judiciary in the country. It's nine magistrates are elected by the Senate, chosen from a list put together by the President, the Court and the 'State Council' (Cardenas et al. 2005). While the independence of the Court has increased since 1991, critics argue that the influence of President Uribe on the Court remained strong through close alliances with decision-makers surrounding and within the Court.[23] Nevertheless, the decision not to allow him to run for a third time in office, after a second term had been approved in 2006, demonstrated the limits of his influence.

Finally, the relative power of regional governments has also been increased by the 1991 Constitution. Specifically, the power of the Presidency has been reduced by specifying that certain competencies fall within the jurisdictions of regional governments (Alcaldía Mayor de Bogotá 2004c). Accordingly:

> Art. 287: Territorial entities enjoy autonomy for the management of their interests within the limits of the Constitution and the law. By virtue of this they will have the following rights:
>
> 1. To govern themselves under their own authority.
> 2. To exercise the jurisdictions appropriate to them.
> 3. To administer their resources and establish the taxes necessary for their operation.
> 4. To participate in national revenues.
>
> Art. 288: The Organic Law of Territorial Organization will establish the division of jurisdictions among the nation and the territorial entities.
>
> Art. 311: As the basic entity of the political-administrative branch of the state, it is the responsibility of the municipality to provide those public services determined by law, to build the projects required for local progress, to arrange for the development of its territory, to promote community participation, the social and cultural development of its inhabitants, and to perform the other functions assigned to it by the Constitution and the laws [. . .].

As we will be discussed later, the Mayor of Bogotá unsuccessfully tested the veto power of the regions during the negotiations.

Peru

As pointed out by Morón *et al.* (2006) since the 1980s the national policy agenda was largely set by the Executive in the country. Most policy decisions, particularly in relation to macroeconomic policy, social policy, social reform and state reform, were taken by Presidents, supported by personally chosen cabinets and personal advisors. The overall system is highly centralised and, unlike Colombia, the country's regions do not play a strong role in national policy-making.

Presidents cannot be immediately re-elected but have to stand down for at least one full term before they can run for office again. They enjoy strong pro-active powers, including the right to dictate 'decrees of urgency' for economic and financial issues, which are as strong as the law (Art. 118(19) of the Constitution). Such power may be assumed by the Executive or delegated to the Executive by Congress. They have been frequently used in Peru. Until 2001, 77 per cent of legislation was passed through such decrees. Under President Toledo the use of emergency decrees for law-making went down to 20 per cent (Morón et al. 2006).

Peru's Constitution of 1993 addresses the negotiation of treaties. Like Colombia, the principal power to negotiate treaties lies with the President of the Republic.

> Article 118. The powers of the President of the Republic are: [. . .]
>
> XI. To direct the foreign policy and international relations; and to celebrate and ratify treaties [. . .]
>
> XIX. To dictate extraordinary measures, through emergency decrees that have the force of law, in economic and financial matters, when required by the national interest and upon notification to the Congress. The Congress may modify or derogate these emergency decrees [. . .]
>
> XX. To regulate tariffs.

Furthermore, all Presidential Acts must be validated through a process of ministerial oversight by the Cabinet obliging Ministers to take responsibility for the Presidential acts that they countersign. Members of the Cabinet are appointed and removed by the President and are accountable to Congress. Traditionally, Cabinet Members have frequently taken the blame for unpopular policies. The average time Ministers spend in office since 1980 has been 13.7 months (Morón et al. 2006).

Furthermore, in the case of Peru the President is also responsible for the ratification of a treaty, although in certain cases, including the FTA, a treaty also has to be approved by Congress. The Constitution states:

> Art. 56: Treaties must be approved by Congress before their ratification by the president, whenever they deal with the following subjects:
>
> 1. human rights;
> 2. the nation's sovereignty, dominion, or territorial integrity;
> 3. national defence; and
> 4. financial obligations of the government.
>
> Congress must also approve treaties that create, modify, or eliminate taxes, those requiring the modification or derogation of any law, and those requiring legislative measures for their application.

Peru's Congress was downsized to a one chamber Congress with the 1993 Constitution and its 120 members are elected with the President for a five-year term. It has considerable formal powers including the debating and passing of legislation, questioning, censuring or impeaching ministers, creating investigative commissions or impeaching the president. However, the use of these veto rights has been limited (Morón et al. 2006). Congress in Peru has been traditionally unpopular, with polls suggesting that 60 per cent of the public perceives legislators as corrupt or ineffective. The turnover of individual representatives has been very high with an average time of 4.4 years in office since 1980 suggesting that those in office often have very little experience. Confidence in legislators tends to be low and voters do not tend to follow their voting patterns but rather turn to the Executive. This can be partially explained by a history of executive decrees where Congress was bypassed either as a result of Presidential decree or by congressional delegation (Morón *et al.* 2006). This situation has been slightly improved in the post-2001 Congress under President Toledo.

Analogous to Colombia, the role of Congress is at the end of the FTA negotiation process, limiting its power as a veto player. Nevertheless, some representatives followed the negotiations in the side rooms. During the 18 months of negotiations 39 Congressmen and women travelled to at least one of the rounds. Furthermore, the Ministry of Commerce held 15 Congressional meetings and 13 information meetings to provide an update to Congress on the advances made in the negotiations (El Peruano 2005g; El Comercio 2006).

In theory congressional veto power increased when the loose coalition backing Toledo's Administration started to fall apart half way through his presidency at the time negotiations started (Morón et al. 2006). Opposition parties could have subsequently undermined the process. Due to Peru's fragmented multi-party system such opposition never developed a unified position on the negotiations. Towards the end of Toledo's administration he became increasingly unpopular while confidence in Congress fell so low that some Congressmen questioned to what extent it still had the legitimacy to approve the FTA given that elections were imminent (El Comercio 2006). Indeed, as we will see below, when the FTA was eventually passed in Congress only a few weeks before the newly elected Congress would take office, it led to major infighting.

While not as powerful as Colombia's Judiciary, Peru's Judiciary functions as an additional potential veto player. However, according to Morón *et al.* (2006), Peru's judicial system has been historically underfunded, inefficient, corrupt and subject to political manipulation. Some improvement was achieved through the 1993 Constitution and a judicial reform undertaken in 1995 where the role of the President in appointing magistrates and judges was eliminated. The Constitutional Tribunal was appointed to rule on the constitutionality of laws and an ombudsman was introduced to defend and protect civil rights. Congress elects the seven members of the Tribunal rather than, as previously, the President. However, in practice President Fujimori frequently intervened in the Judiciary leading towards an institutional culture susceptible to political and economic pressure (Morón *et al.* 2006). Since 2003 under Toledo a judicial reform process is taking place. This has led to a number of positive steps slowly leading to more confidence into the institution (Morón et al. 2006).

A number of cases were launched by the Tribunal after the FTA negotiations had been finalised, raising possible conflicts of the agreement with the country's constitution. All of these cases were rejected by the Tribunal, however, arguing that only once the agreement was implemented it would become subject to the Court's jurisdiction.[24]

Institutional hierarchy and the composition of the negotiation teams

Colombia

The head negotiators in Colombia were picked by President Uribe and the Minister of Commerce, Humberto Botero. Hernando Jose Gomez, former Ambassador of Colombia to the WTO, was appointed to head the negotiations. Gomez, with Botero, then identified a range of individuals from the Ministry of Commerce, Industry and Tourism (from now on Ministry of Commerce) and put them in charge of individual negotiation tables. Other ministries could send their staff to contribute to the negotiation team, but they had to finance their participation in the negotiations. This included staff time and travel to different negotiation locations. Each issue specific 'negotiation table' was headed by someone from the Ministry of Commerce, but included technical experts from other relevant ministries.[25]

The technical negotiation teams were expected to find a consensus with respect to developing the interests and position put forward during the negotiations. Decree 2314 clearly established a hierarchy in which the head negotiator was directing the team. He in turn had to report irresolvable conflicts to the Vice Minister, who then would report to the Minister of Commerce. If still no resolution could be found the issue was brought to the President.

The FTA was the largest and most important commercial negotiation in the history of Colombia so the ministry in charge of the negotiation process was under a lot of pressure. Most attention was focused on Gomez and the individuals in charge of specific negotiation tables. They were responsible for the technical elaboration of the individual chapters that would jointly form the FTA. Each of these sub-negotiations was to have a large impact on the economy of the country, whether in form of tariff levels, labour and environmental standards, investment agreements or the setting of new IPRs standards. All of the sub-negotiation tables were headed by representatives of the Ministry of Commerce, appointed by the head negotiators as elaborated by Decree 2314 (Semana 2004).[26] The same Decree gave the head negotiator the power to remove any negotiator at any time during the negotiations if the person was considered to challenge the coherence of the team.

Colombia health authorities participated both in the preparation and in the actual negotiations of the FTA. As INVIMA had already been active throughout the FTAA negotiations, their involvement preceded that of the Ministry of Social Protection (in charge of health – from now on Ministry of Health). However, soon after negotiations started, Minister Diego Palacio took the issue very seriously and sent two additional health experts to participate in the negotiations next to the two from INVIMA who already participated in the negotiations. All four were well prepared for the negotiations, familiar with the US expectations in the field of patents and test data protection. Furthermore, in addition to the negotiators, Palacio also hired a range of international advisors who further advised the health negotiators through their technical and negotiation expertise.

The Colombian health team was stronger than its Peruvian counterpart and possibly the strongest ever health team representation in any of the new generation of US-led bilateral trade agreements. It was well equipped, had technical experts who included doctors, pharmacists, economists and lawyers, and was very dedicated in maintaining a strong public health position throughout the negotiations. From the beginning they were prepared for the key issues and knew where the conflict areas would lie. For them it was clear that no compromise was to be made in public health. 'Public health is non-negotiable' was a position that was repeatedly stated by the public health authorities. Furthermore, the health authorities had the official backing of the negotiation principals that certain concessions in the field of patents would not be made. These no-go areas were referred to as 'lineas rojas', 'red lines' in Spanish.[27]

As will be seen in the next chapter, throughout the negotiations the 'lineas rojas' were step-by-step crossed by the Ministry of Commerce, in particular towards the end of the process when negotiations went from the 'technical' to the 'political' level. This led to friction within the negotiation team, in particular between the representatives of the health authorities and those of Commerce. Health negotiators turned increasingly suspicious that the 'lineas rojas' had been a political farce from the beginning and were only ever meant to reduce domestic resistance to the negotiations. Indeed, the collaboration of the Ministry of Health was important for the Presidency in order to demonstrate policy coherence across the ministries, in particular with those agencies whose constituencies were likely to lose out from the FTA such as public health and agriculture.[28]

Peru

In Peru, the Ministry of Foreign Commerce, Trade and Tourism (henceforward Ministry of Commerce) was in charge of FTA negotiations. The appointed chief negotiator was Vice-Minister of Trade, Pablo de la Flor. The head negotiators from each negotiation table were appointed by him directly, and mostly Commerce staff. One exception was the head of the IPRs negotiation table. Given the lack of technical experts in the field of IPRs at the Ministry, a representative of the national conjoint IPRs office and competition authority, INDECOPI, was put in charge of IPRs negotiations.

Soon after negotiations started, a conflict arose between the Ministry of Commerce and INDECOPI. The reason for the conflict was that newly appointed president Roca of INDECOPI was an outspoken critic of the nego-tiations. Roca commissioned a total of six studies by a group of leading Peruvian scholars on various aspects of industrial policy that he felt should have been the basis for the negotiation mandate in the field of IPRs. All of the studies were published around March 2005, nearly 10 months into the negotiations.[29] From his arrival at INDECOPI, Roca argued that IPRs nego-tiations should be based on the wider industrial policy objectives of the country and not vice-versa. He claimed the necessary groundwork to prepare for the negotiations had not been done and that he wanted to ensure that the position put forward in the negotiations represented the institutional position of INDECOPI based on a broad set of stakeholder consultations, rather than a position that was drafted by individuals within the negotiation team. In his criticism against the FTA, Roca was not alone, but supported by other govern-ment officials.[30] The studies were extremely critical and recommended against an IPRs chapter in the form found in US FTAs. Because of his criticism, Roca was attacked by other senior members of government calling for his resigna-tion.[31] However, two months after the studies were published, Garcia resigned from INDECOPI and was temporarily assigned to the Ministry of Commerce to continue leading the IPRs negotiations from there (El Comercio 2005a). While INDECOPI continued to provide technical assistance for the remainder of the negotiations, its institutional role was severely marginalised with this move.[32]

The Ministry of Health in Peru and DIGEMID, the domestic drug regula-tory authority, were also invited to participate in the IP negotiations. It was the first time that the Ministry of Health had participated in any international commercial negotiations. The Minister of Health herself, Dr Pilar Mazzetti, followed the negotiations closely and regularly spoke up critically during the process, even though this isolated her in Cabinet. Her political capital was raised, as the officials from the Ministry of Commerce looked on in horror at the publicly unfolding conflict between health and commerce in neighbouring Colombia.[33]

The Ministry, in collaboration with the WHO and the World Bank, also conducted a range of studies on the possible impact of TRIPS-plus provisions on medicine prices in Peru throughout the negotiations. By August 2004 at the beginning of the negotiations, the Ministry published the 'lineas rojas' that were jointly developed with the Colombian health team on the Ministry's website, again raising the political profile of the Ministry in the negotiations. Peru benefited tremendously from the work of the Colombia Ministry of Health in establishing their negotiation preferences for the FTA.[34] By 2006 the Ministry had put together a thorough analysis of the impact of raised IP provisions on access to medicines in the country.

Developing a domestic win-set and preparing for the negotiations

The development of a domestic win-set is essentially a political process that is, in varying degrees, directly or indirectly determined by the different stakeholder groups affected by the agreement. The varying degrees of influence of these groups, or their power as veto players, is in turn driven by the nature of the domestic policy-making process. As we have seen, in Colombia, as in Peru, foreign economic diplomacy is centralised with power resting above all in the respective Presidencies and Ministries of Commerce.

In both countries the principals in charge of the negotiations aimed to finalise the FTA within eight negotiation rounds, or 'rapidito, rapidito'[35] in the words of President Uribe, before the end of 2004. The objective was to have short but intensive negotiations.[36] Three key factors were critical for pushing for a short negotiation time span.

First, Colombia, Ecuador and Peru were scheduled for Presidential elections in 2006, and the hope was to sign and ratify the agreement well before this date so that the negotiations would not be affected by the domestic election campaigns, and vice versa. Second, the US Trade Promotion Authority (TPA), an essential prerequisite for finalising an agreement in the US, was set to expire in July 2005 (USTR 2005a). The Agreement had to be presented to the US Congress at the very latest 90 days before the TPA expiry. While the TPA expiry was later extended to July 2007, there was no guarantee that this would be the case at the onset of the negotiations. Like the expiry of the ATPDEA, the TPA expiry was a pressure point that was actively used by the US negotiation team during the negotiations.[37] Finally, the US also had scheduled Presidential and Congressional elections for November 2004. While the TPA would remain in place and with it the mandate for the USTR to negotiate even if President Bush was not going to be re-elected, a change in Presidency in the middle of the negotiations could have resulted in unnecessary hurdles. Conflicts during the negotiations, however, particularly in relation to IPRs and agriculture, ended up delaying the finalisation of the negotiations by an additional year (Campodónico 2004).

The Colombian Government tried to prepare thoroughly for the negotiations.[38] Preparations started soon after the government decided to enter into bilateral trade negotiations with the US during the collapse of the FTAA talks in Cancun. Among the first steps taken by the Ministry of Commerce was to talk to other governments that had negotiated with the US, namely Chile and Singapore, and to thoroughly study the 2002 trade mandate given by the US Congress to the USTR. Also, some representatives of WIPO went to Colombia to help them prepare.[39] Closer to the actual start of the negotiations other government institutions were invited to join the preparations.[40] As per Decree 2314, the negotiation strategy of the country was kept confidential throughout the negotiations.

As discussed above, a noticeable absence of Congress in the development of a negotiation mandate can be attributed above all to its traditional role at the ratification stage of economic negotiations. This was criticised by Colombian academics who argued that only through the inclusion of Congress a democratic elaboration of the national win-set could have been established, and that in such absence specific interest groups enjoyed much greater access to identifying national preference. The interest of the wider public, they argued, would not be reflected (Alvarez Zarate 2004).

In Peru, even though the Peruvian government also studied previous US FTAs, communicated with the Chileans and Central Americans prior to the negotiations, and internally evaluated different negotiation options, preparations were less elaborate. Not surprisingly, the IP negotiation team had in most aspects a very defensive negotiation position as its level of protection was lower than that of Colombia at the onset of the negotiations. However, Peru was particularly keen on some offensive position in the field of IPRs, above all related to the protection of traditional knowledge and genetic resources into the agreement.[41]

Impact assessment

In both countries a range of very specific impact assessments attempting to predict the impact of the FTA on particular stakeholder groups were undertaken. The studies can be separated among those that focus on market access, those that focused on the most controversial sectors of the agreements, such as IPRs and agriculture. Sometimes the assessments would focus on a particular region, such as the City of Bogotá (Zerda Sarmiento 2005b). However, according to many critics there were insufficient comparative studies outlining real scenarios and cost-benefit analysis across sectors, which would form the basis for the development of a national win-set in preparation of the negotiations (Zerda Sarmiento 2004). In Peru critics argued that most studies were commissioned during the negotiations and in some cases seemed to be more targeted towards calming domestic criticism rather than providing actual input to the negotiations.[42]

Furthermore, and not surprisingly, the outcomes of the impact assessments differed widely, depending on the respective methodologies. In both Colombia and Peru several impact assessments were commissioned by the health authorities (Valladares Alcalde *et al.* 2005, 2006), the generic industries,[43] the Ministries of Commerce[44] and in the case of Peru, by INDECOPI (2005, 2006), and NGOs (Holguin Zamorano 2007; Cortes Gamba *et al.* 2004)[45] with the aim of predicting the impact of TRIPS-plus provisions on the domestic cost of medicines. Further impact studies were commissioned by the regional WHO office (PAHO) (Cortes Gamba *et al.* 2004). Some of the studies only focused on past drugs, certain therapeutic groups, or certain IPRs provisions such as data exclusivity, while others tried to integrate possible future demand for newer drugs, such as second and third-line ARVs. Some of the studies predicted none or very little impact, such as the Ministry of Commerce studies in Peru and Colombia, the study on the impact of Decree

2085 by the 'Colombian Association for Pharmaceutical Research-based Laboratories' (AFIDRO). Others, such as the Colombian-based foundation 'Institute for Medicine-research in Health Systems' (IFARMA) study, a range of academic studies by the Peruvian INDECOPI and Health Ministry study, predicted substantial impact (Zerda Sarmiento 2005a, 2005b; INDECOPI 2005, 2006; Cortes Gamba 2006; Ministerio de Salud 2006).

While it is beyond the scope of this thesis to analyse the appropriateness of the different methodologies used and their accuracy,[46] it seems as if often the studies were primarily used for strengthening certain political positions rather than providing a quantitative basis for the development of an overall domestic win-set. On several occasions during the interviews, negotiators pointed towards the studies, arguing that apart from one particular study, which confirmed their political position, none of the other studies held any merit.

In spite of these and other studies undertaken as part of academic research projects,[47] neither the Peruvian nor the Colombian government carried out a thorough sector-by-sector cost-benefit analysis that would account for the impact of the deep regulatory integration brought about by the FTA. Such an exercise was repeatedly demanded by domestic stakeholders (Campodónico 2005; Acosta Medina 2006) and called for by the Executive Secretary of the UN Economic Commission of Latin America (ECLAC), Jose Luis Machinea (La Republica 2004b). In Peru senior government officials, such as former Minister of Justice Baldo Kresalja, also lamented the fact that not enough understanding of the consequences of the agreement existed. He noted that while there is awareness of the impact of the FTA on specific sectors, such as asparagus, there is not enough clarity on the consequences of chapters like that on IPRs, highlighting the need for an impact assessment that would cover all aspects of the agreement (CEPES 2004).

An impact assessment of this kind would have been useful for a number of reasons. First it would have helped to calculate costs and benefits better and to predict the extent to which some sectors would lose or gain and what type of long-term structural implications the new regulatory environments would signify. Second, the numbers would have facilitated budget reallocations that could have distributed some of the gains across sectors. Third, such budget real-locations could have been based on real evidence rather than on the lobbying capacity of particular stakeholder groups, reducing controversy within the government.[48] And finally, engaging in such an exercise would also have led to a more transparent development of a domestic win-set, which could have strength-ened the negotiation team. Instead, critics in Colombia claimed that whenever an impact assessment was demanded, the government would refer to the economic impact of NAFTA on Mexico[49] to demonstrate the potential of the FTA.[50]

Lineas rojas – or the boundaries of the win-set

The concept of the 'lineas rojas' (or red lines) as ultimate resistance points to the domestic win-sets in the field of IPRs of the Andean countries was introduced as a result of the commitments made by the negotiation principals to ministries that were critical of the negotiations. The fact that at the time nearly half of Colombia's population did not have sufficient access to medicines because a lack of health coverage or not being able to pay for medicine themselves[51] gave health authorities a strong leverage in pushing for these lineas rojas with respect to IPRs. Due to the precedence set by the FTAA and other US FTAs in the region the negotiation team was fairly clear of what would be in the IP proposal by the US. At the beginning of the negotiations the 'lineas rojas' in the field of IPR/health, developed by the Andean health teams and publicly confirmed by the respective Ministries of Commerce, were the following:

- A mention of the Doha Declaration in the text of the agreement.
- No increase of the CAN 486-level of protection apart from:
  - data protection: for no longer than three years, based on the formulation of Decree 2085; including a maximum grace period of 18 months between the data's original registration and registration in Peru/Colombia; emphasising that data exclusivity would not apply when compulsory licensing was issued; and that the provision would only be introduced after 2014.
  - compensation for patenting delays: only if those are a result of the inefficiency of the domestic patent administration, and only if they extend to seven years after filing, or five years after granting.
  - linkage: only to the extent that the Andean countries would commit themselves to transparency in the sense that they informed on marketing approval through a means of their choice but would not be held accountable to the patent holder for any marketing approval granted.
- No reduction of any other TRIPS flexibilities.
- No prevention of parallel import.
- No limitation of compulsory licensing.
- No patenting of plants and animals.
- No patenting of diagnostic, surgical and therapeutic methods for the treatment of humans and animals.
- No watering down of the 'industrial applicability' criteria to the concept of 'utility'.
- No acceptance of 'use' or 'second use' patents.[52]

They were agreed upon jointly be the inter-ministerial IPRs negotiation groups. They were not considered as bargaining chips but 'make it or break it' deals. Under no circumstances were the negotiators to cross these lines. In addition, the Ministry of Health in Colombia had asked the Ministry of Commerce to sign a memorandum confirming the 'lineas rojas'. Several congressional representatives also approached both the Colombian Minister of

Commerce and the head negotiator on the question of public health and were similarly assured that the level of protection of CAN 486 would not be passed.[53] In Peru a similar assurance took place.[54] Finally, as per Decree 2314, they were backed up by the Council of Ministers.

The public commitment of the highest political level to the 'lineas rojas' led the Ministries of Health in Colombia and Peru to believe that these resistance points were taken seriously. Thus, they entered the negotiations with the confidence that they would not be breached, even if this meant the negotiations would not go forward. As the negotiations proceeded, however, these 'lineas rojas' were consistently adapted until they reached a level of protection in some provisions higher than what was found in CAFTA at the end of the negotiations, a level of protection that the health authorities were promised would not be acceptable to the Colombian and Peruvian negotiation principals.[55] Furthermore, the concept of 'lineas rojas' itself changed during the negotiations. While representatives of the health authorities continue to refer to them as real deal breakers, negotiators from Commerce started to refer to them as 'sensitive issue areas' but not as absolutes.

TANDEM *and the negotiation matrix*

As it was pointed out repeatedly in national media and by policy-makers such as Senator Acosta Medina, the Colombian negotiators were much less experienced in negotiations, which was believed to be a major hurdle to the upcoming negotiations (Acosta Medina 2006: 130). In order to strengthen the domestic negotiation team, the Colombian Government hired a group of consultants, Tandem Insourcing,[56] to help them to formulate the national win-set and prepare for the negotiations. As a group specialising in negotiation and conflict resolution they supported the negotiation team in three principal ways.

First, they helped the government develop a matrix containing all the issues that were to be negotiated, mostly extracted from the CAFTA Agreement. The team then allocated different levels of priority between the respective issues. For this, national industrial associations were also allowed to give input (Silva Solano 2007). This allowed the negotiators to familiarise themselves with the relative importance of all issues at hand and would help the government bargain more effectively. They also helped define the 'lineas rojas' that were not to be crossed under any circumstances. The matrix did not only contain the Colombian preferences but also aimed to identify the American negotiation preferences.[57] This important exercise lasted over two months and with each negotiation team working together to establish the government's priorities in the respective negotiation matter, while building trust and confidence within the team.[58]

Second, Tandem provided negotiation strategy advice. The Colombian negotiating team felt that while their negotiators had very good technical skills, their relatively little negotiating experience would be detrimental throughout the negotiations. All of the negotiators were therefore given a short crash course in negotiation strategy that would prepare them for face-to-face negotiations.

Third, Tandem supported the Colombian negotiation team throughout the actual negotiations. This included a regular update of the matrix as well as observing and commenting on the ongoing negotiations. The Tandem consultants were the only ones that, next to the head negotiator's assistant, had constant access to the head negotiator and walked in and out of all negotiation groups. Most of the negotiators would only be in one or two groups, depending on their institutional affiliation.

There were a range of problems that arose as a result of the matrix, for example health negotiators pointed towards the fact that it legitimized the negotiation of certain subject areas, merely by their inclusion in the matrix. They argued that certain provisions, such as 'second use patents', should not even have been included, simply because, from their perspective, they were non-negotiable.[59] A further problem was related to the methodology put forward by Tandem, which was based on conflict negotiations where principles rather than precise wording are needed. In economic negotiation, technical language has a lot of importance, as in the exact formulations of the IPRs provisions included, or the precise tariffs values (Zerda Sarmiento 2004).

Nevertheless, the matrix seemed to set a useful basis for negotiations for the Colombian team. Peru, that had not engaged in a similar exercise, would later on adopt large parts of it for its own win-set, at least at the onset of the negotiations (Silva Solano 2007).

Developing a regional negotiation objective

The development of a regional IP negotiation objective constituted another layer of negotiations for both countries. Indeed, the Andean Community is a project of regional integration to the extent that its legislative framework, one of which relates to a common regime on IPRs, supersedes national law. Any conflict with CAN is thus considered unconstitutional in Member States (Pulecio 2005). Thus developing a regional negotiation objective went beyond examining whether the FTA would be in conflict with CAN in the field of IPRs but also included the impact the FTA would have on the dynamics among Member States given that Venezuela was not included in the negotiations. The US explicitly stated that it wanted to negotiate an FTA with the ATPDEA countries, which did not include Venezuela but the other CAN countries and Bolivia participated only as an observer to the negotiations (Pulecio 2005). From the beginning it was clear that the agreements would undermine the future of CAN as a project of regional integration.

Colombia and Peru approached the IP negotiations jointly, not only because of the joint regime on IPRs but also because they were well aware that it would increase their bargaining power.[60] Furthermore, the Andean countries had joint IPRs negotiation experience as part of the FTAA process. Developing a joint position in the field of IPRs, however, was not easy, as they entered negotiations with different levels of IPRs protection. While Colombia had previously raised its level of IPRs protection as part of the APTDEA extension negotiations in 2002, Peru had not. The level of data protection provided for through Decree 2085 only existed in Colombia, and not in Peru or other countries in the region.

In order to enter negotiations with a joint position on IPRs, Colombia and Peru agreed to put forward the lowest common denominator, namely the level of protection in CAN 486. Yet, it was clear among the negotiating teams that at some point during the negotiations Peru would have to accommodate data protection along the lines of the 'lineas rojas'. What was not clear was when this would happen. Aware of this, the Peruvian negotiators from the beginning emphasised the need to make good strategic use of data exclusivity as a bargaining chip.[61]

However, Peru and Colombia did not share the same objectives in all subjects. Other non-IP-related aspects of the negotiations, particularly in relation to market access, as well as differences in timing with respect to when to end the negotiations undermined a strong regional alliance, leading to an eventual separation of the teams (Silva Solana 2007).

The role of non-state actors

National industry

The most important national industry actors in Colombia during the FTA negotiations was a group of industry organisations, referred to as *gremios*. Gremios play a powerful role in Colombia and, similar to their counterparts in the US, lobby their governments through supporting political campaigns and fund think tanks developing the intellectual basis for their positions. According to Edwards, such *gremios* traditionally focused on short-term economic issues, which are of immediate interest to its members (Edwards 2001). Export-oriented national industry groups such as those represented by the National Industry Council (CGN), the National Council of Exporters (ANALDEX) or the National Association of Colombian Businesses (ANDI) as well as domestic affiliates of international businesses had two key roles: first to provide the government with useful information on specific negotiating items which were of interest to its members, and second to inform domestic industry how the FTA negotiations were likely to affect them.[62]

Naturally, there was infighting within the *gremios* as they represented members which held diverging negotiations objectives. The infighting went to an extent that some of the national industrial groups started accusing one another of being difficult and unnecessarily extending the negotiations. Such accusations were directed above all against industries that were critical of the negotiations, such as certain agricultural groups or the generic industry. One way of controlling such anticipated criticism was the strategic strengthening of some of the *gremios*, such as the CGN, by the government in anticipation of the negotiations. They in turn would call for extreme discipline among its members highlighting that none of them could consider themselves losers until the negotiations were finalised. 'Nothing is agreed until everything is agreed' was a common message brought to the Councils' members (Pulecio 2005).

Another way of appeasing industry groups that were likely to lose out from the negotiations was through the offer of side payments in anticipation of their resistance. In Colombia, for example, large compensation packages were offered to the agricultural sector,[63] accounting for anticipated losses through reduced tariffs. With the exception of certain export groups such as cut flowers or asparagus producers, the agricultural sector was one of the most outspoken against the FTA negotiations. They also enjoyed close links to many *Uribistas* in Congress and had substantial political influence. With the side payments the government strategically increased its national win-set and managed to reduce the deadlock in the agricultural negotiations (Silva Solana 2007). Notably, no official side payment of this kind was offered to the national pharmaceutical industrial sector. However, after signing the agreement a reform process was initiated within government with the aim of introducing measures that would alleviate the health budget (Restrepo Velez 2007).[64] Other critical sectors or industry groups either left uncompetitive sectors or accepted that the FTA was inevitable and that the only thing to do would be to align national production to the imminent changes while hoping that some benefit would emerge due to increased US investment in the country in the future (Pulecio 2005).

Similarly, Peruvian negotiators consulted with a range of domestic stakeholders in preparation for the negotiations. This included the Industry Council for International Negotiations (CENI), made up by a mix of small, medium and large-scale companies, as well as a range of national export groups. Most of the consultations were part of the 'sala adjunta' meetings[65] as well as being through the so-called 'Consultative Council' to the negotiations (SPDA 2006). Unlike in the case of Colombia, however, interviewees from the private sector complained about their lack of interaction with the Peruvian Government throughout the negotiations. They felt that their interests were not sufficiently taken into consideration and the positions put forward were often academic and removed from the real needs of industry.[66] The decline of industry influence in policy-making under Toledo was also observed by Morón *et al.* (2006), who argue that the private sector's strong political affiliation with Fujimori and his associates has undermined their credibility in the public eye.

The generic industries in both countries opposed the IP-related FTA negotiations. The pharmaceutical market in Peru is fairly small. At the onset of the negotiations its value was around US$600–650 million per year (US$150 million of which is public sector procurement), which represented approximately 0.0002 per cent of the global market and about 0.0004 per cent of the US market at the time. More than 60 per cent of national health consumption was spent on generics, accounting for 98 per cent of all drugs consumed (Valladares Alcalde 2005; Mincetur 2005).

The Colombian pharmaceutical market is about double the size of Peru's. In 2004 it was worth US$1.3 billion, US$410 million of which was public sales (Cortes Gamba 2006). The market was expected to grow to US$2 billion by 2010, with the national industry accounting for 38 per cent of sales in monetary terms and 67 per cent of total units sold. The national generic industry, including the chemical and petrochemical sector accounted for 8.6 per cent of Colombia's GDP in 2004 (Business Monitor International 2006; Bravo 2004). At the time of the negotiations there were approximately 134 pharmaceutical manufacturing firms in Colombia, also exporting to the region (Econometria 2005).

Irrespective of their size, the generic industries in both countries had a purely defensive negotiation interest, arguing that additional layers of patent/test data protection would delay the market entry of their products. As an industry they had nothing to gain but only to lose from the negotiations. As a result, they were very critical and outspoken during the process and causing considerable rupture within the *gremios* (Pulecio 2005). The generic industry in both countries called for the exclusion of IPRs from the FTA negotiations (SPDA 2006). Nevertheless, in particular some of Peru's generic industries were impacted by the fact that they were members of the same *gremios* that were also exporting products, which had become dependent on ATPDEA market access. Some of Peru's generic industries' position was also affected by the fact that they invested in 'natural remedies', an increasingly popular niche market in the US, and hoped to benefit from the agreement.[67]

Due to its size, the Colombian industry was more powerful in its lobbying than Peru's.[68] Represented by national industry association ASINFAR, it argued that the level of IP protection in Colombia should not exceed TRIPS. ASINFAR was very critical of the FTA negotiations, constantly questioning negotiators on their actions.[69] According to negotiators, ASINFAR also met with them in more personal meetings in which the industry expressed its explicit concerns and make suggestions with respect to the negotiations. However, according to the generic industry, these concerns were not taken seriously or integrated into the domestic negotiation proposal.[70]

An interesting aspect of the lobbying of the generic industry was that they based their objection to the agreement above all on health-related grounds, something that the negotiators from the Ministry of Commerce heavily criticised. They accused the generic industry of borrowing the 'public health argument' for an end that was essentially driven by commercial motives, namely the relative share of the generic industry in the domestic pharmaceutical market.[71] When interviewed on this matter, the generic industry referred to this as a 'marriage of convenience'. With respect to patents on medical products, both the generic industry and the public health community and respective government institutions, shared a similar objective: reducing monopoly rights as much as possible so that generic competition could enter the market driving down product prices.[72]

It was a strategic move, which originated from the discussions surrounding Decree 2085 in 2001/02 (Rodriguez-Franco 2008). While only a few politicians took to the plight of the industry, no politician could ignore public health arguments. The alliance between the generic industry and the Ministry of Health diminished, however, when the Minister of Health decided to back the agreement despite the continuous trespassing of the 'lineas rojas'. While the Ministry in the end gave its public support to the agreement, civil society organisations and the generic industry never did.[73]

International industry

International (US) industry, particularly the pharmaceutical industry, had a considerable role in preparation of and during the negotiations and their direct influence on specific aspects of the negotiations, such as the removal of people from their positions as advisors to or members of the negotiation team, reached well into Colombia and Peru's decision-making.[74] In the case of Colombia, most of their influence was expressed either through domestic industry representation, such as the American Chamber of Commerce or AFIDRO, through domestic law firms or through the US Embassy. In Peru international industry was represented primarily by the American Chamber of Commerce, ALAFARPE or domestic affiliates of international businesses.[75]

The proximity between private and public sector, a particular characteristic of US commercial policy, was very apparent to both Peruvian and Colombian negotiators during the negotiations, claiming that they felt a constant communication between the US negotiation team and private sector representatives. Chapters 6 and 7 of this book will go into further detail on this issue.

NGOs

In both Colombia and Peru, health-related NGOs were very active during the negotiations. Their link to the respective Ministry of Health was direct and collaboration effective. The assistance they provided was either through technical advice or the mobilisation of events that would raise awareness on the IPR/ health issues. They would also criticise the ongoing negotiations in domestic newspapers, regularly hold their government accountable for previously made commitments or raise the political profile of certain issues through their international NGO counterparts. Often international NGOs or parties would support them financially to ensure their participation in all negotiation rounds.

In Colombia, one of the most active NGOs was Recalca, a civil society network that covered the whole negotiation process and summarised the outcomes in each negotiation table at the end of each round. An NGO working purely on health issues was IFARMA, which supported the health authorities primarily through technical assistance as well as through the carrying out of a range of impact studies on the likely impact of TRIPS-plus provisions. The collaboration between the Ministry of Health and NGOs ended towards the end of the negotiations when it became evident that the Minister of Health was going to endorse the agreement.[76]

In Peru, the two most active health-related NGOs were Foro Salud, which is a membership association of health groups, and Acción Internacional para la Salud (AIS), the Peruvian counterpart of Health Action International. Throughout the negotiations they collaborated with the Ministry of Health. Similarly to Colombia this collaboration lasted until it became evident that the Ministry of Health was going to endorse the agreement. When a possible compensation to the Ministry was discussed, the NGOs pulled back from their collaboration with the government.

In both countries civil society organisations on several occasions called on the government for greater participation and integration referring to the negotiation process as untransparent and undemocratic (Ortiz 2005b; Foro Salud *et al.* 2005).

Another active opponent to the negotiations, particularly in Colombia, was the Church. Archbishop Rubiano of Bogotá was very concerned about the public health aspect of the negotiations and asked Misión Salud, a faith-based NGO, to follow the negotiations on its behalf. Misión Salud became one of the most active civil society organisations during the process, collaborating closely with other NGOs and faith-based organisations, medical associations and the generic industry (Marulanda Lopez, 2007).

The Role of US Congress and Embassies in the Negotiation Process

The US Embassies in Colombia and Peru were primarily working as ground agents during the negotiations, lobbying for the agreement among domestic government agencies. Some of their staff also participated directly in the negotiations. Embassies are important players in the US policy-making in the region, especially in Colombia, home to one of the biggest US Embassy in the world.

The Embassies also facilitated domestic visits of US government officials. Frequently US officials visited the Colombian and Peruvian governments to get an update on the negotiations and to exercise a little additional pressure on issues that were of particular importance to their constituents. These visitors were not only members of the Executive but also the leaders of those Congressional Committees that hold responsibility for trade policy-making. These delegations would hold meetings in the Andean countries to express their minimum expectations of the FTA in order to pass ratification (Committee on House Ways and Means 2005). By doing so, the US government aimed to directly influence domestic preference setting in Colombia and Peru. In these visits the ATPDEA and TPA expiries were regularly mentioned. Other communications would also take place in written format. For example, a letter was sent by the Senate Finance Committee to the Colombian head negotiator outlining precisely what it is they wanted to see in the agreement if it was to pass Congress.[77]

Finally, the embassies also hosted events to address particular aspects of the negotiations that seemed stagnated. On one occasion during the height of the IPRs/health conflict the US Embassy in Peru hosted a special lunch for USTR staff and a range of Peruvian key policy-makers. Some negotiators suspected that the event was targeted at putting pressure on Peru's Minister of Health, who received the honorary seat next to Regina Vargo, head of the US negotiation team.[78] The same Embassy also launched an 'IPRs Kit' shortly before the end of the negotiations in November 2006, emphasising the economic benefit of increased IPRs protection to Peru (El Peruano 2006).

Summary and conclusion

This chapter has outlined the domestic negotiation scenarios in Colombia and Peru and a range of particular factors that characterised the negotiation process became apparent.

First, the *perceived* short-term BATNA by the negotiation principals in both countries was mostly driven by market access considerations. As a result the BATNA was perceived as very low driven by the fear of ATPDEA expiry without exploring alternative options with other negotiation partners such as the EU. External pressures from the US government, including the US Congress, repeatedly reaffirmed the lack of alternatives if current market access was to be maintained.

Second, the linkage between IPRs and other trade issues outside of the WTO was not new. At least Colombia had experienced such pressure through previous ATPDEA negotiations. However, the deep economic integration that characterises US FTAs superseded both in scope and intensity any previous economic agreement that went beyond purely market access negotiations (Shadlen 2005).

Third, in both countries the respective Ministries of Commerce were responsible for the negotiation team. Nevertheless, and possibly for the first time, representatives of the national health authorities formed an integral part of the negotiation teams raising their apparent profile as veto players. While this was truly remarkable, it was still the Ministry of Commerce, driven above all by market access questions, that remained in charge of all negotiation tables.

Fourth, in both Colombia and Peru the negotiations were driven by the Executive, and the role of possible veto players was either structurally weak or to a certain degree undermined by the Executive. In both countries the respective Congresses did not act as an active veto player. In Colombia it was a majority Congress and in Peru no coherent opposition was formulated in a minority Congress. Other possible veto players such as regional governments in Colombia where undermined by the Executive.

Fifth, domestic industry groups had different positions towards the FTA depending on the extent to which they would be affected by it. Those export groups that had become dependent on the ATPDEA lobbied in favour of the FTA. Especially in Colombia, this tended to be groups that had close relationships with the government and which strongly supported Uribe in the negotiations. Other political powerful groups who were more critical of the FTA such as those stemming from the agricultural sector were comforted through side payments. Other critical industries with less political influence, such as the generic industry, were isolated from the support of the *gremios* but tried to borrow power through linking the plight of the industry to arguments related to public health.

Sixth, NGOs and church groups in both Colombia and Peru followed the negotiations closely and constantly reminded the negotiation principals of their commitments with respect to public health.

Finally, the negotiations were influenced by a neo-liberal ideology that had been developing in both countries since the early 1990s. The development of the national win-set was driven above all by market access deliberation and not by a cost-benefit analysis that would account for the real costs of deep economic and regulatory integration. As will be seen in the next chapter, this played an important role, particularly towards the end of the process. By then the horizontal nature of the negotiation process was replaced by a very centralised decision-making. This eventually not only ended the Colombian and Peruvian joint negotiation strategy, but also led to a break within the teams between health and commerce authorities.

5 The US-Peru and US-Colombia FTA negotiations

The negotiations

Negotiation overview and process

Format and venues

There were 16 rounds of FTA negotiations, which lasted from two to nine days each. Their venues rotated between Colombia, Ecuador, Peru and the US. The negotiations were split into 14 different working groups[1] which negotiated separately with representatives from Colombia, Ecuador, Peru and the US, and Bolivia as observer[2] (Garcia 2006).

Table 5.1 Overview over US-Andean FTA negotiation rounds

Rounds	Dates	Location
1st	18–19 May 2004	Cartagena de Indias, Colombia
2nd	14–18 June 2004	Atlanta, US
3rd	26–30 July 2004	Lima, Peru
4th	13–17 September 2004	Fajardo, Puerto Rico
5th	25–29 October 2004	Guayaquil, Ecuador
6th	30 November–4 December 2004	Tucson, US
7th	7–11 February 2005	Cartagena de Indias, Colombia
8th	14–18 March 2005	Washington, US
9th	18–22 April 2005	Lima, Peru
10th	6–10 June 2005	Guayaquil, Ecuador
11th	18–22 July 2005	Miami, US
12th	19–23 September 2005	Cartagena de Indias, Colombia
Progress Meetings	17–21 October 2005	Washington, DC, US
13th	14–22 November 2005	Washington, DC, US
14th	25 January–3 February 2006 (only Colombia – US)	Washington, DC, US
Continuation 14th	13–17 February 2006 (only Colombia – US)	Washington, DC, US

In the first rounds of the negotiations the appointed negotiator in charge for each negotiation table led the discussions. The rest of the teams communicated through them rather than participate directly in the negotiations. This scenario changed throughout the negotiations. After the third round the technical negotiators, such as those sent by the health authorities, engaged directly in the negotiations process, a participation that was again restricted towards the end of the negotiations when decisions were taken away from the 'technical' to the 'political' level.[3]

Negotiations usually lasted from 9am to 6pm at which point the negotiation teams convened to report on the status quo of all the negotiation tables. In this meeting they also discussed what to present in the side room meetings, which took place at about 8pm each day. The day would end at about 10pm and start again the next day at 7am with a daily press briefing given by the head negotiators.[4]

As well as specific negotiation tables there was a negotiation table that was referred to as the 'Mesa de los Jefes', the 'table of the bosses'. This table only included the head negotiators of each country, namely, Hernando Jose Gomez from Colombia, Pablo de la Flor from Peru, Cristian Espinosa[5] from Ecuador and Regina Vargo from the US and their direct assistants. It was here that all the issues, which could not be resolved on the technical level, were addressed again and necessary political decisions were made. The technical negotiators had no access to this room and only at the discretion of the head negotiator were they informed of what was being discussed there. During the negotiations, the head negotiators tended to meet every second day.[6]

Negotiations were held in English and Spanish, with simultaneous translators present. However, the document that served as the immediate negotiation text was in English, even though an informal Spanish version would appear soon after new wording entered the discussion. The final agreement was always based on the English text. Language concerns were ongoing during the negotiations and even after the final text was signed.[7]

Government consultation

During the negotiations in Colombia and Peru, the executives and legislatures were kept informed in varying degrees about the progress made. The executive was primarily consulted through the Council of Vice-Ministers in Colombia and Council of Ministers in Peru. In addition, most relevant ministries had sent staff to form part of the negotiation teams, who directly updated their principals on the state of the negotiations.

With respect to the legislature, Colombian Senators interviewed claimed that only very few of their colleagues actually ever read the entire agreement, and generally felt that Congress was not sufficiently informed about the negotiations. Negotiators, in turn, pointed out that Congressmen hardly showed an interest in the negotiations. In fact many of those that did accompany them abroad to the negotiations rounds often did not follow the side room meetings as much as they should have and instead attended to other matters. This lack of engagement, the Senators argued, was previously seen in other negotiations. According to Senator Lopez, the failure to integrate Congress due to its traditional and constitutional constraint was one of the principal reasons for the reduced negotiating power of the Colombian government (Lopez 2007). Those members of Congress who were active during the negotiations tended to be from opposition parties and primarily lobbied against them.

Stakeholder consultation

All three Andean countries had a side room, referred to in Spanish as the 'cuarto de al lado' or 'sala adjunta' in which the negotiating teams would regularly meet their stakeholders to update them on the status quo of the negotiations. These stakeholders included private sector representatives, civil society groups and government officials that were not within the negotiation teams. The objective of the side room was two-fold. First, for the stakeholders to get information about the state of the negotiations, and second, for the negotiators to get input from the stakeholders. It was an attempt to facilitate participation, as enshrined by, for example, Colombia's Constitution, between negotiators and all other relevant stakeholders, including Congress (Tangarife Torres 2004). However, many of the more critical voices towards the negotiations claimed that only little real dialogue took place in these meetings and that the information shared was superficial. The audience was provided with a general idea of the issues discussed, but not with the precise wording of proposals.[8] Conflict was largely avoided in these meetings. In the sixth round this led to the expulsion of Roberto Lopez, director of HAI Peru, after he circulated material on the possible negative consequences of TRIPS-plus provisions among the participants (Ortiz 2004d).

The side rooms varied in size depending on the engagement and size of the domestic stakeholder groups following the negotiations. The Colombian side room was by far the largest. It was jointly chaired by head negotiator Gomez and the president of the National Business Council, a way of further integrating the industry councils into the process. The meetings usually included approximately 200 participants ranging from domestic industry, civil society organisations, to public servants of regional municipalities, parliamentarians and academics (Puentes 2007). Notably, journalists were not allowed in the side rooms as a press briefing was organised every morning.[9]

Participation in the side rooms was subject to conflict, particularly with respect to some industry associations that also represented the national affiliates of international businesses. Both national businesses and civil society organisations argued that through these associations international companies had access to strategic debates meant for domestic constituencies. In both countries this led to protest and even litigation. In the Peruvian case some of the groups representing international industry, such as ALAFARPE and AmCham Peru, were subsequently not allowed in the side room. In Colombia the court rejected the allegations arguing that any affiliate that paid taxes and employed Colombian nationals should be considered a national business and thus granted access to the side room.[10]

In both countries, critics complained about the overall lack of transparency of the actual negotiations and the proposals that went back and forth between the negotiation teams. These critics were told that the US had insisted on confidentiality with respect to the negotiations and that negotiators had signed confidentiality agreements prior to the negotiations. The confidentially agreements had been attached to the first proposal that the US team sent to the Andean countries, just before negotiations commenced.[11] Furthermore, the negotiation text and different proposals were accessible in the Ministries of Commerce in both countries if interested parties could demonstrate that they had a stake in the negotiations. However, printing or copying the text was not allowed, and in each ministry there was only one computer available on which the text could be accessed.[12] In practice that meant that much information was withheld from the wider public and critics argued that in Colombia this constituted a constitutional breach, specifically with respect to the right to information, the principle of democratic discussion and the processes by which international negotiations should take place (Alcaldía Mayor de Bogotá 2004a).

Inevitably the text leaked. The initial proposal made by the US was passed to civil society groups. Also, groups such as AmCham and ALAFARPE were regularly updated about the precise wording of the proposals during the negotiations. For the wider public, the text was largely out of reach. Indeed, in Peru after the negotiations were finalised it still took three weeks for the actual text to be published.[13]

Who is who in the negotiations

Overview of negotiation teams

The sizes of the negotiating parties differed widely. The US negotiation team consisted of approximately 100 people. The Colombian team was larger than the US team, its size affirming its leadership in the Andean group. In the fourth round of negotiations in Puerto Rico, for example, the team including negotiators and advisors consisted of 125 public servants, 165 members of the private sector and 17 Members of Congress. The Peruvian team consisted of 85 public servants and 80 private sector representatives and the Ecuadorian team of 95 public sector representatives and 100 private sector employees (Pereira 2006). The IPRs negotiation table was always one of the largest of the negotiations with about 30 people present. This included about six people from the US, about ten to 15 from Colombia, four to six from Peru, two from Ecuador and one observer from Bolivia.[14]

The teams were comprised of technical and political negotiators. The technical negotiators formed the majority of negotiators and were mostly considered to be implementers of negotiation objectives put forward by the head/

political negotiators. In Colombia and Peru this included officials from the Ministries of Commerce and the other ministries that sent their staff to participate in the team. Their role was primarily to work on specific wording or make proposals to the head negotiators, but limited to providing technical input to the negotiations. They were not involved in the political and strategic decisions made in the negotiations. Most of them had very little negotiation experience, if any.

The political negotiators or negotiation principals were responsible for strategic decisions in the negotiations, including those that would cross negotiation tables. Usually they included the Minister of Commerce, the head negotiators, and in the case of Peru and Colombia, the actual Presidents themselves given the close attention they paid to the negotiations. While it is not uncommon in complex negotiation to have heads of states involved towards the end of the negotiations, in the case of Colombia and Peru they engaged from the beginning of the process. This constituted a problem for the negotiators as they felt that their strategy was often undermined by statements made by the two Presidents.[15] Their expressed enthusiasm for the agreement reduced the negotiation power for the countries' negotiation teams in the negotiations, which aimed for later trade-offs with issues that were sensitive to the US.[16]

Indeed, from the beginning the Presidents indicated that 'no agreement' was not an option for both countries. In an article, named 'FTA: The sharing of a dream' President Toledo emphasised that the agreement was every Peruvian's dream and that all sectors would be involved in the negotiation process out of which a joint agreement would emerge that would allow every Peruvian to embrace this opportunity (Toledo 2004). And soon after the negotiations started he claimed that 'My name is not Toledo if I don't sign the agreement', and that 'We will sign the agreement – si o si!' (Wiener 2004). Later, Toledo tried to soften his statement by saying that 'si o si' only meant to demonstrate his administration's political will to engage in the negotiations, but not to sign any agreement no matter what its content (Agencia Peru 2005b). During meetings with US government representatives Toledo further communicated his eagerness to conclude the FTA as fast as possible. To a delegation of US Congressional Representatives in July 2005 he said that he:

> . . . wants to conclude an FTA with the United States as quickly as possible [. . .]. [He then] urged his Minister of Trade to conclude the FTA with the United States by the end of September and asked for the [US] delegation's help in meeting this goal. President Toledo expressed concern that the longer the delay in concluding an agreement, the more politicized the issue would become. [. . .] [He also said] he would do everything he could to work with Colombia and Ecuador to conclude a cohesive Andean FTA. He also noted that if a broader Andean FTA is not possible, Peru is prepared to sign a U.S.- Peru FTA [independent of Colombia].
>
> (Committee on House Ways and Means 2005)

Similarly, the Minister for Production in Peru compared failure to sign the FTA in light of the expiring ATPDEA, to 'holding a Damocles Sword over more than a million workers' (Agencia Peru 2005a). The perceived willingness of Peru to sign an agreement was confirmed by US negotiators, stating that in their view Peru would have signed virtually any agreement.[17]

In Colombia the political journal 'Semana' described the negotiations as an 'institutional scaffolding' headed by the President himself (Semana 2004). Uribe at one point in the negotiations said that there would be an FTA at all costs otherwise it would rain 'rays and flashes' on them and the Minister of Congress referred to it as the development plan for the coming 50 years (Acosta Medina 2006). Only a few months later in October 2005 Botero announced that the Uribe Administration would take over the political responsibility of the negotiations acknowledging some sectors would be harmed in the process, predicting that they would not be able to defend all 'lineas rojas' (Lopez 2007).

Extent of negotiation slack

A major difference between the US and the Andean teams in the negotiations was the extent of negotiation slack, which the negotiators possessed in the negotiations. In addition to the fact that the US negotiators were negotiating on the back of a more powerful economy, as will be described in the next chapter, they were operating within the realms of a strict negotiation mandate. The mandate was based on a statuary negotiation framework and on the specific instructions which they had received from Congress and those stakeholder groups that for a number of reasons enjoyed proximity to the USTR. Thus, the US negotiators had very little slack, which, according to the Schelling Conjecture, increased their bargaining power.

In contrast, in Colombia and Peru there was little limit to executive power from influential domestic veto players that tied their hands during negotiations. Furthermore, given the direct involvement of their Heads of State in the negotiations the principals could make far greater concession at any time in order to move the negotiations forward.

Relationship within negotiation teams

The relationship within the negotiation teams, in particular in Colombia, was not smooth. In no negotiation team was this more prevalent than in the IPRs team due to the friction between the trade and health authorities. Indeed, the negotiation table was often referred to as a 'source' of, rather than a 'solution' to, controversies. In the beginning when belief in a joint win-set still existed among the team members, the relationship was fairly smooth, further drawn together by jointly facing a very powerful negotiation party. This common concern also bound Colombia and Peru together as a team and allowed them to act jointly and coherently until the final stages of the negotiations. However, with the increasing crossing of the 'lineas rojas', friction between the Colombian health and trade representatives grew to the point that the health team publicly resigned. While the same friction between the health and trade authorities also existed within the Peruvian team, the conflict was not as apparent and managed much more discretely.

The collaboration within the US team was much smoother in comparison. This is primarily because the team itself had a clear and pre-defined negotiation mandate, especially in the field of IPRs that was insisted upon by external negotiation 'principals', consisting of Congress and certain stakeholder groups. With respect to IPRs the primary function of the negotiation team was to achieve the maintenance of the IPRs template. The efficiency of the US negotiation machinery was well reflected in the smooth functioning of the negotiation team and much admired by the Andeans.

Relationship across negotiation teams

The relationship across the negotiation teams, particularly between the Andean teams, was very amicable. They got to know each other well in the run up to and during the negotiation process. Travelling together and the joint confrontation against the US team formed bonds that soon turned into friendships. Most of the bonds across the negotiation teams, however, would be formed along ideological lines depending on their institutional background, often being stronger than the actual governmental ties among the negotiators. For example, the health negotiators from Colombia and Peru formed a very strong interpersonal unit, stronger than the ties between the health group and the commerce group within the same government.[18]

Negotiation phases

Conditions for entering into negotiations

Before the initial launch of the negotiations, the US government sent both Colombia and Peru a list of so-called 'trade irritants'. These irritants were outstanding legal disputes between a range of US investors and the governments of Colombia and Peru mostly in relation to infrastructure projects.

In the case of Peru some of the conflicts had already been resolved in the course of the 2002 ATPDEA extension negotiations. Others remained unsolved, jointly representing investment interests of about US$300 million (Mohme Llona 2004). The US government insisted that all had to be resolved by the time that the negotiations started, or latest by the conclusion of the agreement (Committee on House Ways and Means 2005). During the negotiations US Congressmen and US Undersecretary of Commerce Walter Bastian called for Ecuador and Peru to be excluded from the negotiations if these issues were not settled (Ortiz 2004f; La Republica 2004a). While the US Ambassador to Peru emphasised that this should not be considered as pressure on the Peruvian Government to move on these open litigations, the link to the FTA did precisely that[19] (Mohme Llona 2004). Yet, President Toledo soon sent clear signals indicating Peru's willingness to deal with these irritants (Acosta Medina 2006).

The visits of USTR Ambassador Robert Zoellick to Colombia in 2003 was considered by many as the beginning and end of the FTA negotiations. Zoellick, on invitation from President Uribe, met with key decision-makers on his visit and essentially laid out the scope and depth of the anticipated negotiation (Sek 2005). The broader aim of the visit was to secure the success of the negotiations before they had even started, including through the mentioning of expectations in the IPRs chapter (Alvarez Zarate 2004). He made clear reference to the US-Chile FTA and emphasised that the USTR expected an agreement along these lines. According to Senator Robledo Zoellick 'We will do the agreement, but we will set the conditions. Either you take it or you leave it' (Robledo 2006: 41–2).

Only when the government affirmed its commitment to the FTA were the official negotiations launched.[20] Later the basis for the IP negotiation text was changed from the US-Chile to that of CAFTA, which at the time of Zoellick's first visit to Colombia had not been finalised.[21] After the visit and commitments from the Andean countries to endorse the negotiations, Zoellick formally notified Congress on 18 November 2003 of his intent to begin FTA negotiations (Sek 2005). Testing the commitment of future negotiation partners and possible veto players is a common criterion for the US government in deciding on FTA partners (Schott 2003).

Setting the scene – rounds 1–5

A few days before the first negotiation round started, the USTR sent the Colombian and Peruvian Governments a draft proposal (in English) on all negotiation subjects, including IPRs (Silva Solano 2007). In contrast to earlier suggestions, the level of protection put forward did not equal the IPRs chapter of the Chilean FTA, but contained levels of protection that substantially exceeded any of the previously US negotiated agreements.

The US original proposal on patents included provisions on:

a   patenting of plants and animals;
b   patenting of surgical and therapeutic methods;
c   patents on any new uses or methods of uses;
d   limiting the use of compulsory licences to cases of public non-commercial use or in the case of national emergency or other circumstances of extreme urgency;
e   prohibition of parallel imports;
f   compensation for delays in the patenting system, whereas delay is defined as: the issuance of the patent of more than four years from the date of filing of the application in the territory of the Party, or two years after a request for examination of the application, whichever is later;

g   compensation for the delays of commercialisation due to drug marketing approval processes through an extension of the patent term, even if the delays are caused by the marketing approval in another country;

h   five years of data protection provisions for pharmaceuticals and a reformulation of the existing Colombian legislation, including: the protection of *information* rather than *undisclosed information*; allowing for a five-year delay of registering the data submitted for the original marketing approval in another territory before submitting it in Peru and Colombia; defining NCEs as an entity that was previously not submitted in the territory of the party; three years of additional data protection for information submitted for new uses; allowing for a three-year delay of registering the data submitted for the original new use approval in another territory before submitting it in Peru and Colombia;

i   linkage provisions between the patent office and the drug regulatory authority which oblige the drug regulatory authority to prevent the marketing of products that are still under patent protection and notify the patent holder; and

j   increased enforcement for patent infringement.[22]

Sending the proposal was an aggressive entry into the negotiations. While some of these provisions were clearly integrated as bargaining chips because they did not feature in CAFTA (such as parallel import or the patenting of surgical and therapeutic methods), the Colombian and Peruvian negotiating teams had not expected the early submission of a proposal before the negotiation started. They themselves had not prepared such a detailed document. While Colombia was better prepared than Peru, with explicit advice from Tandem, they had only put together a list of principles and positions, including the 'lineas rojas'. The hope of the Andeans had been to present these principles to the US at the beginning of the process before entering into text specific debates. The Andean negotiators expressed their preference for a process in which all parties would state their positions and expectations on individual negotiating items rather than immediately enter into text-based negotiations. The US team indicated their willingness to listen while insisting that eventually the negotiations text would have to be the basis of the negotiations.[23] For the next two rounds the Andean countries therefore presented their positions on the different negotiating items and the US team listened, refusing to engage in a principle-based negotiation.

Then in Round 3 the Andean countries made a specific counter proposal in IPRs, which basically reflected CAN 486 level of protection, or the TRIPS level of protection with an addition on genetic resources, technology transfer, collecting societies and a reference to the Doha Declaration in the actual text of the agreement.[24] This proposal was developed by the joint negotiating teams and approved by all relevant ministries, including Health and Commerce. As well as proposing a lower level of IPRs protection, this proposal reflected an attempt by the Andean countries to actively influence the basic negotiation text.

The US negotiators would not accept either the format or content of the Andean proposal. Thus in Rounds 3 and 4 they continued to listen to the Andean proposals put forward but refused to use them as a basic text for negotiating and maintained their position by only accepting specific comments based on the wording as put forward by the US proposal. Eventually, they suggested fusing the two documents based on the format of the US proposal, with the suggested wording of both parties. This, they argued, would allow for a better comparison on the respective positions. This was agreed upon in Round 5 and the US proposal, with inputs from the Andean side, served as basic negotiation text[25] (Alcaldía Mayor de Bogotá 2004a; Ortiz 2004b).

In spite of this early defeat in influencing the format of the negotiations, in a publication named 'FTA: Political Position of the Presidency' by the Colombian Government published, more than five rounds into the negotiations, it was still stated:

> We are not negotiating an adhesion contract here. The point of reference of the negotiations is not the proposal of the United States, but Colombia has equally contributed in all negotiation topics.
> (MinComercio 2004; translated by author)[26]

In Peru, similar statements were made. In March 2005 a publication by the Ministry of Commerce stated:

> The FTA that Peru will sign with the USA will not be a mere copy of the FTA with Chile or CAFTA, nor other agreements previously negotiated. Every country has to defend its own objectives, interests and sensitive areas in the negotiations. Peru has presented text proposals that put its interests in each of the negotiation tables forward. The final text of the FTA will reflect a space which allowed the formation of interests that are mutually satisfactory to both parties.
> (Mincetur 2005: 14; translated by author)

In the same publication the Ministry also claimed:

> The IPRs provisions put forward through the US FTA will not restrict public access to generic products nor will they raise their prices. In fact the opposite will take place. The reduction of tariffs on medicines from the US will benefit consumers, who can access these products more cheaply.
> (Mincetur 2005: 23; translated by author)

Another basic tone of the negotiations was set in this first phase, namely the overall nature of the bargaining process. While the Andean teams aimed to negotiate in packages linking certain issues to each other, the US team refused to do so. They would only negotiate item per item, thus preventing any trade-offs. While this negotiating difference re-emerged throughout the negotiations, it was in these first rounds that it became eminent. It led to the frustration of many of the Andean negotiators that had prepared themselves for package deals, as advised by Tandem.[27]

The first real scandal that hit the IPRs team in this phase was Allan Angell's resignation from government in August 2004. Angell, originally the principal advisor of Peruvian IPRs head negotiator Luis Alonso Garcia, left the Peruvian Government three months after the beginning of the negotiations to join Pfizer. By that time Angell had been included in all of the strategic preparatory meetings among the Andean countries. The scandal was inevitably fuelled by the political sensibility surrounding the IPRs negotiations and the public health debate. As an IPRs negotiator, joining one of the biggest US pharmaceutical companies, while negotiating an FTA with the USA, his decision provoked a public outcry. It led to many discussions on whether a law should be drafted that prevented public sector employees from joining the private sector without grace period (Pereira 2006).[28]

Notwithstanding the difficulties in confronting the US team, the health and trade authorities still collaborated well during this first phase of the negotiations. An example of the power of the health team in Colombia in this phase was demonstrated when the Minister of Commerce was planning to employ Amir Attaran as an official advisor to the negotiations.[29] Attaran, a former Harvard professor, had published widely that IPRs had no impact on questions related to access to medicines.[30] His work had subsequently been referred to by the US Government in related negotiations as 'Harvard Studies' that demonstrated that IPRs and access to medicines were not correlated (Sell 2006). The health authorities successfully opposed his appointment, concerned about his biased position on the relationship between IPRs and access to medicines.[31] Thus, at this point health authorities still had a strong influence in the negotiation process. The preferences put forward by commerce and health still overlapped (Pulecio 2004).

Similarly, in Peru, domestic health authorities became very active during this first negotiation phase by publishing the 'lineas rojas' on their website. Minister Mazzetti's further continued lobbying among the Council of Ministers and negotiating principals. The case of Peru's health authorities was further strengthened during this phase through the visit of the UN Special Rapporteur on the Right to Health, Paul Hunt, urging the government to maintaining TRIPS flexibilities in their FTA (Bridges Weekly 2005).

Towards Round 3, the beginning of a rift emerged with respect to the participation of Carlos Maria Correa as an official member of the Colombian negotiation team. Palacio had hired Correa, an IPRs expert from the University of Buenos Aires, to participate as part of health authorities' team at the IPRs negotiation table. The US team, however, refused to participate in IPRs negotiations if Correa was part of the official delegation (Diez Canseco 2004; Ortiz 2004a). To remove him from the negotiation table they argued that only government officials should be allowed to participate in the official negotiations. The matter essentially halted the negotiations until the end of the round when Palacio agreed to have Correa sit in a side room to the negotiations, accessible to the negotiators but not at the actual negotiation table.[32] The Colombian generic industry subsequently accused their government of 'dejarse pisar el poncho' – allowing the US to 'trample on their poncho' by influencing domestic affairs (Ortiz 2004a).

Some of the Colombian negotiators characterised this first phase as one of very little overall movement. They primarily blamed the US for this, accusing them of not wanting to make any commitment before the presidential election in November 2004. While informally[33] the US team had shown some flexibility with some of the IPRs provisions, in Round 5 the US team entered the IPRs negotiations with a renewed proposal that was exactly the same proposal that they had sent at the onset of the negotiations (Ortiz 2004c). Frustrated Andean negotiators described the negotiations as a tango dance. For each step forward, two were taken backwards.

At the end of the phase, negotiators had started what was referred to as 'cleaning up the text', in which issues which were satisfactory to both parties would be set aside from the negotiation tables. It should also be noted that negotiations in this phase still remained to a large extent within individual tables, thus trade-offs were sought within the same subjects based on technical negotiations. It was only when negotiations got stuck in individual tables they were moved up to the 'political' negotiation table of the head negotiators, who then had to decide on trade-offs (Silva Solano 2007).

A widening of the rift between health and commerce: rounds 6–11

IPRs negotiations continued to stagnate in this second phase of the negotiations, while many other negotiation tables slowly saw advances made. Negotiations in IPRs continued with the US insisting on their initial proposal and the Andeans on their 'lineas rojas'.[34] The stagnation reached such a level that Colombian President Uribe himself got involved. Three days before Round 6 of the negotiations in Tucson he held a meeting in Bogotá, which included Members of the Council of Minister and the country's head negotiator, in which Palacio explained to him the background to the 'lineas rojas'. Jointly they agreed on the following.

- After studying the CAFTA and the US-Chile FTA they agreed that the IPRs provisions of these agreements were inappropriate for the country.
- That compensation for delays with respect to the working of the national patent office and national drug regulatory agency would only be acceptable if it was based on internal delays of the patent office, not delays that occur due to other parties.

- While they would agree to data protection in the FTA some modification from the traditional US proposal would have to be agreed to, such as through the integration of an 18-month grace period between the original date of registration and the initiation of the five years of protection in Colombia.
- That the linkage proposal put forward by the US team was complicated and that all negotiations on this matter had to be guided by making government more efficient and transparent and not by the interests of right holders.
- Finally, the President insisted on having a text prepared for the round in Tucson which reflected the limits agreed to in this meeting.[35]

In spite of this Presidential commitment, Colombian negotiators from the Ministry of Commerce in Round 6 started indicating their willingness to move away from their commitment to the 'lineas rojas', provoking the health team to walk out of the negotiations. It was the first direct confrontation between the Ministries of Health and Commerce and led to Botero seeking their removal from the negotiation team, which was prevented by Palacio.[36]

In Round 7 the IPRs negotiations were hit by another controversy surrounding data exclusivity. As mentioned earlier, Colombia already had data exclusivity legislation, unlike Ecuador and Peru. For the US data exclusivity was of utmost importance, to the extent that it could become a deal breaker for the entire FTA. Aware of this, the Andean negotiation teams had agreed that, subject to certain conditions, they would eventually have to consent to data exclusivity. Peru, however, requested in the regional preparation meetings of Rounds 4, 5 and 6 that they should not give in on data exclusivity at that stage in the negotiations but use it as a bargaining chip for the integration of issues related to traditional knowledge and genetic resource into the FTA at a later stage. The other teams agreed to this.[37] Furthermore, Colombia's health negotiators had been given a guarantee that when data exclusivity was going to be accepted, it would only be introduced in 2014, while making Decree 2085 obsolete. This would mean that essentially Colombia would not have any domestic data exclusivity legislation until 2014, a point that was of particular importance to the Colombian health groups and the generic industry.[38]

Nevertheless, on 9 February 2005, Colombia's IPRs lead negotiator presented the US negotiators with a proposal on data protection that would maintain Decree 2085 until 2014 when the FTA model of data protection was to be introduced. The provision also failed to make reference to the grace period of 18 months that had been agreed upon previously. With this move he not only broke the commitment to the domestic health authorities with respect to the nature of the provision but also the regional alliance with Peru with respect to the timing of the proposal. Peru subsequently did not sign the proposal and for the first time in the IPRs negotiations the Andean nations split (Correa C. 2005; Ortiz 2005a). The fact that at the precise moment in which the negotiator made the proposal the health representatives of the Colombian team were absent from the negotiation table further scandalized the incident. The gravity of the rift became imminent when at the end of the day Colombia's head negotiator attempted to hide the scandal claiming in the side room meeting that the reason for the absence of the health team was the fact that originally copyright was put on the negotiation agenda (Correa C. J. 2005).

The incident immediately erupted the tension that had been mounting within the Colombian negotiation team. Publicly the generic industry referred to it as 'treason'. Alberto Bravo, president of ASINFAR, said:

> I feel betrayed by the negotiating team. In the seventh round in Cartagena they presented a proposal on test data protection that is very different to the one that we had discussed before, and that aims to maintain the controversial decree 2085.
>
> (Bolpress 2005; translated by author)

The tension grew to such an extent that the negotiator in question soon after resigned from his post. Opinions on why he prematurely offered this particular deal on data exclusivity to the US team differ. He claims that it was a miscommunication as he had understood that he should protect the Colombian norm on data exclusivity and that the mistake was not to ensure that all were consulted. In this sense, he claims his mistake was one of process and management (Cubillos and Santamaría 2005). Other negotiators, however, claimed he was made a scapegoat for the incident (Acosta Medina 2006). If this was the case then it is likely that Gomez was at least aware of the impending proposal, but blame was shifted exclusively on the IPR negotiator to reconcile with the health team.[39]

Apart from the conflicts on the domestic level, particularly in Colombia, during this period, the international IP negotiations in turn were still marked by an overall lack of real progress in spite of many informal commitments made by the Andean side. The lack of progress in this but also other fields was blamed primarily on the outstanding ratification of CAFTA in the US Congress. Policy-makers on both sides were aware that if CAFTA did not pass this would mark an end to ongoing negotiations. Minister Botero highlighted this to the US Congressional visitors in July 2005. He:

> . . . stated his belief that while Colombia has demonstrated political will to move the agreement forward, he has not seen comparable will on the part of U.S. negotiators due to the CAFTA approval process. Botero [. . .] pointed out that the United States has yet to respond to many offers on the table.
>
> (Committee on House Ways and Means 2005)

The resignation of the health teams – round 12

With this in mind the Andean teams were surprised in Round 12 by being confronted by an entirely new US IPRs negotiation team. It saw the exchange of a US IPRs team under the supervision of Brian Peck, who had gained some trust with the Andean teams. The new team that arrived showed no awareness of the informal compromises made by their predecessors and returned to the original proposal text presented by the US team at the onset of the negotiations.[40]

The position with which the new team entered represented a major setback to the formal and above all informal discussions that took place during and parallel to the previous rounds. It included all the original proposals on 'use patents', patents on surgical, therapeutic methods, plants and animals, compensation for all kinds of patent delays, adoption of the US criteria of 'utility' and patent term extension, among others with which the US had entered the negotiations. Furthermore, there was no reference to the Andean proposals on data exclusivity, the integration of the Doha Declaration or the protection of traditional knowledge and genetic resources (Villar Lopez 2005).[41]

Colombia and Peru's health negotiators alike objected to a continuation of this path of negotiations, whereas the respective Ministries of Commerce insisted that the negotiations had to continue. Soon it was announced in both countries that the technical negotiations had come to an end and political negotiations had begun. At the same time President Toledo confirmed that the negotiations had to be finalised by the end of the year, even if this meant leaving the Andean alliance and finalising the agreement alone (Villar Lopez 2005).

As a result the health teams of Colombia and Peru resigned in succession. The Colombian team did so most publicly by writing an open letter to their ministry, referred to as 'Carta Bomba':

> There has been no significant advances in those matters that were of interest to Colombia. To the contrary, the representatives of the US government maintained a position of inflexibility [. . .].
>
> Furthermore, on 21 September, the head negotiator to Colombia has announced at an internal meeting of the technical negotiation teams that [. . .] from now on political decisions will determine the final period of the negotiations and that the work of the technical negotiators was finished [translated by author].
>
> (Portafolio 2006)

Health negotiators suggested that without their resignation they would have been excluded from the next rounds of negotiations anyway, given the move from technical to political negotiations. The reaction of the Colombian commerce negotiators to the public resignation of the health team was critical, claiming that they had failed to understand their role during the negotiations. Accordingly, their open protest of the negotiations was not supporting the overall objective of finalising the agreement. 'They did not know what it means to be part of a team' was often mentioned in the interviews, referring to the health negotiators as 'fanatics' and 'paranoid'. One of the interviewees mentioned that:

> . . . they were constantly arguing on the basis of what could happen, rather than what was likely to happen. They always used the 'conditional tense' in their argumentation – such as IF the wording is so and so then it COULD be abused by the patent holder and subsequently lead to an increase of medicine prices. But they never provided any real evidence or data that this really WILL be the case. So their arguments do not have real value nor did do they offer any alternatives.[42]

The end of the Andean collaboration and a resignation from government: rounds 13 and 14

Rounds 13 and 14 took place in Washington, DC and constituted the ultimate break between the health and commerce teams in Colombia. After having resigned as official negotiators the team continued to work as advisors to the Minister of Health, based on a last minute compromise found between the Ministers of Health and Commerce. The position put forward, while trespassing the original 'lineas rojas', was a last compromise by the health negotiators for the sake of saving the negotiations.[43] When in Round 14 of the negotiations in Washington, DC the agreed proposal was again bypassed, and this with the blessing of the Minister of Health, the technical team withdrew from their position as advisors. One of the three, Luis Guillermo Restrepo, went even further and also resigned as a public servant to the government. He did so with an additional open letter in which he accused the government of never having taken the public health objectives put forward at the onset of the negotiations seriously. He wrote:

> Today I would like to publicly state my decision to withdraw from government as a result of my total disagreement with the latest decisions taken during the negotiations in the field of IPRs and the form with which the Ministry of Commerce, Industry and Tourism has conducted the process.
>
> My decision is a result of what in my opinion constitutes the most serious incident of the negotiations so far, which took place in this latest round in Washington, DC. Here the coordinator of the negotiation group on IPRs [. . .] abandoned in an unilateral manner the proposal that was put together jointly by the Andean countries, and presented a proposal on data protection based on the text of the USA, containing dispositions with levels of protection that exceed the level of protection in the FTAs

with Chile and CAFTA. This ignores all the compromises made with the health sector, similar to an incidence that occurred with an official of the same ministry earlier this year, and we still do not know whether this was result of an order from above or on his own account. [. . .]

With respect to how the Ministry of Commerce, Industry and Tourism has conducted the process, it would have been much more transparent to tell the country that the work over 18 months on IPRs and health failed, that negotiations as such never existed and that in order to sign a FTA with the USA it is necessary to pass the 'lineas rojas'. [. . .] This would have maybe saved us much conflict, time and resources [. . .].

I am certain that from the beginning of the negotiation they knew of the rigid posture of the US negotiators and that the US team would not accept a deal that was not equal or better than CAFTA.

(Restrepo Velez 2005; translated by author)

It was also in this round that the entire Colombian negotiation team walked out of the negotiations, primarily because of a continuing lack of advances in patents and agriculture and the respective domestic opposition on these issue areas. Peru, however, decided to remain in the negotiations, with the target of terminating them by early December 2005, aware that this would erode the country's negotiation power (Francke 2005).

Indeed, Peru did finalise the agreement with the US on 7 December 2005, with a Presidential promise that it would bring six million jobs[44] within ten years and would not affect consumers (El Peruano 2005e). The final negotiation round was marked by the participation of politicians of the highest political rank. Present were the Ministers for Production, Commerce, Health, and Economy as well as the head negotiator Pablo de la Flor. Most of the conflicts surrounding the IPRs chapter were resolved at the penultimate negotiation round, with the exception of patents, data exclusivity and genetic resources[45] (Garcia 2006). These outstanding issues were among the last issues to be resolved and were done so in the presence of the Peruvian Minister of Health Mazzetti and some of her closest advisors. Her participation was crucial, primarily for domestic political purposes and indeed after finalising the agreement Toledo publicly applauded her work assuring Peruvians that medicine prices would not be affected. He then extended his gratitude to the Bush Administration for demonstrating flexibility on this matter (El Peruano 2005e).

According to members of her staff, Mazzetti only agreed to endorse the agreement under the condition of a side payment. Realising that she could not prevent the ratification, she used her political leverage to assure the commitment of the Presidency to compensate the public health authorities for the expected price increase of medicines. A study done by the Ministry of Health calculated the costs of data protection alone would exceed US$170 million per year by 2017, a figure that was published widely (El Comercio 2005b). Indeed, in a public meeting just two weeks before the finalisation of the agreement, Mazzetti stated that if the Peruvian Government had to agree to higher IPRs standards affecting the price of medicines, a compensation system for national health authorities would ensure that this would not have an impact on access[46] (El Peruano 2005c). NGOs, however, did not back her in this move. The day after her announcement a statement was published in 'La Republica' calling on the Minister not to endorse the FTA (Foro Salud 2005). Notwithstanding the differences between the Ministry and the NGOs it should be noted that unlike in Colombia, there was a public acknowledgement that there would be an impact on medicine prices as a result of the IPRs chapter.

Colombia closes the negotiations – rounds 15 and 16 in Washington, DC

With Peru's finalisation of the agreement the negotiation flexibility of the Colombian team was even further reduced. The US negotiators made this clear to the Colombian negotiation team, saying: 'Look, this is the deal now. Peru signed this, you may as well, too.' Most of the Colombian negotiators said that with the signature of Peru the US margin of flexibility was virtually zero.[47]

At the same time health-related NGOs were still battling for an FTA with as little as possible TRIPS-plus provisions. Thus, in a last-minute discussion one day prior to his departure to the final rounds of negotiation in Washington, DC, President Uribe agreed to a short meeting of 20 minutes with the key representatives of the health NGOs in Bogotá, again getting directly involved in the domestic conflict within the health and trade groups. In order to reduce the tension Uribe demanded a number of key issues that the health community wanted him to ensure were integrated in the final agreement. To underline his commitment, President Uribe invited German Holguin from Mision Salud to his upcoming meeting with the USTR in Washington, DC, scheduled for 16 December 2006.[48]

In this meeting President Uribe formulated jointly with his Ministers of Health and Commerce as well as members of the USTR, a so called 'Ayuda de Memoria' – a Memory Aid – that confirmed (a) that the IP chapter would not inhibit Colombia from any public health protection measures, (b) 'second use' or 'use' patents would be avoided in the agreement and nothing in the agreement would ever be interpreted as 'second use', (c) that the level of data protection as put forward by Decree 2085 would satisfy the country's obligations under the FTA (Mincomercio 2006). He then confirmed that this document was to be signed by the Colombian Government as well as the USTR.[49]

However, upon returning to Bogotá it became clear that the 'Ayuda Memoria' had only been signed by the Colombian Government and the USTR had refused. Nevertheless, it was celebrated as a success by the Colombian Government in terms of demonstrating its commitment to its different stakeholder groups. The disappointed public health community, however, argued that the initiative was abused by the government on both levels. First, on the international level to demonstrate to the USTR that its health authorities would endorse the agreement, and second, on the domestic level to demonstrate that no health-related compromises had been made.[50] As a legal document, however, it was meaningless (Ministry of Commerce 2007).

Outcome of the negotiations and the 'first' final negotiation text

The negotiations were eventually brought to an end on 27 February 2006, after a final round that lasted four weeks and under the close watch of President Uribe, frequently in Washington, DC at the time. When the negotiations were closed[51] the agreement included an IPRs chapter along the lines of CAFTA, with some minor differences. Also, the Colombia and Peru FTAs included two 'side letters' or 'understandings' that related to the field of public health. The two IPRs chapters of Colombia and Peru were virtually identical, with just two small differences. The outcome of the chapter was to the overall satisfaction of the major stakeholder groups that lobbied in favour for it to the US Congress and the USTR. The USTR's Industry Trade Advisory Committee on Intellectual Property Rights (ITAC-15) noted:

> [The Colombian Trade Promotion Agreement] takes into account the significant legal and technological developments that have occurred since the TRIPS and NAFTA agreements entered into force and mirrors, and, in many areas, improves upon, the Singapore, Chile, and CAFTA-DR in order to establish clear precedents in most key areas of IP protection for future FTA negotiations, many of which precedents were also followed in the FTAs with Morocco, Bahrain, and Oman.
>
> (ITAC-15 2006)

However, ITAC-15 also notes certain disappointment with the outcome of the agreement, as it did not include all the TRIPS-plus provisions they had put forward, some of which could be found in other agreements, such as the FTAs with Bahrain and Oman. These include, for example, higher standards on what is the definition of 'unreasonable delay' for patent term extension or additional data protection for clinical test data for the new application of already introduced chemical compounds (ITAC-15 2006). In addition, when compared to the initial proposal by the US to the Andeans, a range of issues, that were included in the initial proposal, were missing in this final negotiated text. These include: (a) limitations on compulsory licensing; (b) limitations on parallel import; (c) second use/new use patents; (d) diagnostic, therapeutic and surgical procedures for the treatment of humans or animals; and (e) patents on plants and animals.

While the Ministry of Commerce in Colombia pointed to these as clear negotiation successes, others suggested that because none of them featured in CAFTA, they were likely to have only been included as bargaining chips in the original US proposal. Furthermore, as has been pointed out by the US-ITC, on some of the matters, such as on parallel imports, no consensus had been found even within the US Government explaining its withdrawal from FTAs (USITC 2006). On the other hand, what was of particular importance to the US was a harmonised system on data exclusivity, due to its value to national pharmaceutical and agrochemical industries. As one interviewed lawyer put it: 'Data exclusivity provides immediate protection; it's effective, easy and cheap to register.'

In the end the Colombian Minister of Health endorsed the agreement. His Ministry's official position defended the Ministry of Commerce, confirming that the IPRs chapter will have no impact on medicine prices. The unconditional support in Colombia and the somewhat conditional support in Peru, by their respective Ministries of Health, was important for sending a strong message to the US that the whole government endorsed the agreement.[52]

The reason why Palacio finally and so unconditionally supported the government in spite of his initial outspoken criticism remains unclear. The majority of interviewed negotiators and other experts close to the negotiations suggested that it is likely he received a Presidential order forcing him to endorse the agreement if he wanted to continue in his post.[53] This would also explain his abrupt change of position on this matter.[54] Others were less sceptical, arguing that his change of position was a result of him understanding towards the end of the negotiations that the newly negotiated IPRs chapter would not have serious implications on drug prices. They blamed his late 'turning around' on the fact that he had originally surrounded himself with 'extremists' who misinformed him about the real implications of the FTA. Finally, they argued that Palacio, unlike some of his technical negotiators, was a politician who judged the FTA in its entirety and not only based on health-related negotiation objectives.[55]

Unlike in Peru, in Colombia no official compensation system for the health authorities was discussed in public. As the government's official position was that no negative impact would result from the increased level of IPRs provisions no official compensation was possible (Lopez 2007). In fact the official stand of the Ministry of Trade remained until after the negotiations that no direct link between patent protection and drug prices could be made, but that other variables exist that have a larger impact on price differences (Mincomercio 2007). As mentioned above, however, some internal reforms were discussed after the negotiations that would take some weight of the public health budget.

Post-agreement negotiation

The reopening of agreement – a new US trade agenda

In November 2006, elections in the US led to a change in majority in Congress. As we will see in the following two chapters, the newly gained Democratic control over both Houses had an immediate impact on the country's trade policy, and soon Democrats announced that changes had to be made in the finalised FTAs with Peru and Colombia if they were to pass.[56]

On 10 May 2007 Democrats and Republicans came to an agreement on trade policy that aimed to define the future trade policy of the country. In a document referred to as 'A New Trade Agenda for America', new norms were put forward primarily in the chapters on environment, labour and also on IPRs (see Appendix III) (Gestion 2007). The content of the 'New Trade Agenda' was then transferred into specific text amendments that were included in the texts of both agreements. Many of these changes were similar to those originally put forward by the Andean health negotiators, such as including the Doha Declaration in the actual text of the agreement. While this was good news for Colombia's and Peru's health authorities, the situation in Colombia after the announcement of the new trade policy was paradoxical. Essentially, the US Government, as a result of domestic political change, acknowledged that the original IPRs chapter posed a threat to access to public health and subsequently changed its IPRs template. Meanwhile the official position of the Ministry of Health in Colombia continued to argue that there was no impact. Later this was reversed and the negotiators celebrated the change as a negotiation success.[57]

Ratification by Peru and Colombia

The ratification of the FTAs in Colombia and Peru took place in two steps. First the respective Congresses approved the initial negotiated text, and then ratified the FTA amendment, that, among others, introduced changes in the IPRs chapter. This process was criticized, arguing that the government was signing a treaty in spite of knowing the nature of the amendment at the time. In Colombia, in particular, the government was accused of 'negotiating on knees, singing on knees and . . . renegotiating on knees' (Suárez Montoya 2006).

In Peru, the principal ratification took place on 28 June 2006 in a late night session put together at the last minute by the Peruvian Government. The FTA was ratified with an overwhelming majority of 79 versus 14 votes. It was important to Toledo's Administration to ratify the agreement before the newly elected Members of Congress would take office in late July 2006, which included a large block of FTA critical politicians.[58] This action was considered by many critics as highly illegitimate. As stated by Health Action International:

> An outgoing Congress with a minimal level of public approval and a vision of short-term benefits for a handful of business sectors, has dared to approve an agreement with serious risks for the development of the country and serious consequence for large sectors of the population.
>
> (Health Action International 2006: 1; translated by author)

Indeed, some of the newly elected members of Congress were so upset with the last minute vote that they disrupted the debate in the middle of the night, leading to physical fighting and a break in the session (CNN 2006).

Once the US Democrats' 'New Trade Agenda' was announced in May 2007 the Minister of Commerce in Peru, Mercedes Araoz, was quick to welcome the suggested changes, indicating that they reflected the interests of Peru. Without seeing the final document, she suggested that an additional discussion in Congress was not needed (Gestion 2007). On 25 June 2007 USTR Susan Schwab announced that the changes indicated by the 'New Trade Agenda' were translated, in collaboration with Araoz, into a legally binding document that would serve as an amendment to the already signed and, in the case of Peru, ratified, FTA. Two days later this amendment was also ratified in the Peruvian Congress with a majority of 70:34 votes (Villarreal 2007).

In Colombia the FTA agreement was ratified in both houses on 6 and 15 June 2007, respectively. Similar to the case of Peru, at the time of ratification the Colombian Government had not received the final outline of the additional changes put forward by the US Democrats. Those were passed in the form of an amendment on 25 September 2007 with an overwhelming majority of 84:3 (El Tiempo 2007).

Reflections on the negotiations

No negotiation flexibility

If the interviewed negotiators had one thing in common, it was their emphasis on the lack of negotiation flexibility from the US side. Throughout the negotiations the US team either refused to move its negotiation position or would simply say: 'That is an interesting proposal, we will get back to you' but in fact maintained their original position. The lack of movement was particularly strong in the negotiations surrounding the IPRs chapters. While during the course of the negotiations sometimes movement was often informally indicated, the exchange of the negotiating team resulted in moving back to the original US proposal. The inflexibility to reach anything less than what was in CAFTA became so evident during the negotiations that most of the Andean negotiators speculated that the US team had in fact very little negotiation flexibility on the matter. As we will see in the next chapter, they were given very narrow negotiating margins by the US Congress and other stakeholders, and thus negotiated with extreme rigour.

The rigour of the US negotiation strategy was further emphasised by the fact that nothing in the negotiations was confirmed until the agreement was ratified. In fact, as has been mentioned above, negotiations continued even after they were officially concluded: 'Nothing is agreed until everything is agreed' – a concept familiar to many negotiations and which also applied to the US-Andean FTA negotiations. Therefore the original Andean strategy of making package deals was not successful. The US team would not agree to this form of 'petty issue-linkage'. Nevertheless, the US negotiators during the process never failed to make use of the 'grand issue-linkage' to unrelated matters, such as the expiry of the APTDEA, or the ongoing parallel litigation in Colombia and Peru. Given the fact that the presidents of both countries never failed to emphasise that there was no question of *whether* there would be an agreement, but *when* there would be an agreement, a gentle reminder from the US team of 'you wanted to negotiate with us in the first place' was very effective. The Andean negotiators were in the uncomfortable position of having to bargain not only against a more powerful party, but constantly being reminded by their own leadership that 'no agreement' was not an option. Essentially their win-sets were publicly declared as very flexible and the US negotiators were well aware of it.

'Which negotiations?'

Thus, when asked about the nature of the negotiation process some negotiators from the Andean countries responded: 'Which negotiations, there were no negotiations.'[59] For them the whole process had been predictable from the very beginning, both domestically and during the actual negotiations.

On the international level, critics claimed that even though the US team would listen and communicate expressed concerns back to the capital, they actually remained absolutely inflexible in modifying their position. Some, such as the Colombian Senator Lopez from the Liberal Party, went as far as saying that certain negotiations subjects, including IPRs, were arranged from the very beginning (Lopez 2007). And Senator Robledo, also from Colombia, refers to the negotiation process as 'one of the most embarrassing moments of [the] diplomatic history of Colombia' (Robledo 2006: 41).

Equal disappointent, in particular related to IPRs, stemmed from the negotiations on the national level, between the Ministry of Commerce and the Presidency on the one side, and the health authorities, the generic sector and health-related NGOs on the other. The position of the different institutions involved was characterised by a different set of principles that formed the basis of their respective preferences. While the commerce authorities made clear that essentially everything was subject to negotiations, the health authorities insisted (until the change of position of the Minister of Health) that public health was not negotiable (Rossi Buenaventura 2006). While one group emphasised the importance of the overall agreement to secure permanent market access, the other group insisted that certain no-go areas had to be maintained.

The disillusionment, however, was not so much as a result of the dissimilar preferences put forward by the two groups, but more related to process. While at the beginning of the process the head negotiators and the government had presented the negotiations as a full consensus (FC) process in which the Ministry of Health was given equal standing in the establishment of the domestic win-set and its resistance points, this was only going to last as long as a joint win-set seemed possible.

Initially the Colombian Presidency claimed that:

> We want to construct the highest level of consensus among the Colombians. [. . .] In our relation with the ministries, with the regions

[. . .] with the economic sectors, in our relations with Congress, and in the relations with all political parties represented in Congress, with the social groups, with regional authorities and with the unions.

(Ministry of Commerce 2004; translated by author)

However, the real nature of the process emerged when it became clear that the preferences of the health authorities fell out of the perceived win-set of the US. Once this was acknowledged the 'technical negotiations' were over and the 'political negotiations' began and the consensus driven process transformed itself into a 'decide, announce, defence' (DAD) process. By gradually reducing the resistance points defended by the health authorities, the Colombian and Peruvian negotiation principals slowly enlarged the win-set, accommodating the key US preferences in the field of IPRs.

'A waste of time and resources?'

Representatives of the Ministry of Commerce, on the other hand, said that probably their biggest mistake with respect to the negotiations was failed domestic communication on the impact the IPRs chapter would really have on public health. They said that the conflict between the health and commerce authorities got out of control, and did so primarily for reasons of misinformation that resulted from a lack of information or the deliberate spreading of wrong information by a handful of 'radicals'. Accordingly, a better public relations campaign would have prevented much conflict and saved a lot of resources.

Other negotiators who were neither representatives from the Ministries of Commerce nor Health and who observed the conflict from afar argued that more information would not have improved the situation. It was their view that the overall lack of 'soul searching' before the agreement, truly bringing the team together behind a 'real win-set' that was not directed by questions relating to market access but which reflected on the deep regulatory harmonisation brought about by the FTA was the real cause of the friction. Many of the conflicts between the commerce and health teams should have been resolved before the negotiations and real no-go areas agreed upon and maintained and addressed through side payments and other instruments.[60]

Political vs. technical; short vs. long term and producer vs. consumer interests

Some of the interviewed technical negotiators emphasised a range of structural biases that worked against the preferences put forward by health authorities in Colombia and Peru in domestic negotiations. Three principal biases were identified: political vs. technical arguments, short-term vs. long-term considerations and producers vs. consumer interests.

Technical health negotiators were dissatisfied with the importance that political negotiators placed on technical issues. Some of them blamed it on the lack of understanding of the often higher-ranking officials of the consequences of certain technical changes in the medium or long term. For them negotiation bargains that included immediate benefits, such as additional units of flower exports, was much easier to comprehend or grasp than, for example, a new definition of patentability criteria or other IP-related fields. In this sense, some of the technical negotiators felt that political negotiators often either traded in technical changes too easily, or used them as bargaining chips, for gains that would have an immediate impact that was easy to communicate to local constituents and thus avoided repercussions in the next elections. That many of these benefits are only short term did not affect these decisions.[61]

In contrast, the impact of renewed patentability criteria is more complex to comprehend. Stakeholder groups are harder to define and impact is based on theoretic models and a certain amount of speculation. Experts have very different opinions on what will be the precise effects of allowing patents for 'useful' inventions rather than those that are 'industrially applicable'. Furthermore, the impact would not be felt immediately, it would take years, possibly decades, until the full impact of this rewording was understood. Given the length of political cycles through elections, it comes as no surprise that policy-makers will focus their decision-making on the immediate future.

Finally, as mentioned in previous chapters, producer interests tend to be better defended in international negotiations than consumer interests. While IPRs provisions as a whole affect a broad and often indefinable group, the public health authorities argued on behalf of a very specific group. This included the government's own public health institutions, individual consumers who are in need of life-saving medicines, but cannot afford their market price and, indirectly, the generic industry due to its role in driving down prices. While the latter does represent a domestic producer, its political power, even in Colombia, is much less significant in comparison to industry groups representing export groups such as horticulturalists that had become dependent on the ATPDEA preferences.

Institutional learning and the high exchange of negotiators

Some interviewees pointed towards the overall lack of investment in raising the institutional negotiation competence in the two countries. Negotiators in Colombia and Peru have little negotiation experience because in general negotiators do not continue working for the government after (and even during) the process and join the private sector or other institutions.[62] Negotiators tend to be hired for their technical understanding but possess little negotiating experience of their own.

At the time of the negotiations both Peru and Colombia had not invested in building institutional learning capacity to ensure that the experiences of one negotiation are passed on to the next generation of negotiators. Unlike in

Europe, the US and also Chile and Brazil, where young negotiators are trained by a professional civil service programme to then accompany more experienced colleagues to international negotiations before taking over further negotiation responsibility, no such training took place in the Andean region (Morón *et al.* 2006; Zerda Sarmiento 2004).

The vicious circle of strong political affiliation

One senator interviewed for the case study pointed towards a particular problem of the Colombian Government during the negotiations, namely the vicious circle of negotiating with an important political ally. Uribe's policy of 'democratic security' was ideologically closely tied to the Bush Administration, especially in the wake of 9/11. In its alliance to the US, Uribe even decided to send soldiers to Iraq without a UN Security Council resolution legitimising military action. This was further supported by the long-standing relationship between the countries due to US support of Plan Colombia[63] and the well-connectedness of Colombian Ambassador Luis Alberto Moreno in Washington, DC.[64] Uribe even emphasised the geopolitical importance of this tie in a 2005 visit of US Congressional representatives, in which he suggested:

> Colombia is a strong supporter of the United States, while Brazil is trying to supplant American leadership in South America and Venezuela is trying to buy a leadership role with inexpensive oil. The President also emphasized that instability in the region would increase if the United States were unable to conclude an FTA with as strong an ally as Colombia. With so many political uncertainties in the region, President Uribe said, a positive American presence is critical.
>
> (Committee on House Ways and Means 2005: 10–11)

With this in mind, Colombia's negotiation principals expected a more amicable negotiations process for the FTA, linking it specifically to the two countries' political and ideological affiliation (Pulecio 2005). However, this strategy did not materialise. In the same report of the 2005 US Congressional visit, it is stated:

> The [US] delegation believes that Colombia expects special treatment because of its valuable role in counternarcotics and counterterrorism efforts. Despite the strategic importance of the relationship between the United States and the Andean community, the U.S. Congress will judge an Andean FTA on its merits; Congressional support for trade deals – even with Colombia – cannot be assumed.
>
> (Committee on House Ways and Means 2005: 7)

This was also confirmed by USTR Regina Vargo, who in the press conference after the first negotiation round highlighted that the FTA is a commercial negotiation and should not be confused with a negotiation surrounding the fight against drugs and terrorism (Silva Solano 2007). Also, in spite of Colombia's interest to negotiate individually, the US made it very clear that it would negotiate with the Andean countries as a bloc and would not give Colombia a separate treatment (Pulecio 2005). When the Colombian Government realised it had to bargain fiercely in order to defend its national interest in a range of issue areas again the 'good relationship' between the two governments worked to the Colombian Government's disadvantage. Fearing political backlash, they were hesitant to be too demanding in the commercial negotiations so as not to undermine the good relationship between the two parties (Robledo 2006). This situation was further complicated by the 2006 US Congressional elections leading to a Democratic sweep. Uribe's alliance had been built to a large extent on his ties to the Bush Administration. Some negotiators pointed out that the government was not prepared for this change in the US political landscape and should have paid more attention to Democrats to ensure that the finalised agreement would also pass a democratically controlled Congress (Silva Solano 2007).

The role of elections in the FTA negotiations

Elections were critical in the negotiations. First, as mentioned above, all three Andean countries were hoping to terminate negotiations before their national election campaign would begin in 2005. When the negotiations took longer than anticipated, elections in both countries overlapped with the negotiations. This affected the negotiations in different ways. In the case of Peru, by mid-2005 President Toledo held very little popular support, ranging from approximately 5 per cent to the low teens. Throughout the negotiations it was continuously mentioned that it was essential to finalise the negotiations and ratify the agreement before national elections and a new Administration would come into office, fearing that otherwise many of the negotiation subjects would be reopened and Andean collaboration undermined (El Peruano 2005b). Thus, towards the end of his term Toledo wanted to close the agreement and leave behind a legacy of his administration locking in ATPDEA preferences (Silva Solano 2007).

The case of Colombia was essentially the opposite. During and towards the end of the negotiation period popular support for President Uribe was around 70 per cent, with an absolute majority of more than 60 per cent in both Houses. He knew that any electoral losses due to stakeholder groups affected by the FTA would have very little impact on the outcome of the next election in 2006 that above all was still defined by his security policies. In 2006 he won the elections with a majority of 62 per cent after having succeeded in a constitutional amendment that allowed him to run for a second time for Office. As Congress was dominated by 'Uribistas', protests surrounding the FTA by opposition groups had virtually no impact.

In this sense elections only seem to have a real influence on negotiation outcome and process when the outcome of the elections is not well defined. In both cases, Colombia and Peru, where the outcomes of the elections were very clear, the countries' leaders had nothing to lose, and subsequently did not have to adapt their negotiation agenda. In contrast, as we will see in the following chapters, US Congressional elections had a substantial impact on the FTA also because elections took place while the FTA was still waiting ratification.

Centralised policy-making, the Schelling Conjecture and the FTA

As pointed out by Thomas Schelling, a major disadvantage to any negotiations is the lack of a strong level II that limits the negotiating power of its negotiators (see also chapter 1). As was mentioned above, the Andean negotiators had substantial negotiation flexibility and an institutional framework that essentially allowed the countries' negotiation principals to negotiate largely independently, especially when compared to the US. Nevertheless, the systemic weakness of their level II did not go unnoticed and some attempts were made to re-balance this disequilibrium from the Andean side.

The Schelling Conjecture

The US negotiation team made substantial use of the Schelling Conjecture, mostly referring either to the content of the TPA of 2002, other administrative hurdles, or by making use of it in domestic constituencies. As will be demonstrated in the next chapter, the US level II negotiation framework provided the negotiation team with ample opportunity to do so. For example the US team constantly reminded the Andean negotiators that the TPA was going to run out in 2005 (original deadline), and subsequently put time pressure on the negotiations which were initially scheduled to terminate by the latest in February 2005. Similar pressure was made with respect to the expiry of the ATPDEA preferences that were scheduled for December 2006. A 2005 report of a US Congressional visit to the Andean countries, says:

> The delegation in particular emphasized that current unilateral trade preferences under the [. . .] (ATPDEA) are set to expire in December 2006, and the only way that the Andean countries can replicate their access to the U.S. market after these benefits expire is through a comprehensive bilateral free trade agreement providing reciprocal market access.
>
> (Committee on House Ways and Means 2005: 6)

Bearing in mind the dependence of a range of Colombian and Peruvian export groups on the existing preferential market access, this threat concerned Colombian and Peruvian policy-makers. Yet, according to the Mayor's Office, there was never an attempt made by the government to actually extend these deadlines, in order to reduce some of the time line pressure, imposed by US domestic policy (Alcaldía Mayor de Bogotá 2004a).

Ley Espejo

The power of the US negotiation framework did not go unnoticed in the Andean countries and a range of Andean-based initiatives emerged that sought to strengthen their negotiation teams with similar processes. In May 2004 Senator Rivera from Colombia tabled a bill that would mirror the US negotiation system and pass some power from the Executive to the Colombian Congress. The bill was thus referred to as 'ley espejo' – 'mirror law' as it aimed to mirror the US system. Its aim was to define the parameters within which the Executive would negotiate international treaties. It set a framework for foreign diplomacy that would reduce the risk of the Executive's unilateral decision-making by introducing a set of checks and balances, among others, that Congress would have to be consulted on before commercial negotiations were initiated. Rivera realised that the strength of the US negotiators lay in the precise limits of their win-set and that Colombia ought to develop a similar negotiation framework (Caballero Argáez 2004; Arboleda Zapata 2004).

The law was criticised by a number of people, however, including Colombia's Minister of Commerce, arguing that it was unconstitutional, and intruded into the political sphere of the Executive (Arboleda Zapata 2004; Tangarife Torres 2004). Furthermore, given the majority of 'Uribistas' in the Colombian Congress, and that the bill would have led to a power shift from Uribe's Administration to Congress, the bill was never likely to succeed.

The Mayor's office in Bogotá

The Mayor's office in Bogotá also had a very interesting role during the negotiations. Many consider the Mayor of Bogotá to be the second most powerful person in the country, primarily because of the city's contribution to the country's GNP (25 per cent). Furthermore 37 per cent of the country's industry is located in the city, which is also the country's political and financial centre and with its 8 million inhabitants it constitutes the biggest domestic market (Alcaldía Mayor de Bogotá 2004c).

Mayor Lucho Garzon was not against the FTA as such, but against an agreement that was badly negotiated. 'We are not against the treaty but we want to be treated well' the Mayor emphasised in a published statement, in which he complained about the breach of the Federal District's constitutional right to play a larger role during the negotiations (Alcaldía Mayor de Bogotá 2004b). Similar to Senator Rivera he and his team observed that the US negotiation framework was much stronger than the one of Colombia, which essentially placed all the power in the hands of the central government. His attempt to strengthen the country's negotiating position, was to raise the profile of the capital's administration in the negotiation process. His aim was to provide negotiators with a real option of stating in the negotiations: 'We would like to agree to X, but this will not pass the approval of the City Government of Bogotá' (Alcaldía Mayor de Bogotá 2004b). He identified Colombia's federalist characteristics as credible enough reasons to convince the US of this tying of hands.[65]

As a result, between March and September 2004 the Mayor's office developed a negotiation objective for the Federal District on all of the different negotiation topics. To do so he commissioned studies that analysed the impact of the FTA on the region,[66] held meetings with regional industry groups, provided analytical updates and produced a range of other material that were to serve as input to the negotiations.

In addition, he demanded the City Government be represented at the actual negotiation table. He based his argument on Colombia's Constitution of 1991 and the newly developed National Development Plan. One of the principal objectives of the constitutional changes in 1991 was to integrate regional governments further into national policy-making (Alcaldía Mayor de Bogotá 2004a). In this the Mayor considered the FTA as a golden opportunity for generating greater regional capacity in engaging in national and international negotiations (Pulecio 2004). It was argued that the Constitution obliged the President to consult and coordinate with the regional governments before the treaty was signed to ensure that regional interests and rights were not compromised through the treaty (Alcaldía Mayor de Bogotá 2004c; Alcaldía Mayor de Bogotá 2004a).[67]

His request was rejected by the central government on the basis that if they allowed entry for the Federal District, all of the other regions of the country would also demand participation. Thus, he was referred to the side room, where the Mayor's office was subsequently represented.[68]

CAN

A final example of the use of the Schelling Conjecture in the FTA negotiations was highlighted by Luis Alonso Garcia, head negotiator of Peru's IPRs team. In an article on the negotiations Garcia stated that the existing IPRs norms and legal instruments in the Andean community supported them in the negotiation process. He claimed that during the negotiation the Andean teams successfully made reference to CAN to strengthen their negotiation position, an advantage the Chileans or Central Americans did not have (Garcia 2006). An example of such a case was the explicit prohibition of 'use patents' in CAN Decision 486, a provision that the US included in its original proposal. Andean negotiators on several occasions said that 'use' or 'second use' patents were explicitly prohibited under CAN, and could thus not be included in the FTA. While they were successful in preventing the inclusion of 'use patents' in the agreements it did not succeed in preventing other provisions that remained in the finalised text and also conflicted with CAN 486. Furthermore, some private sector representatives hinted that it is likely that the US from the beginning used it as a bargaining chip, aware that 'new use protection' could also be introduced through a lowering of the patentability criteria.[69]

Centralisation

In spite of these attempts there were few real veto players who voiced their concern with respect to the direction of the negotiations. In both countries, albeit for different reasons, the Ministry of Commerce in close collaboration with the respective Presidency were largely in control of the negotiation process and implementation. As mentioned above, Peru's negotiation framework was nearly exclusively based on the Executive, which repeatedly emphasised that no agreement was not an option, driven by the fear of losing preferential US market access. The country's institutions that may have opposed the agreement, such as political opposition parties or the Ministry of Health, were not in a position to exercise real veto power over the negotiations.

While Colombia's political structure in theory allowed for more veto players than Peru's, Uribe's overwhelming support and very centralised style of policy-making undermined their capacity to influence the process. In turn, it provided his administration with the freedom to design and defend a win-set that was largely based on their preferences. Given the importance Uribe placed on attracting investment and locking in existing market access, it was unlikely that negotiation principals would risk failing to come to an agreement with the US negotiators by insisting on the 'lineas rojas' committed to the Colombian health authorities. As it became increasingly evident that the US would not show any negotiation flexibility in key issues such as IPRs, the Uribe's rhetoric shifted. While in the beginning it was claimed that everybody would be a winner as a result of the FTA, it was now acknowledged that there would be losers (Pulecio 2005). Some of these losers such as the agricultural sector in Colombia and the Ministry of Health in Peru were offered side payments that would not turn them into allies, but at least reduce their critical stance towards the negotiations. Others, such as the health authorities in Colombia were slowly side-lined leading eventually to a break within the negotiations team.

Regional implications

Bilateral politics in the American hemisphere have led to a fragmentation of South American integration. Many of the strong regional blocks, such as Mercosur and CAN, have been threatened as individual members have engaged in FTAs with outside parties. After the collapse of the WTO negotiations in Cancun, Colombia and Peru among others decided to withdraw from the G-21, a group of large developing countries that includes Argentina and Brazil, considered by the US as a group of trade liberalisation obstructionists

(Campodónico 2003). The underlying reason for this move was to facilitate FTA negotiations. According to the Peruvian Minister of Commerce, Ferrero:

> Clearly, the impact of a future FTA with the world's largest economy and Peru's main trading partner surpasses the benefits of any agreement derived from mere geographical or political interests, like the G-21.
> (Wing 2004; Merino Roman 2003)

However, regional integration within CAN Member States has historically been very deep and supported by powerful institutions, such as a communal tariff, a regional court of justice, or a common legal regime on IPRs. Furthermore, it is stated in Decision 598 (2004) of CAN on Trade Relations with Third Countries:

> Article 2: If it is not possible to conduct community negotiations for whatsoever reasons, the Member Countries can negotiate bilaterally with third countries. In such event, the participating Member Countries should:
>
> a   Preserve the Andean legal system in the relations between the Andean Community Member Countries.
> b   Take into account the commercial sensitivities of the other Andean countries in the trade liberalization offers.
> c   Maintain within a transparency and solidarity framework an adequate exchange of information and consultations during the course of the negotiations.[70]

The FTA with the US has certainly undermined some of the spirit originally foreseen by the Andean integration project, above all because from the beginning the FTA negotiations only included some of the Andean nations. Furthermore, Peru's legislative package included nearly 100 decrees to see to the implementation of the country's new obligations under the FTA (El Comercio 2008). Emerging conflicts with Andean norms in IPRs and other fields severely destabilised the community (Fairlie 2005a). Indeed, both Ecuador and Bolivia have distanced themselves from the neo-liberal policies of Colombia and Peru (de la Flor 2010) and Venezuela left CAN altogether, claiming that Colombia and Peru's FTA move has left CAN 'deadly wounded' (Anderson 2006). Indeed, some authors have highlighted that it is time to acknowledge that CAN has outlived its political objectives for Peru, and that it is time to look beyond the region for economic opportunities while distancing itself from its Andean neighbours (Paredes 2010).

Apart from the geopolitical implications of the FTAs, a number of IPRs provisions in the finalised text of the negotiations and subsequent implementation in Peru have led to conflicts with the countries' commitments under CAN Decision 486, requiring modifications to the common IP regime. Peru's subsequent lobbying for its modification led to substantial friction among the then four CAN members, namely Peru and Colombia on the one side and Ecuador and Bolivia on the other. Only Ecuador's final support eventually brokered a resolution among members, leading to Decision 689 which allows Members to make certain adjustments in their national IP laws to accommodate the changes brought forward by the FTA (de la Flor 2010). Relations between Peru and Bolivia, however, have deteriorated substantially over the matter (*Peruvian Times* 2008). More analysis is needed to understand whether in the long term the bilateral treaties negotiated by Member States have become not an addition to regional trade policy but a threat to it (Paredes 2010).

Conclusion

In comparison to previous developing countries' FTA negotiation partners with the US, the Andean health authorities were very well prepared and held a high level of technical expertise. They had access to previously negotiated agreements, knew what would be expected of them in the negotiations and had access to a range of international experts that supported them in the negotiations. In addition to that, commitment to the preferences expressed by the public health authorities had been made from the highest political level. In spite of that the negotiated agreement contained the same if not higher levels of IPRs protection as previous FTAs. As it was demonstrated, throughout the negotiations bit-by-bit the commitments made to the public health authorities were let go.

The explanation for this can be found on both the domestic as well as the international level. On the domestic level the centrality of the decision-making process reduced the local bargaining position that was already weakened by the countries' dependence on the ATPDEA. The repeated public statements that 'no agreement' was not an option for the heads of state led to a substantial erosion of bargaining power in front of US negotiators. Furthermore, although the technical negotiations were highly decentralised with an integration of all ministries once the negotiations moved to the political level, the trade-offs were to a large extent decided by negotiation principals and above all driven by motivations related to the maintenance of preferential market access.

On the international level the US negotiators left the Colombian and Peruvian teams very little flexibility and were extremely aggressive in the negotiations, particularly in the field of IPRs. The extent of the US negotiation advantage, however, would have been substantially lower without the solid level II negotiation machinery that forms the basis of all US trade negotiations. This not only established a very narrow and well defined win-set, but also provides specific stakeholder groups with direct access to US negotiation principals and subsequent influence on the negotiations. It is here that the reasons for the inflexibility with respect to the IPRs negotiations mandate can be found.

The next chapter will examine precisely these processes.

6   The domestic framework of US economic diplomacy

Introduction

This chapter will describe the domestic sources of US economic diplomacy, starting with the motivation of the US Government to enter FTAs and then elaborate on the Constitutional framework for trade policy-making and its actual implementation. Particular emphasis will be placed on the notable role and influence that private sector interest groups enjoy in the formulation and execution of US trade policy through formal and informal channels. It will be argued that lobbying groups in Washington, DC have become such an integral part of US policy-making that the government itself relies on them for both campaign contributions and the services they provide. This chapter will provide the background for the next chapter, which will demonstrate why the US negotiation team demonstrated such inflexibility when in the FTA negotiations, in particular related to the IPRs chapter, and how a change in the domestic political landscape led to a re-formulation of trade policy, including in the related IPRs negotiation template.

US motivations for entering into FTAs

There are different reasons for the expansion of FTAs on a regional and bilateral level. A central factor is the overall disillusionment with the multilateral trading system. In many fields, including IPRs, WTO Member States feel that progress is very slow, and that it is easier to move forward in smaller negotiation circles. Given the weight of the US economy, the country has been in the forefront of driving the global trading framework. Stagnating global trade talks did not prevent the country from pursuing its envisaged trade agenda. As Ambassador Zoellick, then USTR, said after the collapse of the trade talks in Cancun 2003:

> Many countries – developing and developed – were dismayed by the transformation of the WTO into a forum for the politics of protest. Some withstood pressure to join the strife from larger developing neighbours.

Of course, negotiating positions differed. But the key division at Cancun was between the can-do and the won't-do.

For over two years, the US has pushed to open markets globally, in our hemisphere, and with sub-regions or individual countries. As WTO members ponder the future, the US will not wait: we will move towards free trade with can-do countries.

(Zoellick 2003)

The economic value of bilateral agreements from the perspective of a larger economy, such as the US, depends on the size and nature of the negotiating partners' domestic market. Most of the FTAs ratified since NAFTA have been with small economies, apart from the notable exceptions of the FTAs with Australia and Singapore. Trade with countries that are not FTA partners with the US still accounts for 84 per cent of US trade. Most of the larger economies do not want to enter into FTAs with the US because they shy away from the deep economic integration template that the US seeks abroad fearing the backlash from domestic constituencies in sensitive economic sectors (GAO 2007b). One such example is Switzerland, which a few months after entering into informal FTA negotiations with the US, soon decided that domestic stakeholder groups would (and could) veto such agreement (Inside US Trade 2006).

However, the intensive pursuit of FTAs, coined by former USTR Robert Zoellick and often referred to as 'competitive liberalisation',[1] has more far-reaching objectives than reducing the US trade deficit but often involves foreign policy objectives. Since the attacks of 9/11, strengthening economic ties has been considered a national security priority, which led to FTAs with Bahrain, Jordan and Oman. Many FTA partners support the US in its policy objectives in the Middle East. Others are of other strategic importance such as supplying oil, combating narcotic cartels or forming alliances with the US in multilateral settings (VanGrasstek 2008a). It is primarily the White House and the State Department who decide on FTA partners. Their choice is frequently not based on economic rationale but on securing specific foreign policy objectives.[2]

A further stated objective of FTAs is the spread of democratic values and the promotion of 'free market reforms' in the partner countries. According to the USTR, FTAs lead to improved democracy, the rule of law, anti-corruption and good governance (GAO 2007b). In this spirit FTAs are often used to promote a much deeper economic integration package through regulatory reform, which is tied to the commitments made on market access. The standards put forward are based on US law and are presented as templates in the form of FTA chapters on a range of subject matters. The IPRs chapter is one of these 'gold standards' templates.

In the case of Colombia and Peru, the countries' economic significance is relatively small for the US. Nevertheless, the FTAs increase US market access in the Andean region. As at the time of the FTA negotiations Colombia and

Peru already enjoyed most of the preferential US market access through the ATPDEA,[3] the FTAs reciprocal nature put the US on equal terms. For example, in the case of Peru, the FTA was expected to lead to an abolishment of tariffs on approximately 80 per cent of US exports of goods to Peru (USTR 2007). From the US perspective this will put the Andean countries into the line of FTA partners that have decided to move out of Trade Preference Programs into reciprocal and comprehensive trade deals.

Of further importance, in the case of the Andean countries, is their signifi-cance in opening up the Latin American region for a future FTAA. Starting on a smaller scale with a range of the FTAA economies such as Colombia and Peru and the CAFTA countries is one step towards greater hemispheric inte-gration (GAO 2007b).

Domestic integration of IPRs into US Trade Acts

The integration of IPRs into the US trade policy-making framework was initiated in 1974 by the endorsement of the US Trade Act. Industrial groups representing software, motion picture, information technology and pharma-ceutical industries played a dominant role in this development. As was explored in chapter 2, the 1974 US Trade Act was given additional teeth through the 1988 OTCA. Its specific goal was to build on the 1974 Trade Act and strengthen US industrial competitiveness, particularly through the devel-opment and protection of new technologies. One of the Act's most notable features was the provision of unilateral trade tools that targeted violations of US IPRs abroad.

These efforts resulted in the integration of IPRs into the new WTO and the 'Single Undertaking' resulting from the Uruguay Round. However, as previ-ously suggested, the final TRIPS Agreement did not fully meet the expecta-tions of some industry groups (UNCTAD-ICTSD 2003). Increasing political awareness on the impact of IPRs, particularly on developing countries, and the related drafting of the Doha Declaration further intensified this disillu-sionment.[4] Efforts to raise IPRs standards towards the US level of IPRs protec-tion continued to be one objective of US foreign economic policy-making.[5]

Additional disappointment emerged in the US towards WIPO, the UN-specialised agency that seeks the progressive development of global intel-lectual property law. The stagnation of the negotiations of the SPLT that aims to harmonise the substantive provisions on patent protection among Member States, lowered the country's confidence in the institution (ICTSD 2005). In particular, government and industry were frustrated with the lack of enforce-ment of IPRs standards abroad. As it was emphasised in USTR's Special 301 Reports of 2004:

> The most significant piracy and counterfeiting problems require meas-ures that may go beyond the minimum standards of TRIPS to ensure effective enforcement at the national and local levels [. . .]. This is why

USTR seeks through our FTAs and our bilateral consultations to ensure that criminal penalties are high enough to have a deterrent effect, both in the law and as imposed by the courts and administrative bodies, as well as to ensure that pirated and counterfeit products, and the equipment used to make them, are seized and destroyed.

(USTR 2004: 2)

At the onset of the Andean FTA negotiations, the USTR claimed annual economic losses of US$200–250 billion (USTR 2004) in developing countries due to lack of enforcement. However, a number of critics have highlighted the arbitrary nature of this figure, which seems to date back to the early 1990s (Sanchez 2008). Similar observations have been made in the medical field with respect to cost estimates of counterfeit products by trade associations, government and even the WHO arguing that after a little bit of further research, 'the "data" begins to resemble a house of mirrors as each group cites the other as the source of the information' (Outterson and Smith 2006: 2). Whatever the precise figures[6] the great majority of such losses originate from larger developing economies, such as India or Korea. Therefore, the gains made from agreements such as the US-Peru FTA or US-Colombia FTA in terms of strengthening enforcement provisions or introducing new levels of protection such as data exclusivity are likely to be insignificant and in many cases unrelated.

The preservation of the 'gold standard' IPRs template was considered crucial in order not to set precedents of flexibility for future negotiations. Since NAFTA, the US has been consistently pursuing the export of its domestic legal IPRs framework to the international level. While the economies of individual FTA partners often do not justify the aggressive pursuit of specific TRIPS-plus provisions, future FTA partners may do. FTAs, and the IPRs chapters within them, have thus had to be understood in their incremental nature. Each agreement improves the level of protection by bringing it closer to US law.[7] Over the years the USTR developed a template that serves as the basis of all negotiation texts and each agreement uses slightly modified language to close the loopholes of previous texts.

In this sense the primary function of the IPRs provisions within the original Andean FTAs was to refine and maintain a blueprint, as a precursor to other agreements.[8] Any concession of the US negotiation team to the Colombian negotiators in the field of IPRs would have set a precedent for future negotiation templates. Furthermore, coalition partners in bilateral agreements are also likely to become political allies during the respective multilateral negotiations, especially in a system that is based on minimum standards (Crawford and Fiorentino 2005; The World Bank 2000).

The US domestic trade policy-making framework

The US Constitution gives the President the authority to negotiate international trade agreements. If the agreement in question demands changes in US laws, then both Houses of Congress have to approve the implementing legislation of the said agreement. In order to provide a *modus operandi* for the collaboration between the Presidency, the Senate and the House of Representative a 'fast track' procedure was introduced in 1974. It is today known as the Trade Promotion Authority (TPA; see below) and understood as a Congressional, Executive- Agreement. Essentially it defines the relationship between the Executive and Congress as one in which the Executive is able to negotiate a trade agreement which is then in the form of implementing legislation passed to Congress for an up or down vote. Upon receiving the legislative proposals, Congress has 90 days to consider the bill. The House must consider the bill first as it affects revenue (Devereaux *et al.* 2006; Baker 2006; Lee 2007).

While this procedure is similar to approval processes in other jurisdictions, one aspect to this distinguishes the US system. When providing the Executive with a TPA, Congress sets precise negotiation guidelines and defines the objectives of the negotiation in advance. Therefore, unlike for example in Peru and Colombia, the Executive is assigned agent, while Congress takes the role of a principal (Devereaux *et al.* 2006; Baker 2006; Lee 2007).

While positions on trade agreements differ from agreement to agreement, traditionally, of all the US Government institutions, it is the Presidency that is most open to trade liberalisation. The Presidency judges the impact of trade on the country as a whole. He evaluates each agreement in its wider political and economic BATNA and accepts trade-offs in one field as long as they are sufficiently outweighed by benefits in others.

In contrast, Representatives in the House tend to represent much smaller municipalities, whose local constituencies and economic sectors may be negatively affected by trade liberalisation and thus often critical of any new trade agreement. A possible long-term political benefit that may arise from FTAs is of little importance to them. Representatives of the House are faced with a two-year election cycle and are thus constantly campaigning. They are subsequently primarily concerned with the immediate impact of FTAs and have to listen more carefully to their constituents' interests. Thus, very generally speaking, the House tends to be more critical of liberalising trade, with the exception of those Representatives whose municipalities include key stakeholders that have specific interests in particular issues subject to negotiations.

The Senate tends to represent an in-between position between the Presidency and the House. Enjoying a six-year election cycle and usually larger constituencies than their counterparts in the House, they are also in a better position to balance out possible trade-offs while considering long-term benefits (Devereaux *et al.* 2006).

Finally, as will be seen in the next chapter, Democrats tend to be more trade averse[9] than Republicans, especially since the 1990s. As a broad rule of thumb, therefore, within Congress House Democrats are usually most opposed to market liberalisation whereas the Senate Republicans tend to be least opposed.[10]

The TPA and the USTR

The aim of the TPA is to provide the Executive with the capacity to negotiate international agreements without the interference of Congress until the agreement has been finalised. Its origin dates back to 1934[11] when Congress delegated some of its constitutional authority to regulate commerce to the Executive because tariff regulations had become too complex and detailed for many legislators. Furthermore, Members in Congress felt that a more centralised agency would be able to deal better with the unbalanced pressure from stakeholder groups (exporting producers versus producers fearing international competition) that sought to influence trade policy leading to exceedingly high levels of protection, that contributed to the devastating experience of the Great Depression in the late 1920s (GAO 2007b).[12]

However, at that time foreign commerce was primarily related to tariffs. The need for further reform became evident during the troubled Kennedy Round in the mid-1960s of international trade negotiations, when negotiations increasingly included non-tariff barriers to trade. During negotiations it was found that US officials would not receive sufficient credibility as they did not have the power to implement the changes in domestic law needed to fulfil its newly made negotiation commitments. At one instance during the Kennedy Round Congress refused to implement two non-tariff measures that were previously agreed upon in international negotiations. As a result the Executive found it increasingly difficult to fully engage in international negotiations, as they never knew what they could commit to on the international level. Naturally other negotiating parties lost confidence in commitments made by the US during the negotiations (Devereaux *et al.* 2006).

It became evident that a 'fast track' procedure was needed, one that would balance on the one hand the role of Congress in reviewing and approving trade agreements while on the other providing US negotiators with a good chance of actually securing Congressional approval in a reasonably timely manner (Devereaux *et al.* 2006). The subsequent Trade Act of 1974[13] substantially revised the US trade negotiation framework, and provided the President with a first 'fast track' time framework from 1974 to 1979. The Act also established the basic consultation framework with both technical agencies and Congressional committees, set up the required notification system and accredited 10 Members of Congress to serve as official advisors to US negotiation teams permanently integrating them into the negotiation process (GAO 2007b; Falke 2006). Fast track was extended on a regular basis until 1993. During that year it was further extended to allow for the termination of the Uruguay Round of negotiations, after which it was not renewed until 2002[14] (Devereaux *et al.* 2006; Lee 2007).

The TPA conceptually confines the role of Congress to the beginning and the end of negotiations. This mainly includes drafting the trade mandate, linked to a certain extendable time frame, and the final up-or-down vote to approve the implementing legislation of the negotiated agreements, which endorses changes in US law that the President committed to as part of the negotiations. The final vote of approval cannot address individual parts of the negotiated agreement but only approve it in its entirety through the respective implementing legislation.[15] However, while this has resulted in Congress never having amended any implementing bills for agreements that have been protected by TPA, trade expert VanGrasstek points out how in practice legislators have been savvy in securing ways to influence and modify the results of negotiations. One opportunity to do so comes before the Bill is put to vote in Congress and congressional trade committees are to work out the terms of the agreement with the Executive (VanGrasstek 2008b).

One of the results of the fast track procedure is that it encourages Congress to put together a negotiating package for the Executive branch *before* the USTR embarks on a new series of negotiations.[16] The TPA functions as a trade mandate and precisely outlines which outcomes Congress wants to see in a finalised agreement. Thus, the TPA puts together a win-set based on which the Executive then enters into negotiations. While it is not necessary to deliver on all the objectives included in the TPA it has to deliver on sufficient objectives to accumulate enough votes to pass the agreement's implementing legislation in Congress. In this sense the TPA forces Congressional Members to agree on specific guidelines of what constitutes the win-set for negotiations that often have not yet began. This demands a considerable amount of reflection within Congress and its constituents before the start of the negotiations, leading to a well-prepared negotiation mandate and objective.

Furthermore, it also increases transparency in the negotiations and subsequently provides for continuous stakeholder involvement and monitoring to ensure that the negotiators do not lose track of the original mandate. Negotiators know that eventually they will be held accountable for the outcome of the negotiations, measured against the original mandate through the up or down vote of the Congress. They are aware that the closer they come to the objectives put forward in the TPA the higher their chances to pass the final agreement. Finally, the granting of 'fast track' can always be reversed, if Congress feels that the President fails to meet the requirements that Congress delegated to the Executive (O'Halloran 1994: ch. 6). Thus, Congress does not only have veto power when the finalised agreement is tabled for a vote, but can always take the TPA away from the Executive during the negotiations. The power to do so has been demonstrated by legislators in 2008 when President Bush decided to send the implementing legislation for the Colombia FTA to Congress without first working out its terms with the relevant trade committees. Legislators responded by suspending the trade promotion authority for the bill, subsequently abolishing its requirement to vote within 90 legislative days on the bill after it has been submitted by the President (VanGrasstek 2008b).

Fast track and an increasingly broad trade agenda

FTAs today include issue areas that traditionally did not fall under commercial treaties. As it is put by a US trade negotiator:

> America's FTAs break new ground – they establish prototypes for liberalization in areas such as services, e-commerce, intellectual property for knowledge societies, transparency in government regulation, and better enforcement of labor and environmental protection.
>
> (as quoted in Charnovitz 2004: 699)

Charnovitz argues that the FTAs, by including a range of 'non-trade' issues, enter areas of law that traditionally fall under an area of treaty-making that would require the approval of two-thirds of the Senate had they been negotiated outside of a trade agreement (instead of an up or down vote of both Houses necessary for trade agreements). By including them in the FTAs, Charnovitz argues, that policy-makers bypass a different and arguably more complex administrative route (Charnovitz 2004).

Apart from the changed dynamics this implies for passing the agreement, it has stirred up much concern in what this means within different institutions. For example, the Congressional Committees responsible for trade[17] have subsequently been faced with decisions on issues integrated into trade agreements that traditionally fell under the jurisdiction of other Committees. This can include questions on immigration and IPRs that conventionally fell under the Judiciary Committees of both Houses. Once they were part of FTAs, they were addressed through the trade committees.[18] In this sense not all are in favour of a fast track process at a time that sees the emergence of increasingly holistic trade agreements, claiming that it undermines committees that saw their jurisdiction wane to that of trade committees, bypassing inherent steps of the US 'checks and balances' system. Senator Robert Byrd, for example, referred to it as the 'rape of the legislative process' and considered it 'destructive of the sovereignty of the people of this Republic' (Charnovitz 2004: 704).

The role of the USTR and the statutory trade consultation process

The delegation of a precise negotiation mandate from Congress to the Executive does not take place in a vacuum, but is linked to statutory procedures that oblige other agents, such as interest groups, to provide an input in the process (O'Halloran 1994: ch. 4). The USTR, as the Executive agency in charge of international trade-related negotiations, is responsible for a complex consultation process. As such the USTR functions as an agent for all the governmental and non-governmental agencies that provide input into US trade policy. As described by statute (outlined below), the Executive has three different sets of principals it needs to consult with, namely with other Executive agencies,

Congress and industry technical advisory agencies that are affiliated to the USTR. The fact that the consultation process is defined by statute gives the US negotiators substantial leverage during the negotiations. As we have seen in the case study of the US–Andean deliberations, during the talks the US negotiators frequently claimed their hands were tied because of the role other governmental institutions or industry groups played in the process.

Furthermore, the role of the USTR does not end with the signature of FTAs but includes the successful implementation of FTAs and the monitoring of their enforcement. Indeed, as described in the domestic implementation acts that are associated with each FTA the US is not obliged to act on its obligations, such as providing preferential market access, until the Presidency is satisfied with the FTA implementation including the entire regulatory package in the partner countries. It is the USTR that advises the US President on when this process, often referred to as 'certification process', is terminated, and only then does the President initiate the US compliance with the agreement. With respect to IPRs, this traditionally includes an emphasis on the satisfactory implementation of the TRIPS-plus provisions, in particular on data exclusivity, patent term extension and 'linkage' (GAO 2007a).[19]

During the negotiations the USTR tended to present itself as a technical agency that follow through with a pre-defined win-set. As will be argued below, however, the USTR is more of a broker of a range of issues put forward by its three types of principals, namely Congress, executive agencies and interest groups. By picking and choosing, bearing in mind the ultimate need to ratify the agreement in Congress, a number of combinations of the nature of the final agreement are possible. Key in this is the approval in the House of the Representatives as the more trade adverse agency in Congress. As one interviewee put it: 'When the USTR negotiates what they bear in mind is 218 – as this is the number of votes they need to pass a bill through the House.'[20]

This results in some principals being significantly more important than others. It explains why the USTR ignored for many years the concerns put forward by a range of Democrats with respect to the IPRs/public health conflict as they related to FTAs. These concerns, they argued, would at the time only lead to a few additional votes in Congress, if any, while risking the support of the pharmaceutical industry would have meant the loss of a lot of votes in the then Republican controlled Congress. 'The Pharma lobby carries at least 40 votes in the House' the same interviewee claimed.[21] Thus, once the IPRs template was defined through previous FTAs to the satisfaction of the relevant stakeholder groups and interested government officials, there was very little overall consultation on this matter. The USTR did not see any need in it, especially in a field as technical as IPRs. The principal objective remained to confirm the precedence of the US position and, if changes were allowed, use these to close loopholes discovered in previous agreements.[22] As such the USTR has been much more instrumental in setting the tone of trade policy than is often perceived to be the case. In the end, the USTR reports directly to the White House and its key representatives are political appointees that have a sizeable political agenda of their own. Thus, the USTR is not an agent in a traditional sense, but takes control over the issues put forward in the negotiation, depending on which of its many principals is more important to them at that point in time.

The following section describes the consultation process executed by the USTR.

Consulting the Executive

The Executive consultation process that is to be undertaken by the USTR is defined in US Law. 19 U.S.C. § 2152 states:

> Advice from executive departments and other sources:
> Before any trade agreement is entered into under section 2133 of this title or section 2902 of this title, the President shall seek information and advice with respect to such agreement from the Departments of Agriculture, Commerce, Defense, Interior, Labor, State and the Treasury, from the United States Trade Representative, and from such other sources as he may deem appropriate.

More than 18 Federal Agencies, including a range of independent agencies such as the ITC, provide input to the USTR (Huenemann 2002). The consultations take place through a long process of meetings of committees and subcommittees that either represent certain regions, sectors or functions. For example, the executive agencies responsible for patents and their enforcement are the USPTO and the Justice Department, as well as for all pharmaceutical-related IPRs, the Department for Health and Human Service, and its subordinated agency, the FDA (Huenemann 2002; GAO 2007a). On top of that, members of executive agencies form part of the USTR-managed negotiations teams in international negotiations. Reporting back to their departments as the negotiations are ongoing allows them to provide additional input in the process.[23]

The inputs of the executive agencies with respect to IPRs negotiation that are part of FTAs are primarily technical and determine whether the provisions put forward in the IPRs chapter are compliant with US law. As the IPRs template in the more recent FTA negotiations only experienced marginal changes, they remained largely passive. Only during the negotiations of FTAs with Jordan, Oman and Singapore, when the template was still undergoing more changes, did they participate more actively in its development.[24] Concerns related to public health in other countries have never emerged in this process; indeed, the position of both the FDA and Department for Health has always supported the view that IPRs protection is important for promoting access to medicines (GAO 2007a).

Consulting Congress

Two principal committees in the US Congress have jurisdiction over trade policy. The responsible committee in the House is Ways and Means, whereas its counterpart in the Senate is the Finance Committee. These Committees are responsible for all matters related to trade, even though some other Committees, such as International Relations, Agriculture or the Judiciary Committees affected by trade policy will hold respective meetings on specific aspects.[25] These two Committees are considered to be the most powerful committees in Congress, primarily because they also hold jurisdiction over tax policy (GAO 2007b).

Above all, the Committees function as 'watchdogs' on USTR's activities. They frequently call upon the USTR to testify on specific matters, and can pass legislation to force the USTR to act in one way or another. They can withdraw trade negotiating authority, if necessary, block the ratification of signed agreements, limit budgetary allocations or indeed block other legislation in order to push the USTR to act according to their will (Shaffer 2003). Most of the Members in these Committees will have one or more staffers that exclusively work on trade. The Members of these Committees, in particular their Chairmen, are very powerful in steering Congress' position on certain trade policies.

Furthermore, Congressional Members that are not sitting in one of those committees may dedicate staffers to follow certain aspects of trade negotiations that are of particular importance to the Representatives' constituents. For example, states or Congressional jurisdictions that include cotton-producing industries most likely dedicated staffers to closely follow deliberations related to textiles during the CAFTA negotiations.

The Committees, in order to discuss trade policy, also hold public hearings in both House and Senate. This allows them to draw upon constituencies, which are not represented through the actual Representatives themselves and the broader public. The Committees also hold informal meetings in so-called 'Executive Sessions', which seek cross-fertilisation between the two branches of government (Huenemann 2002).

The Congressional Committees responsible for trade have another important responsibility, namely the so-called non-mark-ups and the drafting of the implementing legislation of the FTA. It is this implementing legislation that is finally voted upon in Congress. Thirty days before submitting the Bill the President has to consult with the Committees in 'non-mark-up' sessions that give Members of Congress an opportunity to protect domestic industry from foreign competition. They are called 'non-markups' as technically no changes are allowed within the text of the trade agreements due to the TPA. However, they can make recommendations with respect to changes in domestic law required to comply with the new obligations that may help to mitigate impacts on domestic industry. First House and Senate make their own 'non-markups' and then meet in a 'non-conference' to agree on a joint bill (O'Halloran 1994: ch. 6).

In the end, all Members of Congress will be integrated into trade policy because once the Committees present the agreements on the floor of both House and Senate, they have to vote. As a result it is critical for the USTR to always be aware where Congress positions itself towards ongoing trade negotiations. Therefore, the USTR regularly informs Members of Congress how the negotiations are proceeding. There are three principal levels of engagement that the USTR seeks from Congressional offices.

The first and most intense level of engagement involves all the offices of Members of Congress that are responsible for trade policy, namely all the Members that are represented on the Finance or Ways and Means Committees. Over half of the meetings between the USTR and Congress are held with members and the staff of these two committees (GAO 2007b). These Members will be informed on a very regular basis, often weekly, as negotiations are ongoing. They will have intense sessions before and after each negotiation round and will have access to the actual negotiation text, for which they get security clearance as negotiation material tends to fall under classified information.

The second level of engagement reaches out to other relevant Members of Congress, often involving the offices of Senators or Congressmen that are very influential, such as the late Senator Edward Kennedy at the time of the negotiations. This group also involves Members of other relevant Committees, such as Agriculture or Judiciary, and those Members that have expressed explicit interest in trade. These offices will also be regularly informed, possibly on a monthly basis, and while not enjoying access to the classified text, will be very aware of what is being put forward by the different negotiation teams in general or with respect to their specific topic of interest.

The third level of engagement of Congress involves all the other Congressional offices, which receive a general update of information on a fairly regular basis of what is going on in trade negotiations around the world.[26]

According to a report on the nature of the trade consultation process by GAO, the USTR held 1605 consultations with Congress related to FTAs between 2002 and 2007, over half of them with the two main Committees mentioned above (GAO 2007b). The following graph provides a good overview of the breakdown of consultations undertaken in Congress.

However, as GAO points out, satisfaction with the process and outcome of these meetings is mixed. Many complain about bad timing of the meetings, some about the intentional withholding of information by the USTR and others about the fact that their capacity to influence negotiations is dependent on their relative political importance at the time of consultation (GAO 2007b). Indeed, the USTR is often accused by Congressional staff of being very selective in whose feedback will actually have an impact and whose will not. During a range of interviews in Congress, staffers suggested that especially before the 2006 Congressional elections, if they were from minority offices then their advice was regularly ignored by the USTR.

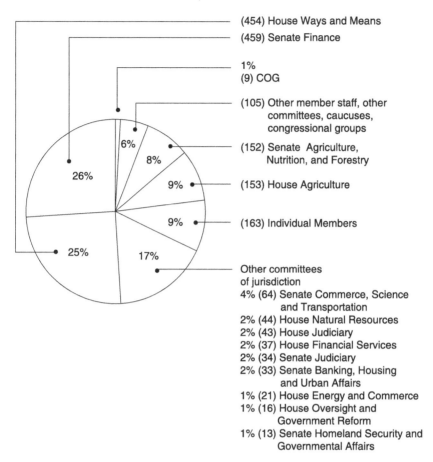

(454) House Ways and Means

(459) Senate Finance

1%
(9) COG

(105) Other member staff, other
committees, caucuses,
congressional groups

(152) Senate Agriculture,
Nutrition, and Forestry

(153) House Agriculture

(163) Individual Members

Other committees
of jurisdiction
4% (64) Senate Commerce, Science
and Transportation
2% (44) House Natural Resources
2% (43) House Judiciary
2% (37) House Financial Services
2% (34) Senate Judiciary
2% (33) Senate Banking, Housing
and Urban Affairs
1% (21) House Energy and Commerce
1% (16) House Oversight and
Government Reform
1% (13) Senate Homeland Security and
Governmental Affairs

Figure 6.1 USTR consultation in congress.
Source: GAO 2007b: 36.

Many of them expressed their frustration that the USTR maintained a heavy partisan bias.[27]

On the other hand the USTR also complained about Congressional involvement during the consultation sessions, arguing that Congressional staff tended to only get involved towards the end of the negotiations when most of the text had already been agreed upon. In this sense, the USTR pointed out that there was a great need for earlier involvement of Congress arguing that the TPA was not detailed enough to clarify all negotiation objectives. Similar complaints were also made about the fact that only few Congressional staffers actually understood the issues at hand, particularly when dealing with technical issues such as IPRs, especially compared to the vast amount of technical expertise that is available in industry (GAO 2007b).[28]

Technical consultations with private interest groups

Private interest groups play a dominant role in US policy-making. The decentralised nature of the system in combination with a political philosophy that encourages strong private-public engagement allows for an enhanced role of interests groups in domestic trade policy-making.[29] According to political scientist Clyde Wilcox: '[i]f [a] political scientist were charged to design a national legislature to maximize interest-group influence, they would be hard pressed to improve on the American Congress' (as quoted in Shaffer 2003: 105). Representatives are primarily driven and held accountable by their local constituents, including a particularly large influence of industry associations. Through Congress interest groups can in turn exercise pressure on Executive agencies, such as the USTR.

There are two types of influence exercised by interest groups. The first, which will be described in this section, is the institutionalised influence through a range of advisory committees. The second is the lobbying that takes place on a more informal basis, which will be described in the next section.

The USTR has been allocated an institutionalised and sector specific advisory committee system that supports the office on a range of its activities. The system was deliberated in the US 1974 Trade Act, and continuously expanded until today. It is designed to assist particularly the technical needs of USTR staff through information and advice on matters ranging from the government's negotiation objectives and bargaining strategy to implementation and administration of trade policy (Huenemann 2002; GAO 2007b).

In 19 U.S.C. § 2155, the need to include non-governmental players in the consultative process with respect to trade policy-making is prescribed:

Sec. 2155. Information and advice from private and public sectors

1   The President shall seek information and advice from representative elements of the private sector and the non-Federal governmental sector with respect to –

A   negotiating objectives and bargaining positions before entering into a trade agreement under this subchapter or section 3803 of this title;

B   the operation of any trade agreement once entered into, including preparation for dispute settlement panel proceedings to which the United States is a party; and

C   other matters arising in connection with the development, implementation, and administration of the trade policy of the United States [. . .]

To the maximum extent feasible, such information and advice on negotiating objectives shall be sought and considered before the commencement of negotiations.

2 The President shall consult with representative elements of the private sector and the non-Federal governmental sector on the overall current trade policy of the United States. The consultations shall include, but are not limited to, the following elements of such policy:

A The principal multilateral and bilateral trade negotiating objectives and the progress being made toward their achievement.

B The implementation, operation, and effectiveness of recently concluded multilateral and bilateral trade agreements and resolution of trade disputes.

C The actions taken under the trade laws of the United States and the effectiveness of such actions in achieving trade policy objectives.

D Important developments in other areas of trade for which there must be developed a proper policy response.

By 2002, based on this statute, 33 advisory committees had been formed, comprising approximately 1000 official advisors. These committees include the Advisory Committee for Trade Policy and Negotiation (ACTPN) that reports directly to the President, six additional policy advisory committees and 22 technical advisory committees, including one on pharmaceuticals and chemicals and one on IPRs. Next to the direct advice they give to the USTR, their positions are also passed to Congress for consideration. Membership on these committees is highly sought after and appointments are often given to those interest groups that have been helpful through campaign contributions. According to Inside US Trade:

[t]he White House rewarded major supporters of Republican candidates in the 2002 midterm elections with seats on a trade advisory committee that meets regularly with the U.S. Trade Representative and provides input to the president regarding trade agreements.

(as quoted in Shaffer 2003: 106)

Figure 6.2, put together by GAO, provides a good overview of the committees and their reporting lines.

The ITACs are in regular communication with the USTR. During the period between 2002 and 2006 the USTR met 729 times with the 16 ITACs providing them with considerable access to the negotiations (GAO 2007b). Most of the technical advisory committees, especially those that advise on provisions that are relevant to IPRs (ITAC 15) and pharmaceuticals (ITAC 3) are filled with private sector representatives. Their role is to provide regular input and feedback to the negotiations. They are also required to produce a report for Congress within 30 days of being informed by the President that he seeks the approval of a finalised agreement.[30] In this report the ITACs will outline their position towards the final agreement, which in turn will influence the respective vote in the Senate and the House.

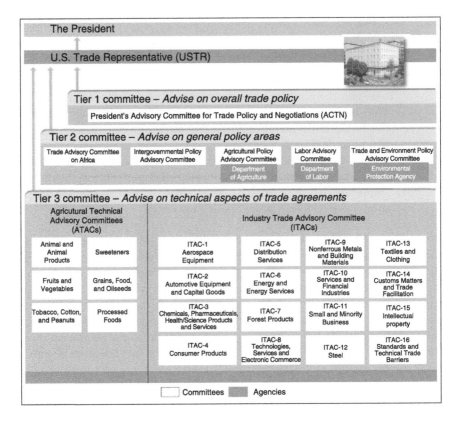

Figure 6.2 US trade advisory system.

Source: GAO (2007b).

The work of these Committees[31] has strong influence on the negotiation and implementation of FTAs. Throughout the Andean FTA negotiations and other previous agreements, their work was the principal driver behind the USTR's refusal to move away from the 'gold standard' IPRs template that is based on the US level of protection and refined through each FTA. Furthermore, they always emphasised that the importance of maintaining the template went beyond the individual FTAs, but to 'improve' IPRs protection on a global level. In its report ITAC-15 (then referred to as IFAC-3) noted:

> While IFAC-3 recognizes that the negotiation of FTAs with individual countries and regions is labor-intensive, especially when compared with the negotiation of a multilateral agreement among the 146 Members of the WTO, FTA negotiations provide the most effective approach currently available to the United States for improving global intellectual property protection. The negotiation of an individual FTA provides the opportunity to deal

with specific intellectual property concerns that U.S. industry may have in the particular negotiating partner. Our goal in the negotiation of an FTA is to set a new baseline for all future FTAs, including the FTAA. This baseline is continually reflected in the model FTA agreements which are constantly changing based on what we learn through negotiating each of the FTAs.

(IFAC-3 2004: 5)

In April 2005 public health advocates requested the participation of public health specialists to both committees. They only succeeded in January 2007 after nearly two years of, what the USTR argued, was security clearance and other administrative obligations. In the meantime the USTR had concluded nine FTAs (GAO 2007a).

The informal role of major stakeholder groups in influencing US trade policy

The institutionalised role of the private sector and other influence groups through the advisory committee system is not their most important contribution to the formulation of trade policy. Of greater importance is the vast amount of informal communication between industry groups and the government. As will be shown below, the work of the capital-based lobbying groups, often referred to as 'K Street' for their location in Washington, DC, is so significant that the government relies on them for a range of services.

Within K Street, the pharmaceutical industry lobby has traditionally been one of the most influential, with a particular height during the years of the Bush Administration. A report by the Center of Public Integrity claims that between January 2005 and June 2006 alone, the industry spent US$182 million on federal lobbying (and more than US$1 billion in the preceeding 10 years). The pharma lobby employs approximately 1200 lobbyists in DC, which equals more than two lobbyists per Member of Congress (Asif 2007). Senator Grassley (R-Iowa) once famously remarked: '. . . you can hardly swing a cat by the tail in that town without hitting a pharmaceutical lobbyist' (Drinkard 2005). In comparison to other lobbying groups, the (research-based) pharmaceutical lobby has historically enjoyed the added advantage that its members decide, to a large extent, on the policy changes they would like to see in government.[32] Many other industries and trade associations do not possess such unity, which significantly undermines their lobbying strength.[33]

Furthermore, the pharmaceutical lobby is very well connected to government officials in Washington, DC. Indeed, many of them are former federal officials, substantially increasing the effectiveness of their lobbying. Central among the pharmaceutical and life science lobbying groups is PhRMA representing the country's largest pharmaceutical and biotech companies. Until 2010 PhRMA was headed by now retired Billy Tauzin, former Republican Congressman from Louisiana. Tauzin spent his previous professional life in the US Government, including as the Chairman of the

House Committee on Energy and Commerce, which regulates the pharmaceutical industry. During his time in office he oversaw the passage of the 'Medicare Prescription Drug Law', which was of great interest to the pharmaceutical industry (Asif 2005; Drinkard 2005; Welsh 2004).

Career moves such as that of Billy Tauzin are common in Washington, DC. Next to the campaign contributions that the industry provides to different representatives and governmental offices, the 'revolving door' between public office and lobbying groups distinguishes the way that policy-making takes place in the capital. Having served in a powerful committee such as W&Ms or the Energy Committee or within the USTR is a useful qualification for entering any lobbying firm that seeks to influence the Federal Government.[34] 'Revolving door' is by no means a new phenomenon in US politics, as Schattschneider observed in 1935 in his study on the importance of pressure groups in influencing domestic tariff legislation (Schattschneider 1935: 196). The expertise and connections that these individuals bring to the lobbying groups is invaluable. As most of their day-to-day work consists of promoting the agenda of their clients with Congress, Executive agencies and the White House, this familiarity with government is vital.[35]

An additional effect of the 'revolving door' is its influence on public servants while still in office. Aspirations to a future career within a lobbying group will influence the behaviour of the respective individual.[36] For many lawyers and lobbyists in Washington, DC, public office is a milestone in their resumé before moving to more lucrative posts in the private sector. Former USTR Robert Strauss goes as far as claiming that lawyers often seek a public service position, not because they are interested in a government career, but because 'they know that [government work] enables them to move on out in a few years and become associated with a lobbying or law firm [where] their services are in tremendous demand' (as quoted in Shaffer 2003: 122). As a result, Shaffer continues to point out, senior agency positions in Washington, DC are often filled by political appointees, who only remain in office for a maximum term of four years. Others come directly from the private sector to the USTR and go back to the same firm after one term in office (Shaffer 2003).

Today private law firms and trade associations are filled with former USTR or Congressional staff, to the extent that during some interviews the interviewees pointed out that it is hard to get a job in the lobbying arm of a trade association without having public sector experience. The more 'trade-related' the public service position was, such as the staff of the two powerful trade Committees or the USTR, the higher the demand by lobbying firms. Party affiliation also matters: after the Congressional elections in 2006 Democrats were most sought after by interest groups, such as the pharmaceutical industry, that previously primarily focused on Republican staff.[37]

Lobbying consists of many more activities than providing campaign contributions. Next to writing memos, providing technical information and analysis, lobbyists spend much time on the phone, email and fax raising awareness of their respective interests within the Federal Government or simply by stating whether they endorse a particular bill or not. Sometimes their activities include accompanying key policy-makers in the private jets owned by companies which are regularly used by policy-makers to travel for business. While the companies receive payment for the trips, this payment represents only a fraction of what a chartered flight would actually cost (Drinkard 2005).

The sheer political weight that an industry such as the pharmaceutical industry carries influences the way that people vote in Congress. At the time of the negotiations, most of the industry's lobbying was targeted at domestic legal reform, as more than 50 per cent of their revenues stem from the US market. Examples included the Medicare Prescription Drug Law or laws that prevent the importation of cheaper drugs from Canada, Indeed, between 1998 and 2004 the top 20 pharmaceutical companies, PhRMA and BIO lobbied on over 1600 bills (Asif 2005).

In addition, a significant section of lobbying efforts is directed towards international trade and policy.[38] A number of authors have analysed the history and nature of the integration of intellectual property rights in trade agreements (Sell 2003; Matthews 2002; Drahos and Braithwaite 2002; Ryan 1998). Many of them claim that industrial interests were paramount in this process, functioning as efficient agents in terms of lobbying their national governments, including formulating actual treaty text. The following section will provide a brief overview over this process.

The role of industry in historical perspective

The first attempt to lobby for the integration of IPRs into trade-policy was made by the so-called Anti-Counterfeiting Coalition, comprised of several trademark holding firms. They attempted as early as the 1973–79 Tokyo Round of the GATT to lobby for the inclusion of a code for anti-counterfeiting. While this attempt was unsuccessful, it set a trend of industrial lobbying groups, primarily in the US, with the aim of presenting the lack, or insufficient, IPRs protection in overseas markets as a trade-related issue. Even though the lobbyists had little success in their endeavours, they resulted in the formation of industry alliances pushing for stronger IPRs protection in all fields, from trademarks and copyright to patent protection. By the time the Uruguay Round was launched, these industrial alliances were well coordinated, pushing their respective governments to include IPRs in the trade deal (UNCTAD-ICTSD 2003).

Later on, industry involvement in actual policy formulation was more direct. The MPAA formulated most of the section of the CBI that made the link between trade and copyright. Associated copyright lawyers introduced the same language in the outline of the GSP, and significantly influenced the wording of Section 301. By 1984 industry groups with primary interest in copyright provisions started lobbying Congress to make the GSP status dependent on the successful protection of US IP. This language was then repeated in the Trade and Tariff Act of 1984 (Drahos and Braithwaite 2002).

One of the strengths of the industrial lobby was their very early formulation and organisation of industry associations, according to specific topics of interests. The most crucial of those was the Intellectual Property Coalition (IPC), formed in 1986, and the IIPA in 1984 (Sell 2003). The IIPA focused exclusively on copyright, and, due to the influential nature of its members, became the most powerful copyright lobby in the world. According to Drahos and Braithwaite, in the 1990s their members accounted for 3.3 per cent of US GDP, representing the interests of some 1500 companies (Drahos and Braithwaite 2002). Of additional importance, related to the organisation of industry associations, was the strategic placement of industry advocates in the above-mentioned advisory committees of the USTR and other official advisory groups.[39]

Not only the US, but also the EC (UNICE) and Japan (Keidanren) had their own lobbying associations. They supported their negotiations, but they never went as far as the US industry groups. As quoted in an interview by Drahos and Braithwaite:

> US negotiators were physically accompanied by US business representatives. They sat with members of the US negotiating team and passed messages to them at crucial stages. We [European Commission] don't work that way, that's not our political system (European negotiators, 2001).[40]
>
> (quoted in Drahos and Braithwaite 2002: 141)

With respect to the Colombia/Peru FTA, PhRMA lobbied over a period of years for Peru to be placed on the US Special 301 Country Watch List, especially for the lack of data exclusivity provisions in the country's legislation. For example, the PhRMA 2006 Report on Peru states:

> PhRMA recommends that Peru remain a Watch List country due to continued ineffective patent enforcement, the lack of second-use patents, data exclusivity (DE) and linkage, and the failure to lift discriminatory measures that unfairly protect local copiers. The U.S.-Peru Trade Promotion Agreement (PTPA) shall provide, if appropriately implemented, effective DE and linkage and a stronger intellectual property framework. PhRMA will closely monitor implementation of that Agreement and assess improvements in the IP environment over the year.
>
> (PhRMA 2006)

The essential role of industry today

The services provided by lobbying groups to foreign economic diplomacy are of that service that the US government has become reliant on them. At the time of the US-Peru and US-Colombia FTA negotiations the USTR was staffed with approximately 75 employees, of whom only about two or three worked on IPRs,[41] which did not give it the capacity to provide all the technical information needed. For example, the issuing of a Special 301 requires the provision of evidence and data from the respective country that supposedly violated its IPRs obligations. This data tends to come from domestic Chambers of Commerce, PhRMA or other industry affiliations.[42]

Furthermore, private sector representatives accompany the negotiation teams in order to provide technical input and feedback during the negotiations. Most new treaty language is discussed with the private sector representatives to confirm the appropriateness of the wording and get the industry's endorsement. In this role the representatives from the pharmaceutical industry have always emphasised the absolute nature of the 'gold standard' IPRs template. They insisted that the negotiation team should avoid any modification to this template to avoid setting precedents for any future agreement. Even though during the Andean and other negotiations non-government officials were not allowed to enter the negotiation room, industry advisors were 'virtually' present in adjacent rooms, by staying in the same hotels, or by phone. Their presence and support particularly in the field of IPRs was of greater importance than, for example, the role of representatives of the accompanying Federal agencies, which tended to remain passive.[43]

Towards the end of the negotiations at the time of trade-offs, the role of industry tends to be particularly important. The integration, for example, of the biodiversity side letter was analysed in much detail by the industry representatives ensuring that it reflected the US approach on this matter in other fora.[44] The importance of private sector advice in this function is also related to the amount of technical expertise that industry groups possess and that Congressional staff, for example, does not. As mentioned above, only a small handful of staffers in Congress truly understand and follow issues related to IPRs and related negotiations, and only a fraction of them will be able to use their time and resources to provide input into the negotiations.

An additional vital role that the private sector plays in US trade policymaking takes place domestically, after the agreement has been finalised. Once the agreement is signed the USTR needs to pass it in Congress. To achieve this, a considerable amount of lobbying is needed, which goes beyond the sole capacity of the USTR, thus depending heavily on the support of groups such as PhRMA. Given the often very tight vote by which trade agreements are passed, every vote matters. In this sense, interest groups that enjoy close proximity to a relatively large share of Congressional representatives, such as the pharmaceutical industry in the Republican Party until the 2006 elections, can be crucial in order to see to the ratification of an agreement.[45]

Finally, private sector representatives also contribute to the monitoring of the enforcement of ratified agreements, often through the domestic US Chamber of Commerce or affiliates of MNCs. Again, the USTR does not have the human resources available to do so and relies on the data and input provided by the private sector to compose, for example, the Special 301 reports. Sometimes industry groups also accompany the USTR when travelling to other countries in order to negotiate the implementation of certain provisions. Their role in this process is to visit government representatives of partner countries on occasions, highlighting the link between local investment and the appropriate implementation of the FTA.[46]

In spite of the fact that the USTR does rely on industry for a range of services, the relationship between industry and the USTR has not always been harmonious. Several instances in the past, such as the withdrawal of the US WTO, claim against Brazil's patent law, was against corporate interest and a result of public pressure on the US Government. Similarly, the Doha Declaration that emerged out of the post-9/11 window to reach out to other nations and to align trade and security policy equally went against the explicit interest of industry (Shaffer 2003). Thus, there are clear limits to industry influence, often triggered by shifts in the domestic policy scenarios leading to a reshuffle of preferences. This can, for example, be due to systemic shocks such as 9/11 or the financial crisis of 2008, which lead to a period of strong government. Alternatively, it could be due to shifts within the systems, such as elections, which may bring to power principals which represent a different set of constituents and interest groups, and which subsequently prioritise a new set of preferences. An example of the latter will be provided in the next chapter.

Conclusion

This chapter has described the domestic nature of the US trade policy-making process and the following observations have been made:

The key objectives of the US-Colombia and US-Peru FTAs were not directly economic but long-term considerations for greater political and economic hemispheric integration. Furthermore, the FTAs were to serve as a means of exporting certain legal frameworks that accommodated US economic interests, including a framework on IPRs.

The US trade policy-making process is well defined by statute which strengthened the US negotiation teams during the negotiations with Colombia and Peru. The USTR is further presented with a pre-defined win-set that is compiled by all relevant stakeholders, from within and outside government.

Although the process is defined in much detail through statute, its actual implementation and execution is heavily influenced by the power distribution in Congress and subsequent interest groups represented. As we will see in the next chapter this may lead to a very biased integration of the preferences put forward by different principals.

Private sector groups, such as the pharmaceutical industry, play a fundamental role in the domestic trade policy-making process, both formally as well as informally. Next to campaign contributions to Members of Congress, the services they provide have become essential to the functioning of FTA negotiations, ratification and subsequent monitoring of the agreements.

The particular strength of the pharmaceutical lobby, especially because of its economic power, its well-connectedness, and the unity among its members in the preferences put forward, also explains the USTR's position of absolute inflexibility during the FTA negotiations when it came to IPRs. The next chapter will demonstrate how substantial institutional change was necessary in order to move away from the traditional IPRs template.

7 The impact of US domestic policy change on the integration of IPRs/health concerns into the US-Peru and US-Colombia FTAs

Introduction

This chapter will elaborate how the domestic trade policy-making framework described in the previous chapter determined the US negotiation position on IPRs in the Andean FTAs. It will be shown how domestic political change had an immediate impact on the nature of the IPRs template traditionally put forward in US FTA negotiations. Particular emphasis will be placed on the way a power shift within Congress changed the domestic win-set, in turn leading to the emergence of a revised IPRs template. To do this the chapter will first describe the nature of the 2002 TPA, which provided the mandate for the Andean negotiations, before analysing the elections in 2006 and their impact on trade policy-making.

A revised 2002 trade mandate

The latest US Trade Act, which also provided the grounds for the US-Andean negotiations, was passed in 2002 after much debate. From the beginning, consumer organisations, trade unions and anti-globalisation organisations criticised the Act, claiming it favoured industry associations and large businesses (Trosow 2003).

During his presidency President Bill Clinton had made several attempts to pass fast track in Congress but had failed, also because from 1994 onwards he was confronted with a Republican majority in one or both Houses. When George W. Bush was elected, he fundamentally changed the image of fast track. First, he gave it a new name by changing it from 'fast track' to 'Trade Promotion Authority'. Strategically, a TPA communicated the 'trade promotion' rather than a 'fast tracking' or bypassing of due administrative process. Second, after the terrorist attacks of 9/11 he integrated national security concerns into the debate. The aim of the Pentagon and White House was to 'counter terrorism with trade'. In a *Washington Post* article, USTR Zoellick said:

[t]he terrorists deliberately chose the World Trade towers as their target. While their blow toppled the towers, it cannot and will not shake the foundations of world trade and freedom.

(as quoted in Devereaux *et al*. 2006: 229)

Third, he linked the TPA to a budget increase of the Trade Adjustment Assistance (TAA) programme, to reduce the voice of critics fearing the loss of American jobs.[1] With those changes he managed to pass the 2002 Trade Act (H.R. 3009) in the House, but only by a single vote margin (Trosow 2003; Devereaux *et al*. 2006).

The fact that the Act passed with such a narrow majority led to concern in the USTR, as it reflected a very hesitant position towards trade agreements (Schott 2003). As will be discussed below, the distribution of votes further indicated an increasingly partisan divide on trade policy. It represented a very narrow win-set, leading to a much stricter interpretation of the TPA by the USTR, which in turn further increased the lack of flexibility demonstrated by the US negotiators during the FTA negotiations. A one-vote majority meant a very critical level II. Thus, in order to keep all the *aye* voters who supported the TPA also supportive of subsequent FTAs they had to ensure that sufficient TPA objectives were met at the time of approval.

The 2002 TPA set three particular negotiation mandates for IPRs. The first two reflected the previously mentioned objectives to use FTAs for the promotion of IPRs standards that were similar to those found in US law:

Section 2102, § 4 INTELLECTUAL PROPERTY–The principal negotiating objectives of the United States regarding trade-related intellectual property are–

A to further promote adequate and effective protection of intellectual property rights, including through–

   i I ensuring accelerated and full implementation of the Agreement on Trade-Related Aspects of Intellectual Property Rights [. . .], particularly with respect to meeting enforcement obligations under that agreement; and

     II ensuring that the provisions of any multilateral or bilateral trade agreement governing intellectual property rights that is entered into by the United States reflect a standard of protection similar to that found in United States law;

   ii providing strong protection for new and emerging technologies and new methods of transmitting and distributing products embodying intellectual property;

  iii preventing or eliminating discrimination with respect to matters affecting the availability, acquisition, scope, maintenance, use, and enforcement of intellectual property rights;

      iv ensuring that standards of protection and enforcement keep pace with technological developments, and in particular ensuring that rightholders have the legal and technological means to control the use of their works through the Internet and other global communication media, and to prevent the unauthorized use of their works; and

      v providing strong enforcement of intellectual property rights, including through accessible, expeditious, and effective civil, administrative, and criminal enforcement mechanisms;

  B to secure fair, equitable, and nondiscriminatory market access opportunities for United States persons that rely upon intellectual property protection;[2]

A third objective put forward in the IPRs mandate referred to the Doha Declaration:

  C to respect the Declaration on the TRIPS Agreement and Public Health, adopted by the World Trade Organization at the Fourth Ministerial Conference at Doha, Qatar on November 14, 2001.

Making reference to the Doha Declaration resulted from an amendment originally proposed by the late Senator Kennedy,[3] who aimed to strike a balance between the interests of IPRs holders and public health. The amendment he sought was to integrate the objectives of the Doha Declaration as a principal negotiating objective into the TPA. His work was supported by other Senators, including Senators Grassley, Feinstein, Feingold and Baucus (GAO 2007a; Lee 2007).

    Yet, bearing in mind the US position on IPRs in the Andean trade negotiations, the reference to the Doha Declaration in the US Trade Mandate was not a driving force behind US foreign IP policy. While the USTR claimed they withdrew on some of the TRIPS-plus provisions, such as parallel imports[4] and a limitation on compulsory licensing (GAO 2007a), we know from chapter 5 on the US-Andean negotiations that both were included in the initial US negotiation proposal, even if only as bargaining chips. In spite of the wording in the mandate, the USTR never interpreted the Declaration as a mechanism that could change any provisions in the IPRs template. The USTR argued that the interpretation of the flexibilities confirmed by the Doha Declaration should not be at the discretion of governments except in scenarios of extreme urgency. In this sense the US Government has historically put forward a much narrower (if not incorrect) interpretation of the Declaration compared to other WTO Member States (GAO 2007a), and has maintained this position through FTA negotiations after the 2002 mandate.[5]

    The USTR was criticised on this matter by the 'Labor Advisory Committee for Trade Negotiations and Trade Policy':

[I]t appears that CAFTA undermines the protections for public health contained in TRIPS and the Doha Declaration. This not only violates Congressional negotiating objectives, it sets a terrible precedent for pending free trade agreements with developing countries in Southern Africa and elsewhere. In countries facing devastating public health crises, governments must have adequate flexibility under international trade rules to provide their people with access to essential medicines.

(as quoted in Lee 2007: 13)

Furthermore, Senator Kennedy also continued to criticise the Administration for failing to include the objectives of Doha into the negotiated agreements, accusing it of defying its statutory obligations. This eventually led to his and Rep. Waxman's call for investigation by GAO 'to help understand how the Administration has balanced commercial drug interests with the health needs of poor people living in developing countries' (Office of Senator Kennedy 2006).[6] The report made a range of conclusions, for example that the USTR only adjusted two provisions that were part of the larger FTA IPRs template to the Doha Declaration (compulsory licences and parallel import, as mentioned above), that the USTR had a very narrow interpretation of the Doha Declaration, that health-related Federal Agencies were not asked to provide input on the matter and that the input of the public health community had not been supported by the USTR. The Executive branch's response was that it primarily followed the first two goals of the 2002 IPRs negotiation mandate, namely to strengthen IPRs standards and implementation through the FTAs, based on US law (Lee 2007), clearly indicating a hierarchy of negotiation objectives (and underlying preferences).

Thus, while the integration of the Doha Declaration into the 2002 TPA was a success for public health advocates, its actual impact on trade negotiations was marginal. The principal reason behind this is the fact that those Members of Congress that promoted the integration of Doha into the FTA were a small group of Democrats that until 2006 were not essential for passing any FTA in the House. In contrast, the USTR was part of a Republican Administration at that time that above all relied on the support of Republicans to pass an agreement in Congress. Thus, opposition from the Democrat side was not important and their power as significant veto players substantially undermined. Given the proximity between the pharmaceutical industry and the Republican Party at the time it is of no surprise that including the Doha Declaration in the 2002 TPA had no real effects when it came to the negotiation of FTAs.

However, the failure to act on the integration of public health objectives into the 2002 TPA did not pass unnoticed. In a clarification[7] filed in the Congressional Record on 16 February 2006 Senator Kennedy pointed out:

Our amendment to the Trade Promotion Authority Act reinforces the Doha Declaration. The Bush administration should be using it to negotiate trade agreements that allow urgently needed access to medicines. Instead, the administration has used trade agreements to promote the interests of the pharmaceutical industry at the expense of access to drugs in developing nations. Again and again, the administration has defied the Doha Declaration and imposed unjustified restrictions on the availability of patented drugs. [. . .] In these agreements, the Bush administration has undermined the very core of the Doha Declaration.

(as quoted in Jorge 2007b: 170)

Power shifts in Congress and the formulation of a new trade agenda

The partisan nature of trade policy

The lack of influence that even powerful Democrats enjoyed in trade policy-making in 2002 can be explained by the fact that from the mid-1990s until 2007 trade has increasingly been divided along party lines. Before that, trade politics were based on subjects and regions rather than party affiliation. The emergence of a more partisan trade policy was a result of a range of factors, not all of which related to trade. Polarisation on issues ranging from security policy to trade grew substantially over the last decade; in particular in the House, Republicans and Democrats were respectively moved towards the left and right of the political centre (Destler 2005). The Committees responsible for trade, accustomed to bipartisanship, also saw an increasing move towards partisan affiliation along issue lines among their Members. This was partially driven by ideological differences on the integration of normative questions related to labour and the environment into the trade agenda, which many Democrats embraced and Republicans rejected.[8]

Additionally, this separation was further cultivated by the individuals in charge of trade policy-making. In the long run up to the 2002 TPA, Ways and Means Chairman Thomas (R-CA) largely excluded ranking Member Rangel (D-NY) and ranking subcommittee chair on trade Sander Levin (D-MI) from influencing the process. Instead, to claim bipartisanship, he allied himself with a handful of junior Democrats. The alienation got so extreme that when the TPA mandate eventually came to a vote, it was passed with the majority of only one Member in the House, 20 minutes after the vote was closed. Congressman Jim DeMint (R-SC) was promised a range of concessions in the textile field, based on which he changed his vote from *nay* to *aye*. It was a very narrow victory, even though the TPA was tied to national security interests post-9/11, as well as with concessions made in TAA (Destler 2005). Only 21 out of 210 Democrats voted in favour of it, meaning that the TPA was nearly exclusively based on Republican support. A few years later CAFTA only passed with a majority of two votes, among them only 15 Democrats, illustrating further alienation of Democrats, even though concessions to the sugar and textiles industries had been made (Destler 2007; Falke 2006; Blustein and Allen 2005).[9]

As a result, with a peak in the run up to the 2002 TPA approval, the USTR at the time was essentially driven by Republican trade preferences. Indeed, over the previous ten years the positions of Democrats, whether in the form of written submissions, or feedback during USTR consultancies, were largely ignored.[10] To make matters worse, some Republicans, most prominently among them Republican Whip Rep. Tom 'The Hammer' Delay used the partisan basis for trade to push trade-interested industry groups to allocate their donations accordingly (Destler 2005). As a result a range of industry groups, among them the pharmaceutical industry in its close affiliation with the Republican Party, reflected the partisan bias in their lobbying efforts at the time.

It is therefore no surprise that the Democrat insistence on the importance of the third IPRs negotiation mandate in the 2002 TPA had little impact in the actual FTA negotiations. The USTR at that time was focusing largely on securing Republican votes in the House. Yet, all this took a dramatic turn in the 2006 Congressional elections.

The 2006 Congressional elections

The elections in November 2006 constituted, with 31 additional seats, the largest Democrat seat gain in the House since 1974, while also gaining five additional seats in the Senate (from the 33 that were open for vote). In the Senate, the final breakdown post-elections was 51 Democrats (including one Independent, that participated in the Democrat Caucus) versus 49 Republicans, and in the House 233 Democrats versus 202 Republicans. Democrats subsequently came to hold the majority in both Houses of Congress. Two scholars at the University of St. Gallen analysed the position taken by the 62 'freshmen' in Congress, and compared their record on trade with the incumbents they had replaced. They found that in the Senate, five trade-friendly Senators were replaced with trade sceptics, whereas in the House 16 seats held by trade-friendly Representatives had been passed to trade-sceptics (Evenett and Meier 2006).

Many of the newly elected Democrat Representatives in the House had used trade policy and the unpopular CAFTA to get support from labour unions in their election campaigns. Thus, their demand for a change in trade policy was great. In an open letter to Rep. Rangel, now Chairman of Ways and Means, in January 2007, 39 of the 42 newly elected Democrats called for a new approach to trade:

> Vital to our electoral successes was our ability to take a vocal stand against the Administration's misguided trade agenda, and offer our voters real, meaningful alternatives to the job-killing agreements, such as CAFTA, that the majority of our opponents supported.
>
> (as quoted in Destler 2007)

The demand for change in trade policy came at a difficult time for the Bush Administration, as four agreements (Colombia, Korea, Panama and Peru now awaited Democrat-approved finalisation and ratification, all of which had been based on a TPA mandate given by a Republican Congress and up until now negotiated by a Republican Administration. Furthermore, WTO negotiations in Geneva were stagnant awaiting a renewal of the TPA. Yet, it was clear that under no circumstances was any move on any agreement possible without change. The USTR could not rely anymore in their negotiations on passing the agreements through Congress based on purely Republican votes, bearing in mind the cultivated partisan feelings towards trade policy.

As Destler (2007) points out, however, the situation could have been much worse, given the different philosophy that was put forward by leading House Democrats with respect to the partisan nature of trade policy. Right from the beginning, new chairman Rep. Charles Rangel reached out to the Republican leadership in 'Ways and Means', minority leader Rep. Jim McCrery (R-LA). By including the Republicans in his negotiations with the USTR, he communicated that the new Democrat leadership was more inclined towards a bipartisan trade policy.[11]

This move can be attributed to two principal reasons: first, Rep. Rangel was a consensus seeker, and did not want to continue Rep. Thomas' partisan trend, and second, Democrats, unlike Republicans, did not have a unified 'party position' on trade. Many Democrats were likely to continue opposing trade agreements in spite of any changes put forward by Reps. Rangel and Levin (at this stage chair of 'Ways and Means' subcommittee on trade). In this new Congress it was clear that even though the USTR could not rely anymore on Republican votes to pass the outstanding agreements, neither could they rely on Democrats only. Equally, if the Democrat leadership wanted to continue putting forward a trade agenda, they relied on Republican support in Congress (Destler 2007).

As of January 2007 the offices of Reps. Rangel and Levin, leading Republicans in the Committee and the USTR under close watch of the White House, started elaborating on a new bipartisan trade policy. Often the negotiations were very difficult, because particularly Reps Rangel and Levin had to negotiate on both 'fronts'. They needed to reach a deal with the Republican Members of Congress and the Republican Administration as well as with the more trade adverse Democrats in the Democratic Caucus. The first indication of change was unveiled in March 2007 when Democrats made public a set of policy principles to be included in those finalised agreements that were not approved to date. With respect to the already negotiated agreements, the principal changes sought by the Democrats were changes in labour, environmental standards, as well as IPRs provisions affecting access to medicines (see Appendix III).[12] While these were all matters that traditionally had been rejected by Republicans and the USTR, the new power distribution in Congress left them no choice but to demonstrate some willingness to compromise (Bridges Weekly 2007b). They knew that without satisfying a sufficient number of House Democrats there would be no trade policy under that Congress.

Even though regulatory templates of previous FTAs such as the one on IPRs remained important to Republicans and their stakeholder groups, the continuation of trade policy was more important. Given the many trade agreements on the table, their hope was that this new template would guarantee the ratification of the pending agreements and see to TPA renewal.[13] This compromise, referred to as the New or Bipartisan Trade Agenda, was found on 10 May after four months of tense bipartisan negotiations[14] between Democrats in Congress and the Administration, chiefly led by Rep. Rangel. A detailed document outlining the precise changes was published a few weeks later,[15] and the final version of the updated FTA with Peru was available by July.[16]

The final agreement constituted a substantial success for Rep. Rangel and his team. Senator Baucus, Chair of the Senate Finance Committee, gave Rep. Rangel the lead in finding an agreement, which he later endorsed. It also meant success for the Republican leadership in the House under Rep. McCrery, distancing themselves from the partisan approach of Rep. Thomas and demonstrating commitment to this new political environment. However, it constituted a defeat for the pharmaceutical industry and lobbyists, as it meant an end to the 'gold standard' IPRs template.

For USTR Susan Schwab, the agreement was a success (Destler 2007). While the USTR failed to maintain its traditional FTA template, it had secured, as it seemed, its principle objective of expanding the US network of trade agreements. The dropping of USTR's commitment to some of its previous allies, was a concession they had to make for a Democrat-controlled Congress. As the composition of one of the USTR's most important principals changed so did the win-set that was being put forward. This led to the inclusion of new (Democrat-promoted) preferences, while others (Republican-promoted) were dropped, including those of the pharmaceutical industry.

The partisan nature of selected key interest groups as they relate to trade policy

Before elaborating on the changes associated with IPRs in the new trade agenda, it is essential to take a closer look at the affiliation of two key lobbying groups, whose preferences were key in determining trade policy with respect to the US-Andean FTAs in general and the IP chapter in particular.

The pharmaceutical industry

Similar to the partisan nature of trade policy-making in general, the industry developed a significant bias towards lobbying Republicans over Democrats from the latter half of the 1990s until 2006. As a study by the Washington-based Center for Responsive Politics reveals, the last 10 years until the 2006 elections saw a tremendous favouritism of contributions by the pharmaceutical industry to members of the Republican Party.

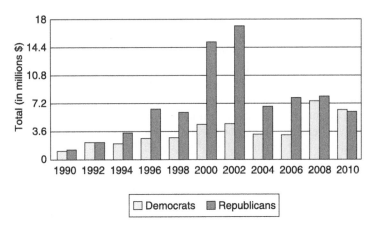

Figure 7.1 Pharmaceutical manufacturing: long-term contribution trends.

Source: Center for Responsive Politics (OpenSecrets.org – accessed 15 March 2011).

The graph demonstrates how in the mid-1990s contributions from the industry moved to a clear bias towards Republicans. This makes sense bearing in mind the political scenario of that time. In 1995, for the first time in 40 years, control over Congress moved from Democrat to Republican hands. The Washington-based lobbying machinery that was previously structured around a Democrat Congress suddenly had to rearrange its affairs. Their previous hiring had focused primarily on Democrats that would lobby the Federal Government on their behalf. At the same time expensive television ads, direct mailing and other instruments had become a crucial aspect of election campaigns and the reliance on campaign contributions by lobbying groups grew swiftly. Compared to the early 1980s lobbying groups had tripled in the mid-1990s (Confessore 2003). Thus, when Republicans gained control over Congress, they immediately put pressure on lobbying groups to realign their party contributions and hire Republicans to the key lobbying positions. In a project referred to as the 'K Street Project', Tom Delay (R-TX), then House Majority Whip, took leadership in regularly meeting with lobbying groups and informing them that they should direct all their resources, including personnel hires, towards Republicans or they would be denied political influence in Washington, DC. Delay famously put together a list of all big trade associations tracking their contributions to Democrats, reminding them: 'If you want to play in our revolution, you have to live by our rules' (Confessore 2003).

While not all Republicans backed this initiative, it had immediate effect and campaign contributions started to shift further towards Republicans. This also included contributions by the pharmaceutical industry, which ideologically already was a more natural ally to the industry compared to

Democrats. Furthermore, the Bush Administration, in power in 2001, further accelerated this trend by aligning the Administration's policy objectives closely with those of the business community. As a result the bias towards Republicans paid off, as they continued to place their political allies in high-level decision-making positions. The lobbying climax in 2001/2002 is reflected in the graph above. Indeed, the pharmaceutical lobby overall spent US$30 million to help their Republican allies to be elected to Congress in 2002. Once elected, the Republican-pharmaceutical alliance was fortified, securing the industry considerable influence in Congress and the White House (Pear and Oppel 2002; Sell 2010). Incidentally, 2001/2002, were also the years of the TPA renewal. Soon after, the Colombia and Peru FTA negotiations were initiated.

Nevertheless, the alliance between Republicans and the pharmaceutical industry was not written in stone. As the 2006 elections changed the power distribution in Congress, and Democrats sought a bipartisan trade deal, which included a move away from the traditional IPRs template, Republicans saw themselves in a position where they either had to back away from their alliance with the industry or risk a failure of the bipartisan deal. While during the negotiations of the New Trade Agenda Republicans backing the positions of the pharmaceutical industry still managed to include some changes, there was a clear move away from the previous IPRs template.[17]

Thus, the final version of the template (see below) constituted a compromise that attempted to reflect on some of the preoccupations put forward by the pharmaceutical industry as well as by a range of Republican allies and the USTR. Most of the compromise made was based on the NAFTA level of IPRs protection. Yet, the compromise was not to the satisfaction of the pharmaceutical industry, which felt that the majority of their comments had been largely ignored in the consultation process and which subsequently voiced deep concern over the Agenda's impact on the industry. Of particular concern was the possibility of setting a precedent for future FTAs by using the new IPRs template as the basis of all future agreements and TPAs (*Inside US Trade* 2007a).

However, for Republicans, above all from the USTR and the White House, it was clear that once a bipartisan agreement on the much bigger question of labour was found, there was no going back, and a bipartisan deal would be made. In their anticipation that the compromise would lead to the ratification of all pending trade agreements, including the TPA, they essentially turned their back on the pharmaceutical industry. They saw the continuation of trade policy as more important than the maintenance of the IPRs template.[18]

While the realignment of party donations post-2006 Congressional election quickly reflected the new political reality in Congress, this development demonstrated the dependence of private interest groups on key policy-makers. Its choice to align itself primarily with Republicans clearly backfired with the 2006 elections and provided a window within which the industry had less influence on trade policy-making until new alliances would be established.

Labour unions

Another equally relevant interest group for this study are labour unions, which tend to be even more partisan than the pharmaceutical industry.

While the sheer volume of donations provided by the labour unions seem to vastly outnumber those of the pharmaceutical industry, it is important to remember that the unions in this chart represent a conglomerate of small unions, such as electrical, chemical, automotive workers or nurses. Most unions work independently of each other. They do not possess the unity on specific trade policy aspects that the pharmaceutical lobby enjoys. What remains constant, however, is their party loyalty. The vast majority of resources that the unions donate are directed at Democrats. Of particular importance here is the American Federation of Labor and Congress of Industrial Organizations (AFL-CIO),[19] which is an umbrella group representing a large range of smaller unions which in turn represent 13 million workers nationwide and which is the key advocate for unions on trade-related matters. It is these numbers that comprise the real strength of unions. They do not only reflect votes, but also contribute with tremendous advocacy work for Democrat candidates in elections, often lobbying with television ads and rallies that strive on the sheer quantity of people. Furthermore, as has been mentioned above, many of the newly elected Members in Congress had relied on the support of unions in their election campaigns, which raised the AFL-CIO's political capital with respect to influencing the Democrat Caucus in this newly formed Congress.

AFL-CIO, like PhRMA, is very active when it comes to lobbying on international trade, in the attempt to protect against job losses for American workers. As such the AFL-CIO's position is to object to any trade agreement largely based on arguments that seek to protect American jobs. One way of

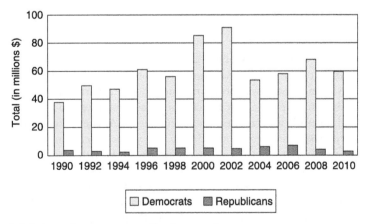

Figure 7.2 Labour: long-term contribution trends.

Source: Center for Responsive Politics (OpenSecrets.org – accessed 15 March 2011).

doing so is through the integration of labour standards or environmental standards into trade agreements as a means of reducing competition from abroad. It was their lobbying power over many years that led to the eventual reform of the labour chapter in the US-Peru FTA. Furthermore, forming alliances with other trade critics, labour unions have also occasionally referred to the public health concerns in FTAs.

The revised IPRs template

With respect to the IPRs chapter the following changes were introduced, as also outlined in Appendix III:

1   Limits in patent term extension provisions.

     The original FTA with Colombia and Peru included provisions on patent term extension. The revised agreement tones these obligations down with respect to pharmaceutical patents by leaving the parties the choice of whether or not to implement it. In exchange the Andeans committed themselves to processing applications expeditiously, with the assistance and cooperation of the US (McDermott 2007; Levin 2007).

2   Limit data exclusivity periods to the term provided in the US.

     Under the original agreement the five-year (10-year for agrochemicals) data exclusivity period in Colombia or Peru would have started when the product was introduced in the market, with a possible grace period of five years between its original introduction elsewhere and when it was introduced in Colombia and Peru. In the new agreement this possible grace period has been abolished under the condition that the approval of the new compound would take place within six months of application. This may reduce the overall period of protection (McDermott 2007; Waxman 2007; Levin 2007; Roffe and Vivas-Eugui 2007).

     Other changes are related to the scope of protection. In the new provision, data protection reincorporates the definition 'undisclosed' to describe the information that is subject to protection, while replacing the broad term 'information' with 'undisclosed text or other data'. This term had been dropped from previous FTAs, applying data protection to all related information, independent of its disclosure status. Other changes include the limit of protection to five years, and not 'at least' five years, while explicitly referring to exceptions to data protection, such as in scenarios of compulsory licences (Jorge 2007a).

3   Rephrasing of 'linkage' provisions in the FTA.

     The traditional linkage provision has been revised by changing the *shall* with a *may* and subsequently allowing Parties not to introduce such provision. Furthermore, the FTA emphasises that Members should provide for procedures or remedies for the expeditious adjudication of disputes concerning the validity or infringement of patents of pharmaceutical products or methods of use (McDermott 2007; Jorge 2007a; Levin 2007).

4   Including the Doha Declaration in the actual text of the agreement.
    Whereas the original Colombia and Peru FTAs mentioned the Doha Declaration in an Understanding on Public Health that was attached to the FTA, it did not feature in the actual text of the agreement, in spite of Colombia and Peru insistence. The revised FTA does include the Declaration in the actual text of the Agreement and subsequently raises its legal importance in case of a conflict that may arise in the future (McDermott 2007; Levin 2007).

When the revised US–Peru FTA text was made available to the public, reactions from the public health and Generic Pharmaceutical Association (GPhA) emerged. For the first time endorsing an FTA, the GPhA states in a letter to Chairman Rep. Rangel and ranking member Rep. McCrew:

[t]he GPhA welcomes the recent changes to the intellectual property protection provisions for pharmaceuticals as an important step forward in ensuring that our free trade agreements reflect the balance contained in U.S. law between the interests of fostering drug innovation and ensuring access to affordable medicines. We urge you to support the U.S.-Peru Trade Promotion Agreement, including the intellectual property provisions for pharmaceuticals.

(letter attached to Rahm 2007)

Similarly, Oxfam, a staunch critic of all previously negotiated FTAs that included TRIPS-plus provisions referred to the revised text in a letter to Nancy Pelosi, Speaker of the House as:

. . . an important [step] toward making trade work for poor people and developing countries . . . We particularly welcome the significant achievement made in reducing the onerous requirements for intellectual property protection for pharmaceuticals . . . This will make a real difference in preserving access to affordable medicines.

(McDermott 2007)

Furthermore, Rep. Waxman who so far opposed all FTAs wrote in an open letter to his colleagues in the House:

I am writing to express my support for the Peru Free Trade Agreement (FTA), based on important changes that congressional leadership has been able to negotiate in the intellectual property provisions for pharmaceutical products. [. . .] [T]his spring the Democratic congressional leadership successfully negotiated substantial improvements to pharmaceutical-related provisions. The revised Peru FTA restores much of the flexibility needed to protect public health [. . .]. With the revision to the Peru FTA, Congress has an important opportunity to embrace a new direction and build momentum for further changes to U.S. trade policy that will do even more to prioritize access to medicines and public health.

(Waxman 2007)

Interesting also was the reaction of PhRMA to the Peru FTA. While they did not lobby against it, they did not endorse it, even though they had been repeatedly asked to do so by the Administration. PhRMA decided not to lobby against the FTA for the same reason that the AFL-CIO did not do so, namely to not alienate themselves from the Democrats and the new bipartisanship found in Congress. In addition, the White House had sent a clear message to PhRMA not to lobby against it reminding them that the Administration had been very supportive with respect to domestic legislation, such as that on biogenerics,[20] or the blocking of legislation that would facilitate the import of cheaper drugs from Canada[21] (*Inside US Trade* 2007c).

While changes with respect to the IPRs provisions were sought over many years by a range of Democrats, it constituted a strategic success to align them with the far larger and older movements of labour and environment. In comparison to the vast majority of Democrats that were keen on seeing certain labour standards in the new agreements, it was only a small handful of Democrats that had repeatedly insisted on seeking changes in the IPRs field. The environment and labour movement were movements that already rose to prominence in seeking to influence previous Administrations' trade policy in the 1990s (Falke 2006). The much younger and smaller Access to Medicines movement did not hold such prominence in Washington, DC. Protecting public health abroad did not hold the same political weight as protecting American jobs at home. Indeed, public opinion, while strong on labour issues, was hardly aware of the IPRs/health issues related to FTAs in developing countries (Destler 2007). While public health activists have been pointing to the IPRs/health issue over many years, supported by repeated letters in Congress, it was always a fringe movement in comparison.

Without doubt, it was the savvy political manoeuvring of a range of public health groups, in collaboration with a handful of dedicated Senators, such as Kennedy, and Representatives in the House, such as Waxman and Levin, that managed to take advantage of the labour and environment movements to raise the stakes on IPRs/public health. The move was facilitated further by the willingness of the Republican Administration to reduce its support for the pharmaceutical industry in order to achieve a bipartisan trade agreement. Also, unlike the labour and environment provisions, which were repeatedly discussed on the floor, the IPRs changes were mostly developed through a consultation process put together by Rangel's and Levin's staff.[22] For most Democrats that supported the agreement, the IPRs changes were not a 'make or break' issue, but simply an opportunity to bring another 'success story' home to its own constituents, while at the same not paying too much attention to the matter.

In the end, many Democrats voted in favour of the New Trade Agenda to show support for the efforts made by the Democrat leadership to integrate their concerns into trade policy.[23] They did not want to be seen as being against trade *per se*, but to make their support dependent on each individual agreement. The US-Peru FTA was a great opportunity to do so for relatively small political costs, given the size of the Peruvian economy. The fact that most possible American job losses as a result of the FTA already took place through the ATPDEA also calmed the unions. Voting *aye* on the Peru FTA meant that the traditionally trade critical Representatives could now say they were not simply against all trade, but only against certain forms of it. This is also likely to be the reason behind the labour unions' decision not to lobby against the ratification of the US-Peru FTA, but focus its political capital on opposing the remaining FTAs.[24]

The domestic politics of ratifying the Colombia and Peru FTAs

As the final US-Peru FTA text was made public it became increasingly apparent that it would possibly be the only agreement that was going to move forward in the medium-term future. While Peru seemed to get the go ahead from Congress (as well as a neutral acknowledgement of the labour unions), the other outstanding agreements did not, mostly for political reasons that were not related to the FTAs. The first indication of a possible delay of the US-Colombia FTA was a letter to Ambassador Schwab attached to the 10 May statement, in which Reps Rangel and Levin referred to systemic and persistent violence against trade unionists, emphasising a broad range of related steps that had to be taken by the Colombian Government before Congress would consider the agreement's ratification[25] (Callan and Guha 2007; Rangel and Levin 2007). On 29 June 2007 the House leadership also made a written commitment to the unions, confirming that the Colombia FTA would not pass in this Congressional period, justified by the continuing violence against unionists and the government infiltration by the paramilitary (*Inside US Trade* 2008a). US labour lobbied fiercely against the agreement. In a statement at a Senate Finance Committee hearing, Thea Lee, Policy Director for AFL-CIO stated:

> We welcome the progress made by the new Democratic leadership in the House of Representatives in negotiating improved provisions in key sections of pending free trade agreements, including the U.S.-Peru TPA. [. . .]
>
> Also, it is important to note that, while the May 10th template represents progress, it is by no means a complete fix appropriate for any country or any situation. Intractable and egregious human rights

violations in Colombia and unequal market access issues in South Korea put these two agreements in a completely separate – and significantly more problematic – category. [. . .] The AFL-CIO will vigorously oppose the FTAs with Colombia and Korea and any renewal of the current fast track authority.

(AFL-CIO 2007)

While some argue that the compatriotism between unionists in Colombia and the US is ideologically understandable, other critical voices claim that human rights abuses in Colombia have been used as a reason to block the FTA for protectionist reasons. 'As if the US labour unions cared about workers in Colombia' one interviewee put it bluntly.[26]

In the meantime the Colombian Government did all in its power to convince Democrats and their stakeholders that violence in the country was reducing. Often President Uribe engaged in lobbying himself, accompanied by leading political figures reporting on the reduction of murder rates. Furthermore, Uribe convinced some of the opposition parties to publicly support him in order to demonstrate that parties without 'para-politicas' scandals were also backing the agreement. The Liberal Party, for example, announced in May 2007, after years of opposition, that they would now favour a ratification of the FTA.[27]

In this endeavour the Colombian Government was strongly supported by the Bush Administration[28] and by Republicans, who demanded from the House Leadership more precision in terms of what kind of improvement they would like to see in Colombia (Hennig 2008). Rangel's response to this was:

I do not put demands on sovereign nations. [. . .] It is below the dignity of sovereigns that members of Congress attempt to negotiate with governments.

(Wasson 2008)

In the meantime, the Bush Administration, with the support of the US Chamber of Commerce, continued to fund Congressional visits, which took Democrats to Colombia to demonstrate how security had improved in the country (Wasson 2008; *Inside US Trade* 2008b). The Administration also repeatedly sought the support of PhRMA to secure the passage of the Colombian FTA in Congress. PhRMA, however, had by then decided to invest its political support in the Korean FTA, indicating to the Administration that it had no intention in supporting the outstanding Latin American FTAs, featuring the revised IP chapters.[29] According to PhRMA spokesperson Mark Grayson:

[w]hile we have long supported free trade in the hemisphere and still believe it's an essential element for enhancing economic prosperity there, and believe that Peru, Colombia and Panama are all key partners in markets that could be key centers for research and development of pharmaceuticals, our board has decided that, given revisions to the recent

agreements, we cannot support passage of the agreements. [. . .] As such, we will be spending our time trying to work in support of the Korea agreement.

(*Inside US Trade* 2007d)

As a result, prospects for the Colombian FTA became even less likely. The lack of definition of circumstances under which an FTA with Colombia was conceivable at the time seemed to support the suspicion of many in the Administration that violence and human rights concerns in Colombia were used as a reason to block the agreement for domestic political reasons.[30] On several occasions, when Colombian Government officials met with labour unions, they were told that independent of how much the situation would improve, the unions would continue lobbying against it.[31]

As was expected, the US-Peru FTA passed the House on 8 November 2007 with a safe majority of 285:132 and a large number, albeit still a minority, of Democrats voting in favour of it (Callan 2007). One month later the agreement also passed in the Senate and on 14 December President Bush signed the respective Implementation Act.[32] USTR Susan Schwab called the passage of the FTA in the House, the traditionally more protectionist Chamber of the US Congress, a 'historic achievement for the U.S. and Peruvian people'. Furthermore, she said:

[t]he conventional wisdom last fall was that the President and Congress could not come together to make progress on a pro-trade agenda. The Administration reached out to build on shared principles and sort out honest differences. At the time – almost exactly one year ago – I said that divided government means shared responsibility, and that we should look forward to the future as partners – because the world is watching.

(Schwab 2007)

However, the passage of the FTA did not take place without further conditions: two other political objectives were tied to it and both had to be satisfied before the FTA was put to vote in the House. The first condition was that Peru had to upgrade its labour laws to the satisfaction of Congress *before* Congress would even consider approving the FTA. The second was the passing of a new TAA bill, which also had to take place prior to the consideration of the FTA (*Inside US Trade* 2007b; Strawbridge 2007; Farnsworth and Hufbauer 2007). While the nature of the former had precedence in the sense that all US Implementation Acts contain a 'certification' requirement before the US enforces its part of the agreement, this 'certification-plus' went a step further. While under the traditional certification system the monitoring of the other party's implementation takes place *after* both parties have approved this agreement, in this case Peru had to adapt its labour laws *before* the US Congress was even willing to consider the vote on the FTA,[33] above all to satisfy US unions.

The birth of a new IPRs template?

One of the questions that remains open at the time of writing this book relates to the new IPRs template's future impact. After the New Trade Agenda was published it was argued that the template would apply not only to Peru, but also the Panama and Colombia FTAs. While they have been signed, at the time of the writing of this book both remain subject to US partisan battles and implementation legislation is yet to be approved (*Bridges Weekly* 2011). Furthermore, new US FTA negotiations such as the Trans-Pacific Partnership Agreement negotiations have come under fire by a number of NGOs highlighting the TRIPS-plus nature of the leaked negotiation documents. The little that is known of the negotiations, which include Peru, indicates that the US is proposing levels of protection that go beyond the IP standard included in the US-Peru and US-Colombia FTAs and possibly other FTAs.[34]

A more immediate question is what will be the impact of the new IPRs template on previously negotiated agreements. While it is unlikely that other agreements, such as the US-Chile FTA or CAFTA will be reopened and changed, it is possible that the new template will have an impact on the enforcement of the existing provisions. Insisting, for example, in CAFTA on patent term extension, but not doing so in Peru due to the new wording, may be a politically difficult inconsistency to justify. Similarly, the new template may have an impact on the substance of the 301 Watch List, and the selection of countries that are being put under 'Priority Watch'.

Reflecting on the US trade policy-making process and the new trade agenda

The nature of the domestic political landscape before the 2006 elections explained the origin of the traditional IPRs template and the firm stance which US negotiators took in the US-Andean FTA negotiations. Similarly, the new domestic political landscape and shake up of interest group influence in Washington, DC, post-2006 election in turn was reflected by a new IPRs template put forward by a group of Democrats. Domestic policy dynamics are without doubt the driving force of how the US negotiated and approved (or not) the Andean FTAs. The way domestic politics characterise international negotiations, however, is defined above all by the structure of domestic institutions, the veto power of interest groups and the preferences they put forward. The following section will reflect on the lessons learnt from this chapter.

Lack of negotiation flexibility on IPRs as a function of domestic political circumstances

As was discussed in the previous chapters, US negotiators remained highly inflexible throughout the IPRs negotiations. The nature of the original IP chapter before its revision after the 2006 elections was based on the traditional IPRs template that had been developed over the course of previous FTA negotiations. The position put forward by health authorities in Peru and Colombia had little effect on the outcomes of the negotiations.

After a closer look at the domestic negotiation scenario of the US system, this came as no surprise. Congress at that time was controlled by Republicans, many of whom in turn were closely allied with the pharmaceutical industry. This alliance was partially a result of a shared ideology between many pro-industry Republicans but further exacerbated by the particularly strong partisan nature of lobbying that evolved post-1995. Any change in the IPRs template would have risked the support of the industry, which in turn would have led to a reduction of Republican votes. Given that the USTR was entirely dependent on Republican support to approve the agreement, US negotiators had to be extremely firm in their stance on IPRs. The near miss of the vote on CAFTA served as a reminder of the tight vote margins USTR was facing.

Therefore, the near absolute inflexibility on IPRs can be explained by the US domestic scenario at the time. Only when the power distribution among the negotiation principals changed were some of the public health concerns integrated into the US win-set.

USTR – agent or principal?

Constitutionally, the overall direction of trade negotiations is set by the trade mandate that is defined by Congress. The trade mandate that provided the basis of the US Andean negotiations was the TPA of 2002. While the TPA was relatively clear in terms of the demands it set in IPRs, it set them broadly and still left the USTR a lot of negotiation space in terms of how it sought to satisfy the objectives put forward. Also, it is important to remember that a TPA is essentially only a list of objectives that guides the USTR in terms of what it has to achieve to get the support of those Members of Congress that have also supported the TPA. It is not an absolute list and the USTR is free to disregard certain objectives while adding on others. The fact that the USTR initially chose to ignore the 2002 TPA's third IPRs negotiation objective, namely the inclusion of the Doha Declaration into the FTA demonstrates this matter. Indeed, the USTR chose to ignore many of the Democrat demands during USTR-Congressional consultations during the original FTA negotiations as has been confirmed by the findings of the GAO 2007 Report.

So essentially the USTR enters into a 'pick and choose' process when engaging in international trade negotiations, in which it prioritises different preferences put forward by different domestic stakeholder groups. It sets these priorities above all according to their importance *vis-à-vis* the final vote in Congress. Thus, as a result the highly partisan nature of trade policy tended to favour Republican above Democrat input during the US-Andean negotiations. All of this of course changed after the 2006 elections severely redefined the possible win-set of any trade agreement that was going to get approval in a Democrat-controlled Congress. The USTR suddenly had to serve a different set of principals and had to demonstrate its capacity to function as a strategic broker to a changing set of preferences.

As a result it can be argued that the USTR, while being an agent in trade policy-making, carefully chooses the principals it decides to represent. It will do so above all based on its calculation off whatever combination will guarantee the 218-vote benchmark needed to approve the agreement in the more trade-averse House. The narrower the anticipated vote will be the lesser policy space the USTR will have to influence what negotiation objectives to put forward and which principals to obey.

This does not mean, of course, that the US negotiators have as little negotiation flexibility as they often state during the negotiations. On many occasions the US team during the US-Andean negotiations referred to the statutory consultation process claiming that it essentially tied their hands for making further concessions in areas where they could easily have done so. However, given the close affiliation between the pharmaceutical industry, the USTR and Republicans, it is likely that, indeed, in the case of the IPRs chapter the inflexibility was to a large extent real.

Public and private sector interaction in US domestic policy-making

Next to the above-mentioned developments influencing the US-Peru and US-Colombia FTA negotiations, the overall public-private relationship within the US policy-making system deserves attention. The particular proximity between the public sector and private interest groups in the US reflects a different philosophy to policy-making compared to other countries in the world. This includes the statutory role of the private sector through the ITACs, the importance of private campaign contributions in local, state and federal elections, and, above all, the 'revolving door' between the private and public sector. The 'revolving door' phenomenon is much more common in the US than in, for example, Europe, where the move from high level public service into trade associations is still less common (albeit increasing). Similarly, in Colombia and Peru, where some negotiators joined international companies during or after the negotiations, their move provoked outrage. In the US, however, the move from public to private sector can in many instances be an expected career move. Inevitably this has an effect on the way that interest groups gain access to, and influence policy-making processes, especially when combined with strategic campaign donations. It equally has an effect on people in public office that aspire to work for certain trade associations later on in their career.

An additional particularity of interest groups in the US is the services they deliver to the Federal Government, and on which the Government has started to rely upon, such as the provision of data on alleged patent infringement to the USTR for 'Special 301' report. The technical understanding of the pharmaceutical industry lobby of IPRs in particular is highly sought after during the negotiations. Finally, lobbying groups also play an important role in securing the passage of trade agreements and other bills in Congress. Their lobbying capacity is powerful enough that their backing of an agreement and subsequent lobbying for it can end up securing a majority in Congress. In contrast, their lobbying against an agreement, such as the labour unions in the case of the Colombia FTA, can severely delay or even block the passage of a trade deal indefinitely.

These services provided by trade associations are essential in the formulation of US trade policy and systemically embedded in the system. While the 2006 Congressional election offered a brief window of opportunity to reverse some of the TRIPS-plus trends, more recent developments such as the TPP negotiations or negotiations of an Anti-Counterfeiting Trade Agreements proved that this window shuts as quickly as it can open. The 2010 midterm elections in which Republicans regained control over the House are likely to further exacerbate the move back towards traditional TRIPS-plus trends.

A bleak future for the pharmaceutical industry's influence in US foreign IP policy?

The political might of interest groups over trade policy is dependent upon the political landscape in Congress, which holds the ultimate jurisdiction over trade. In this sense the victory of Democrats in Congress had an immediate impact on the political access that the pharmaceutical industry enjoyed. The decision to focus mostly on Republicans for allocating campaign contributions over the last decade clearly backfired.

However, the rearrangement of contributions reflecting the new distribution of power in the US Government did not take long. Donation data from the Center for Responsive Politics revealed that already in 2008 Barack Obama and Hillary Clinton were the two highest recipients of campaign contributions from the industry.[35] Respective donations made to Democrats versus Republicans have now evened out. This has allowed the pharmaceutical industry to regain influence in Congress and subsequent trade policy-making as can be seen in above-mentioned developments.

The industry, however, has to confront much larger issues. Next to facing a huge innovation crisis with fewer and fewer new products coming on the market, scandals over the safety of a range of blockbuster drugs, such as Vioxx, and lobbying against cheaper importation of drugs from Canada have shaken its image on a domestic level. Internationally the industry has become increasingly synonymous with bullying developing country governments that are using their domestic legal framework to produce generic versions of expensive patented HIV/AIDS and other drugs. Fewer policy-makers therefore want to fully associate themselves with the position of the industry, as they are seen as bullies who stand in the way of getting HIV/AIDS drugs to poor people in poor countries (*Inside US Trade* 2007c).

Getting rid of this image is likely to take much more than just a re-allocation of campaign donations. More recent activities such as IFPMA's backing of LDCs to extend the deadline by which they have to become

TRIPS-compliant beyond its current deadline of 2013 or technology transfer initiatives are likely moves in this direction (Intellectual Property Watch 2011b, 2011c).

A new trade negotiation framework for the future?

A remaining question relates to the nature of the future of the TPA. Democrats, when re-opening the already signed trade agreements of Colombia and Peru did precisely what the concept of fast track aimed to prevent. With re-entering the text after the signing of the agreements, Congress moved beyond its traditional up-or-down-vote role on implementing legislation post negotiations. While in the past side letters with negotiations partners have sought to clarify certain issues of concern to Congress, Congress is not supposed to reopen the actual text of the finalised Agreement. After doing so Congress placed additional conditions on Peru on the terms under which it would even consider a vote. Finally, as mentioned above, in April 2008 the US House suspended any immediate consideration obligation on a Colombia FTA – distancing itself even further from the TPA of previous years (ICTSD 2008; Hulse 2008). All this indicates considerable dissatisfaction from Congress' side with respect to the current procedures of the TPA and the way it has been implemented at least in the more recent past. The fact that the current TPA has not been extended or a new mandate has so far not been given to the Obama Administration further highlights this frustration.

It is possible that US trade policy-making over the coming years will go through a certain change. This could happen on two levels. First, substantively, through the integration of more or other public policy preferences such as labour standards, environmental protection and/or access to medicines into future TPAs and FTAs – naturally depending on which principals at the time will be driving the TPA extension or developing a new mandate; second, procedurally in terms of redefining the exact rules of TPA procedure in particular in relation to Congress' role in trade policy-making. The treatment of the outstanding FTAs, such as the Colombia, Panama and Korea FTA, and the trade agreements currently under negotiation, such as the TPP and the WTO Doha Round, are likely to shed further light on these questions.[36]

Conclusion

This chapter has demonstrated how domestic political change brought about a considerable turn around in the way that IPRs were integrated in the US-Peru FTA. Ironically, the changes made with respect to the IPRs template included some of those that the Andean health negotiators had aspired to, but failed to achieve during the original negotiations. This was—apart from their own domestic policy dynamics—due to the fact that their negotiators were confronted by an extremely narrow US win-set. As a result of Congressional elections, however, a new set of principals came to power with different preferences, lobbied for by a different set of interest groups. The same principals were then tasked to approve an agreement that was negotiated on the basis of an expired win-set. They thus decide to update the win-set, based on which they subsequently adapted the already signed agreement.

None of this comes as a surprise. Essentially what it demonstrates is that elections can have a big impact in defining whose preferences are included in the formation of the national win-set. To what extent they matter, however, is in turn defined by the national trade policy-making system. In policy-making systems where Congress plays a less important role, congressional elections of this type would have had less of an impact. Additionally, in systems were interest groups are not as closely affiliated to decision-making institutions as they are in the US, the impact may not have had such immediate impact leading to such substantial changes in the trade policy agenda.

While the changes retrospectively introduced into the US-Peru, Colombia and Panama FTAs are a welcome departure from an IP negotiation template that has been increasingly tightened since NAFTA, it is unlikely that it will remain permanent. As private interest groups have wasted no time in realigning themselves to the new political realities, their impact, no doubt, will be felt in future trade policy as the TPP negotiations demonstrate. To permanently reduce interest group influence in trade (and other) policy-making in the US, a more fundamental institutional change is required, which is unlikely to happen in the near future.

8 Conclusion

This book has analysed the interplay between domestic and international factors as they relate to FTA negotiations between Colombia, Peru and the US. It has demonstrated that domestic trade policy-making systems and the forces that shape them are essential for understanding the process and outcomes of international negotiations. Domestic institutions and the political structure in which they are embedded play a fundamental role in determining whose preferences are represented during the international deliberations and how this is done. Any international negotiation analysis that ignores them is, at best, incomplete. At the same time political and economic developments that are outside of domestic reach can have an equally strong impact on how domestic policy-makers engage in negotiations. Thus, a thorough analysis of process and outcome of negotiations needs to engage on different levels of diplomacy and should seek to understand how they influence each other.

The concept of two-level game has proven to be very useful in allowing us to integrate the different levels of diplomacy on which the US-Andean FTA negotiations unfolded and to gain a better understanding of the complex interplay between domestic and international actors that shaped the process.[1] The metaphor of two-level game further provided us with a framework for incorporating other schools of thought in the analysis, such as the study of political structures, institutions and principles and ideas and their impact on the negotiations. Indeed, the case study of the IPRs/public health conflict[2] as it emerged during the Andean FTA negotiations[3] served as a good example to demonstrate the importance of these factors in determining the process and outcome of the original, and then revisited FTA negotiation text. The following observations were made.

In both Colombia and Peru, public health authorities were facing a tremendous bias throughout the negotiations as a result of domestic decision-making processes.[4] Although their full integration into the negotiation teams of both countries constituted a considerable success for public health advocates, their integration turned out to be superficial. As soon as negotiation principals were convinced that a win-set that included public health preferences would not overlap with what they perceived as the US win-set, they decided to move away from the commitments made to domestic health authorities. It is possible that from the beginning negotiation principals knew that this would be the case and that they used the international negotiations on this matter as a means to appease domestic constituents. They were able to do so also because in the end the decision-making process was such that opposition from the health authorities were not in the position to challenge such a move.[5]

Furthermore, any attempt to decentralise the domestic decision-making process was rejected by the Executive.[6] This included, for example, the propositions by Bogotá's mayor, or Senator Rivera's 'ley espejo'. While CAN was used to strengthen regional bargaining power, its success was limited to negotiation items that arguably were only bargaining chips in the US proposal.

Even though a credibly stronger domestic negotiation framework could have strengthened Colombia and Peru's bargaining leverage, negotiation principals did not want to pursue this option. This may be a result of different factors. First, a stronger framework would have meant passing authority from themselves to other governmental fractions; second, it would have taken substantial political will to confront the US team with real no-go areas; and third, and maybe most importantly, Colombia and Peru's negotiation principals did not believe that 'no agreement' was an option. Principals in both countries strongly believed in the necessity of securing permanent preferential access to the US market under any cost. Personal ambitions to do so may also have played a role. President Toledo on several occasions expressed his desire to finalise the agreement under his Administration, even if that meant doing so without Colombia. This did not go unnoticed by the US negotiation team and its principals. Aware that the Colombian and Peruvian governments would not jeopardise the success of the negotiations, they felt free to maintain a position of absolute inflexibility throughout the process.

Being able to maintain a position of absolute inflexibility on the IPRs negotiation template was further facilitated by the fact that it was linked to other crucial negotiation items such as market access.[7] Even though most of the preferential market access included in the FTA was already covered by the ATPDEA, a failure of completing the FTAs could have jeopardised the maintenance of these preferences. This substantially decreased any perceived BATNA for both countries. It also turned those domestic constituents that depended on these preferences, often the large and politically well-established exports groups, into tough proponents of the FTAs. Aware of this, it was used as a powerful negotiation chip by the US negotiators who never failed to remind their Andean counterparts, and indirectly those stakeholders that depended on the market access, of the imminent expiry of ATPDEA preferences.[8] While in February 2011 they did expire for Colombia, bearing in mind the importance of drug eradication in the country it is questionable whether this expiry will remain on a permanent basis.

In order to understand the origin of the position of absolute inflexibility with respect to the IPRs template from the US negotiation team one has to also examine the US domestic trade policy-making framework.[9] While industry groups for a long time have played a strong role in US trade policy-making per statute and the traditional 'revolving door' between the public and private sector, this has been even further exacerbated in the years before and during the US-Andean negotiations.[10] A range of factors worked particularly to the pharmaceutical industry's advantage. The industry's strong alliance with the Republican Party, above all under the Bush Administration, provided it with unprecedented leverage over the US trade policy-making process. Also the USTR and Congress had become accustomed to the services provided by the industry during the negotiations as well as its lobbying capacity for seeing the finalised agreement through ratification. These combined factors turned the industry into one of the USTR's most influential negotiation principals and its preferences among the most important in the US win-set. This relationship, to a large extent, characterised the way that the US engaged in international IPRs negotiations, including those that were part of the US-Colombia and US-Peru FTAs.[11]

All the same, as was seen in the case of the reformulation of the US-Peru FTA (and signed US-Colombia and US-Panama FTAs), the powerful access of the pharmaceutical industry was toppled, at least for a brief moment in time.[12] An institutional shift instigated by the 2006 Congressional elections reshuffled the access different stakeholder groups enjoyed with respect to trade policy-making. With the end of a heavily partisan trade policy in Washington, DC, many of the previously repressed constituents gained new grounds in the process, and with them the different sets of preferences they wanted to include in the domestic win-set. The most powerful interest groups standing behind them included the labour unions, pushing for stronger labour and environmental standards.

A third set of preferences was put forward by those concerned about access to medicine, which were similar to some of those preferences proposed by the Andean health authorities during the negotiations. These preferences were based on principles that had been promoted over some years by public health advocates and a small group of dedicated Members of Congress. While their preferences did not carry much political weight even in the new policy environment after the 2006 elections, the institutional reshuffle provided a window of opportunity to attach the preferences to a pool that was largely put forward by the labour and environment movements. This strategic linkage allowed these groups to 'borrow power' and reformulate some sections of the seemingly untouchable IPRs template that had been developing since NAFTA.[13] While the IPRs chapter of the final US-Peru FTA still includes TRIPS-plus provisions, it constituted a welcomed departure from the previous texts. The new institutional framework, however, also resulted in the blockage of the US-Colombia FTA, which the newly empowered labour unions did not want to see ratified. While to some extent related to human rights violation in Colombia, the ratification of the FTA, at the time of writing this book, has fallen hostage to US politics out of which it is yet to emerge.[14]

The process and outcome of these negotiations demonstrate that principle and ideas (such as the position of the Andean health authorities that public health is not negotiable) by themselves are not sufficient to instigate policy change. They have to be backed by political agents, whose influence is determined by institutions and political structures. In Peru and Colombia the lack of political support for public health objectives was a result of the decision-making processes, which gave way to those principals that prioritised preferences surrounding market access.[15] In the US the particularly strong access of the pharmaceutical industry in a political system that allocates much weight to the private sector in the design of trade policy-making, further suppressed public health preferences.[16] Only after institutional change, which (temporarily) reduced the pharmaceutical industry's influence, could the public health principles be integrated into the domestic win-set.

Indeed, these principles are not new, but have developed over the years since the negotiation of the TRIPS Agreement. They have been continuously lobbied for by international public health networks, resulting among other in the Doha Declaration.[17] With respect to US FTAs, however, they never had the institutional backing needed to truly impact the negotiations until the approval of the US-Peru FTA. Whether it will impact only this FTA or others in the future, or even be integrated into future TPAs, remains to be seen.

This study has examined the integration of public health preferences into the negotiations of IPRs chapters that form part of two recent US FTAs. Yet, the importance of this study goes beyond the public health concerns associated with these agreements. Above all it raises questions about the extent that the political decision-making processes that shape trade policy-making reflect the much longer list of issues at stake. At a time when trade agreements become progressively broader and affect a growing range of public policy sectors over a longer period of time, we have to wonder whether the current institutions in place can echo the issue-linkages that take place during the negotiations. Decisions on environment, health, education and labour law, as they are mantled in a trade agreement's frameworks, are placed in the hands of trade authorities, which are prone to bias in favour of trade-related preferences. Only through a redesigned decision-making procedure that makes the process as comprehensive as the agreements it is mandated to negotiate, can a less biased outcome be made possible.

'Laws and institutions are constantly tending to gravitate,' said Henry Ward Beecher, '[l]ike clocks, they must be occasionally cleansed, and wound up, and set to true time' (Beecher 1859). If trade agreements continue to be of such comprehensive nature, it is time that the institutions and decision-making processes that shape them follow suit.

Appendix I

Overview of US free trade agreements

Year	Signed	Ratified	Under negotiation / Not closed
1988	Canada		
1989		Canada	
1992	NAFTA (Canada, Mexico, US)		
1993		NAFTA (Canada, Mexico, US)	Free Trade Agreement of the Americas (FTAA)
2000	Jordan		
	Vietnam		Ecuador
2001		Jordan	Southern Africa
		Vietnam	Customs Union (SACU)
2003	Chile	Chile	Malaysia
	Singapore	Singapore	Republic of Korea
	Lao People's Democratic Republic		Thailand
2004	Australia	Australia	United Arab Emirates (UAE)
	Morocco	Morocco	Middle East Free Trade
	Bahrain		Area Initiative (MEFTA)
2005	US-Central America and Dominican Republic (CAFTA-DR)	Lao People's Democratic Republic	Trans-Pacific Strategic Economic Partnership Agreement (TPP)
2006	Oman	Bahrain	
	Peru	CAFTA-DR	
	Colombia	Oman	
2007	Panama	Peru	
	South Korea		

Appendix II

Time line of relevant events of US-Colombia and US-Peru FTA negotiations

Rounds	Dates	Location	Key IP events
1st	18–19 May 2004	Cartagena de Indias, Colombia	• US submits IPRs proposal
2nd	14–18 June 2004	Atlanta, US	• Colombian Ministry of Commerce criticises Carlos Correa's participation as part of health team • UN Special Rapporteur to the Right to Health visits Peru and warns on TRIPS-plus provisions in FTA
3rd	26–30 July 2004	Lima, Peru	• Carlos Correa blocked by US team • Andean proposal IPR submitted to US
	In between		• Peru's Alan Angell joins Pfizer
4th	13–17 September 2004	Fajardo, Puerto Rico	
5th	25–29 October 2004	Guayaquil, Ecuador	• US shows no flexibility and maintains a position of no movement with respect to original proposal
	In between		• Presidential elections in US • Intragovernmental meeting in Colombia with President Uribe on the IPRs/health conflicts (27 November 2004)
6th	30 November– 4 December 2004	Tucson, US	• Continuous crossing of lineas rojas – Colombian health team jointly leaves negotiations • Diego Palacio prevents their expulsion from the negotiation team
7th	7–11 February 2005	Cartagena de Indias, Colombia	• Luis Angel Madrid 'prematurely' presents a proposal data protection and is subsequently expelled from team • Javier Gamboa appointed new head negotiator for IPRs

8th	14–18 March 2005	Washington, US	
9th	18–22 April 2005	Lima, Peru	
	In between		• Luis Alonso Garcia leaves INDECOPI and joins the Peruvian Ministry of Commerce
10th	6–10 June 2005	Guayaquil, Ecuador	
11th	18–22 July 2005	Miami, US	
	In between		• CAFTA passes US Congress by two votes
12th	19–23 September 2005	Cartagena de Indias, Colombia	• US IPR negotiation team exchanged • Announcement of the end of technical negotiations and the beginning of political negotiations • Colombian health team writes open letter to Minister of Health withdrawing from the negotiation team – team continues as technical advisors to Ministry of Health • Announcement that Peru will conclude the negotiations by December 2005 • Peruvian health team withdraws from negotiations
13th	17–21 October 2005	Washington, DC, US	
14th	14–22 November 2005	Washington, DC, US	• Colombia walks out of negotiations • Peru continues negotiations on its own
	In between		• Peru concludes Trade Promotion Agreement on 7 December 2005 • Luis Guillermo Restrepo resigns from government • President Uribe holds meeting in Bogotá with domestic health advocates asking them for what it is that is most crucial for them within the IPR Chapter • President Uribe holds meeting at USTR offices on 16 December 2005 to draft the 'Ayuda Memoria'
15th	25 January– 3 February 2006 (only Colombia–US) and 13–27 February 2006 (only Colombia–USA)	Washington, DC, USA	• President Uribe oversees the closing of the IPR negotiations himself at the USTR • Diego Palacio backs the agreement • IP Chapter finalised in separate meeting at USTR (17 February 2007) • Colombia concludes FTA with USA (27 February)

(Continued overleaf)

Rounds	Dates	Location	Key IP events
	April 2006		• Peru signs FTA with US
	22 November 2006	Washington, DC, US	• Colombia FTA is signed in the office of Inter-American Development Bank
	26 June 2006	Lima	• Peruvian Congress ratifies FTA in extra-curricular overnight session, a few weeks before newly elected Members in Congress take over Parliament
	7 November 2006	Washington, DC	• US Congressional elections lead to sweeping victory for the Democrat Party, now holding majority in both Houses
	10 May 2007	Washington, DC, US	• US Congress announces bipartisan New Trade Agenda, including new provisions on IPR/health issue
		Lima, Peru	• Peru receives overview of changes to the FTA that are to be integrated into the environment, labour and IPR Chapters, but not the final text of the agreement
	15 June 2007	Bogotá, Colombia	• Colombian Congress passes US-FTA
	25 September 2007	Bogotá, Colombia	• Colombian Congress passes the changes put forward by the US Congress to the text of the FTA
	8 November 2007	Washington, DC, US	• US–Peru FTA passes vote in US House of Representatives, one month before it also passes in the US Senate
	14 December 2007	Washington, DC, US	• President Bush signs the Peru FTA Implementation Act
	April 2008	Washington, DC, US	• President Bush passes US Colombia FTA to US House of Representatives for consideration • Instead of voting against the Agreement, House Democrats vote against rule, which requires Congress to approve or reject the Colombia FTA within 90 legislative days

Appendix III

A new trade agenda for America: suggested changes to the IPRs Chapters

On 10 May 2007 the Peruvian and Panamanian governments were sent a document indicating the changes to be made in the FTA. The document was specifically directed to the Peruvian and Panamanian governments, however, attached was a letter by Congressmen Rangel and Levin to Ambassador Susan Schwab from the USTR, stating that the same terms must be incorporated in the Colombian FTA, and that the issue of violence against trade unionists still had to be addressed in the latter case.

The documents suggest the following changes to the Chapter:

III. Provisions on Patents/IPRs and Access to Medicines

A. Data exclusivity

As a general rule, where a marketing approval application includes undisclosed test or other data, the FTA would provide for five years of data exclusivity for new chemical entities, taking account of the nature of the data and the person's efforts and expenditures in producing them. However, if a Party relies on marketing approval granted by the US FDA, and if that Party grants approval within six months of an application for marketing approval by a person that produced the data, the five-year period begins when the drug was first approved in the US (a so-called 'concurrent period').

B. Patent extensions

FTAs currently provide that a Party 'shall' extend the term of a patent to compensate for any unreasonable delays in the patent or marketing approval process, provided the delay is not attributable to the applicant. 'Shall' would be changed to 'may' with respect to patents on pharmaceutical products.

FTAs would also provide that a Party shall make best efforts to process patent and marketing approval applications expeditiously with a view to avoiding unreasonable delays. The US and the trading partner would agree to cooperate and provide assistance to one another to achieve these objectives.

C. Linking drug approval to patent status

Amend FTA so that there is no 'linkage' requirement between drug regulator agencies and patent issues: in particular, no requirement that the drug regulatory agency withhold approval of a generic until it can certify that no patent would be violated if the generic were marketed. [. . .]

D. Side letter on public health

The 'side letter' currently included as part of US FTAs should be made a part of the *text* of the FTA. The Parties (1) would affirm their commitment to the Doha Declaration, (2) clarify that the Chapter does not and should not prevent the Parties from taking measures to protect public health or from utilising the TRIPS/health solution, and measures to protect public health in accordance with the Doha Declaration and subsequent protocols for its implementation.

E. Amendments to Chapter based on economic development

The FTA could include a provision calling for the periodic review of the implementation and operation of the IPR Chapter, and giving the Parties an opportunity to undertake further negotiations. The Parties could agree to consider, among other things, whether any improvement in the level of economic development in the territory of the other Party would support amendments to the chapter (US Congress 2007).

Notes

Notes to Introduction

1   Letter to Diego Palacio Betancourt, Minister of Social Protection (Health), Colombia, by Gilberto Alvarez Uribe, Luis Guillermo Restrepo Velez and Luis Fernando Garcia Echeverri, 23 September 2005, Bogotá, Colombia. Available at http://www.aporrea.org/tecno/n66492.html (accessed 31 March 2011).
2   Open letter by Luis Guillermo Restrepo Velez, 2 December 2005. See http://www.bilaterals.org/spip.php?article3189 (accessed 31 March 2011).
3   Art. 25, Universal Declaration of Human Rights: http://www.un.org/en/documents/udhr/index.shtml (accessed 31 March 2011);
      Art. 12 of the International Covenant on Economic, Cultural and Social Rights: http://www2.ohchr.org/english/law/cescr.htm (accessed 31 March 2011);
      Art. 24, Convention on the Rights of the Child: http://www2.ohchr.org/english/law/crc.htm (accessed 31 March 2011).
4   The experience of being passed on from one interviewee to the next was interesting as it demonstrated the personal connections among the different negotiators and stakeholders. I found that the connections made were often based on ideological rather than institutional connection. For example, personal connections between the health authority representatives of Colombia and Peru seemed to be stronger than those within the same negotiation team. I found the 'who recommends whom' worthy of further examination, however, beyond the scope of this book.
5   While I tried to interview all 'sides' to the story, inevitably interview-based research is based on the perceptions of those involved in the process. While such perceptions allow for a rich discussion particularly in relation to political process, it is important to bear in mind that this may lead to exaggerations or even misrepresentation. While I tried to back up what I was told in my interviews as much as possible through additional written sources or by confirmation with additional interviewees, readers should bear in mind that many of those interviewed for this research were directly involved in the negotiations and subsequently often subjective in their interpretation.
6   For further reading into the challenges of implementing FTAs see: Vivas-Eugui and von Braun (2007).

Notes to Chapter 1

1   See, for example, Grieco 1988; Waltz 1979.
2   See, for example, Keohane and Nye 1977; Krasner 1983; Conybeare 1987.
3   According to Milner, the 1960s and 1970s did see some IR theorists, mainly from Marxist and psychological schools, look at domestic factors in order to

explain state action. However, most of these approaches disappeared from IR theory in the 1980s.

4 See, for example, with respect to international economic diplomacy: Lohmann and O'Halloran 1994; Milner 1988; Gowa 1983.

5 Studies on economic negotiations have not only focused on intergovernmental negotiations, but have also ventured into other fields, drawing from the fields of cooperation studies, from mathematical models of bargaining, psychological models and business models as well as law, political science and sociology.

6 Due to the complexity of economic negotiations today no central authority can master all negotiation subjects independently. Most negotiation teams either include technical experts from other agencies or employ external experts to function as advisors to the team. See also Bayne and Woolcock 2003a: 48.

7 For an overview of the role of NGOs in influencing the IPR/public health debate, see Matthews 2006.

8 See http://www.iprcommission.org/ (accessed 1 April 2011).

9 See http://www.who.int/intellectualproperty/en/ (accessed 1 April 2011).

10 Furthermore, many negotiators highlight the relationship among individuals as fundamental for advancing in the negotiations. Trust and credibility are important simply for the fact that one party knows that the other will stick to the compromises made during negotiations. Also, trust is not only important across negotiating teams but also within negotiation teams (Bayne 2003: 77; Zartman and Berman 1982: ch. 2).

11 Odell (2000) defines win-set as a Zone of Agreement.

12 For a psychological analysis on the impact of personality, expectations and perception of the negotiators on the negotiations, see Spector 1978.

13 Issue-linkage is not the only type of linkage that has been analysed. For further reading on other types of linkage see, for example, Sebenius 1983 and Lohmann 1997.

14 http://www.wto.org/english/thewto_e/minist_e/min01_e/mindecl_trips_e.htm (accessed 2 April 2011).

15 Mo (1995) takes this argument even further and analyses the conditions under which the negotiator actually has an interest in imposing restrictions on himself by granting veto power to his domestic constituents in order to increase his bargaining power. In her model she finds that the decision to do so depends largely on the available information to the other party on domestic preferences.

16 For further reading on the EU institutional framework for trade negotiations, see Meunier 2005.

17 Two-level game scholars do not claim that it is in and itself a predictive theory but refer to it more as a metaphor or an approach, which allows for the integration of other theories. See also Bayne and Woolcock 2003a: 37.

18 See, for example, Cowhey 1993, Evans *et al.* 1993, Cameron and Tomlin 2000, Bayne and Woolcock 2003a, Milner 1997, Crump 2006, Mo 1995, Nicolaidis 1999, Meunier 2005, Clark *et al.* 2000, Woolcock 2006.

19 For an overview of how two-level game fits into the broader field of IR theory, see Milner 1998.

20 For an interesting study on how differences in ratification procedures resulted in the failure of international oil negotiations, see Milner 1993.

21 A range of theoretical methods of how to calculate utilities for identifying preferences has been developed; see, for example, Raiffa 1987.

22 For further study on veto-players, see the work of Tsebelis 1995, 2002.

23 For an excellent study on the impact that 'doves' and 'hawks' can have on the outcome of negotiations, see Pastor 1993. For simple analysis of the pros and cons of different levels of negotiating authority, see Fisher and David 1999.

24 For a good overview of the study of institutions from different disciplinary perspectives, see Goodin 1996b. For a good overview of the different definitions of institutions, see Peters 2005: 29.

25 Public choice theorists in particular pay importance to the way that private rent-seeking drives the behaviour of agents. See, for example, Stephan 1995.

26 The basic assumption of rational choice institutionalism reflects this argument, claiming that within institutions there will always be a certain behavioural element that is driven by personal utility objectives. Indeed, sometimes individual leaders within institutions will even use them to maximize their personal gains. The better the institutions the more will such self-maximisation drives be constrained towards socially desirable outcomes. See Peters 2005: 49–55.

27 Discussions with two CAFTA negotiators, one from Costa Rica and one from the Dominican Republic.

28 The term was originally coined by Herbert Simon, for example, Simon 1995.

29 The concept of ideas as used by Goldstein refers to 'shared beliefs'. As such it is very broad and also includes other concepts, such as norms, principles and values.

Notes to Chapter 2

1 Indeed, concepts of the ownership of ideas can be traced back to Greek city states; see, for example, May 2007b.
   For detailed historical overviews, see May and Sell 2006; Dutfield and Suthersanen 2008.

2 On 8 September 2011 the US Senate passed patent reform legislation that includes a 'first to file provision' paving the way for the bill to be signed into law by President Obama.

3 See Paris Convention for the Protection of Industrial Property, 20 March 1883, last amended 28 September 1979; http://www.wipo.int/treaties/en/ip/paris/trtdocs_wo020.html (accessed 2 April 2011).

4 See Berne Convention for the Protection of Literary and Artistic Works, 9 September 1986, last amended 28 September 1979; http://www.wipo.int/treaties/en/ip/berne/trtdocs_wo001.html (accessed 2 April 2011).

5 Art. 33 of Berne Convention, and Art. 28 of the Paris Convention.

6 For a detailed overview of the negotiations on the revision of the Paris Convention, see Sell 1998: ch. 4.

7 The CBERA included: Anguilla; El Salvador; Panama; Antigua and Barbuda; Guatemala; St. Lucia; Barbados; Guyana; St. Christopher Nevis; Bahamas; Haiti; St. Vincent and the Grenadines; Belize; Honduras; Cayman Islands; Jamaica; Suriname; Costa Rica; Montserrat; Trinidad and Tobago; Dominica; Netherlands Antilles; Turks and Caicos Islands; Dominican Republic; Nicaragua; Virgin Islands (British).

8 Chapter 6 will elaborate further on the US institutional trade negotiations framework.

9 The OTCA of 1988 had another important feature in that it changed the administrative authority of Section 301 to the USTR – hoping that the USTR's link with interest groups would allow for a more rigorous use of Section 301; see Mundo 1999.

10 The countries identified as the source of principal losses constitute large developing countries and are unlikely to be representative of the majority of developing countries. Furthermore, the data for the ITC study originated from a survey of 161 US firms that were asked to estimate the losses of their products through what they perceived as counterfeits or illegal practices and business conduct in

developing countries. The direct interest of US firms in this matter also raises some questions on the impartiality of the survey results.

11 While most US technology-intensive firms supported this move, there was some disagreement among them. Notably, the copyright-based industries were split, and the film, music and book producers among them lobbied in favour of maintaining a bilateral approach as the most effective way to increase enforcement. See in particular Ryan 1998.

12 The first time the US tried to include the issue surrounding counterfeit products in the GATT system was 1978 by suggesting an Anti-Counterfeiting Code. While receiving support from Canada, the EC and Japan, the Code was not sufficiently supported to be officially included in the Tokyo Round of negotiations (Primo Braga 1989; Abbott 1989).

13 See http://www.sice.oas.org/trade/Punta_e.asp (accessed 4 April 2011).

14 See http://www.wto.org/english/tratop_e/trips_e/t_agm0_e.htm (accessed 2 April 2011).

15 For a detailed negotiation history of the TRIPS Agreement, see Stewart 1999.

16 See Art. 5, paras 2 and 4 of the Paris Convention.

17 The flexibilities were reaffirmed in the Doha Declaration: 'In this [public health/ access to medicines] connection, we reaffirm the right of WTO Members to use, to the full, the provisions in the TRIPS Agreement, which provide flexibility for this purpose.'

18 See Arts 27.2 and 27.3(a) TRIPS.

19 See Art. 30 TRIPS.

20 See Arts 8.2, 40 TRIPS.

21 See Art. 31, TRIPS, and para. 5 of the Doha Declaration.

22 See Art. 6, TRIPS, which recognises the possibility of Member States to legally admit parallel imports. In this context, see also Commission on Intellectual Property Rights 2002: 42. See also para. 5 of the Doha Declaration that confirmed the importance of parallel import.

23 See Art. 39.3 TRIPS. For a discussion, see UNCTAD-ICTSD 2005: ch. 28.

24 See Art. 66.1 TRIPS, and para. 7 of the Doha Declaration.

25 See, for example, Park and Lippoldt 2003.

26 See, for example, Art. 7 TRIPS.

27 For a range of articles and opinions, see Maskus and Reichman 2005. For a more political economy analysis of the impact of TRIPS, see May 2000.

28 Priority Foreign Country List: China (1991), India (1991–93), Thailand (1991–93), Taiwan (1992), Brazil (1993), Priority Watch Countries: Brazil (1989–92), China (1989, 1990, 1993), India (1989, 1990), Mexico (1989), Saudi Arabia (1989, 1993), South Korea (1989, 1992, 1993), Taiwan (1989, 1993), Thailand (1989, 1990), Australia (1991–93), Hungary (1992, 1993), EU (1991–93), Poland (1992, 1993) Philippines (1992), Turkey (1992, 1993), Egypt (1992, 1993), Argentina (1993). See Stewart 1999.

29 The role of industries leading up to and throughout the IPRs-related GATT/ WTO negotiations has been well documented. See, for example, Sell 2003, Drahos and Braithwaite 2002, Matthews 2002, Dutfield 2003.

30 Named after Arthur Dunkel, then Director General of the GATT. The draft was developed by Dunkel in 1991 after previous negotiations had failed and finally led to the formation of the WTO.

31 According to the UNCTAD-ICTSD *Resource Book on TRIPS and Development* (UNCTAD-ICTSD 2005: 755), the concept of 'pipeline protection' was one 'under which a country that has not provided patent protection undertakes to give effect to patents and/or patent applications from another country(s), notwithstanding circumstances that might otherwise have precluded late-patenting within the former country's territory. This [was] a substantially more ambitious

proposal from the developed country side than was ultimately adopted because it would effectively have required all Members to extend protection to existing patents granted in other Members (with some limitation)'. See also Stewart 1999: 510.

32 The vague language of Art. 39.3 results from a disagreement between the US, the EU and developing countries at that time about whether, and if so how, to include the protection of test data for pharmaceutical and agrochemical products into TRIPS. See also Reichman 2004.

33 Within BITs, IPRs are interpreted as a mode of investment. BITs set a framework that protects this investment. BITs mostly rely on IP standards set in other agreements. For further reading on BITs, see Drahos 2001b; Correa 2004a.

34 For further reading on the interplay between bilateral, regional and multilateral negotiations, see Landau 2000.

35 These include: national treatment for copyrights; encrypted program-carrying satellite signals; pipeline protection for pharmaceutical and agrochemical products; prohibition of dependent patent compulsory licensing; 10-year minimum trademark term; five-year exclusive use of data supporting new chemical entities pending marketing approval; adverse effect on trade; transition periods. For a more detailed review, see Stewart 1999.

36 See http://www.wto.org/english/tratop_e/region_e/region_e.htm (accessed 2 April 2011).

37 For a precise list on all registered trade agreements, see http://www.wto.org/english/tratop_e/region_e/type_e.xls (accessed 2 April 2011).

38 See http://www.upov.int/de/publications/conventions/1991/act1991.htm (accessed 2 April 2011).

39 See http://www.wipo.int/treaties/en/ip/wppt/index.html (accessed 2 April 2011).

40 Part of this section can also be found at Roffe *et al.* 2007.

41 See, for example, Drahos and Braithwaite 2000.

42 See, for example, Helfer 2004.

43 See, for example, Dutfield and Suthernsanen 2008.

Notes to Chapter 3

1 For further reading on the potential impact in other fields, see Fink and Reichenmiller 2005; Rens *et al.* 2006; Roffe 2004. For further reading on TRIPS-plus provisions in the field of trademarks, see Barbosa 2006; Haight Farley 2006. For further reading in the field of geographical indications, see Vivas-Eugui and Spennemann 2006.

2 An example of such an industry is the Indian pharmaceutical sector. While the industry grew in the absence of product patent protection until 2005, some companies are increasingly investing into R&D and are likely to benefit from IPRs protection in the future; see, for example, Lall 2003. For further information on the importance of weak IPRs protection for the creation of domestic industry in developing countries, see Maskus 2003; Branstetter 2005; CIPR 2002.

3 According to the OECD 2007:10 'Triadic patent families are defined at the OECD as a set of patents taken at the European Patent Office (EPO), the Japan Patent Office (JPO) and US Patent and Trademark Office (USPTO) that protect a same invention'. See http://www.oecd.org/dataoecd/5/19/37569377.pdf. (accessed 26 September 2011).

4 Discussions on the impact of IPRs on technology transfer and generating domestic innovation capacity go beyond the scope of this thesis. However, for further reading, see for example Maskus 2004; Branstetter 2005; Correa 2004b.

For broader reading on the impact of IPRs on developing countries, see CIPR 2002.

5 IPRs can also affect access to many non-health-related essential consumer products, such as seeds and education material, or access to environmentally sound technologies. The discussion of those is beyond the scope of this book, however, for further reading, see Wilkinson and Castelli 2000; Tansey 2002; Hepburn 2004; Tansey *et al.* 2008; CIPR 2002; Okediji 2006; Rens *et al.* 2006.

6 For further information on the technicalities of compulsory licences and the waiver, see UNCTAD-ICTSD 2005: ch. 25. For further discussion on the 30 August Mechanism and its negotiation, see Abbott 2005b.

7 Not only US but also EU-FTAs include TRIPS-plus provisions. See, for example, Santa Cruz (2007)

8 This section is based on von Braun and Pugatch (2005).

9 The FDA defines priority review drugs as: 'The drug product, if approved, would be a significant improvement compared to marketed products in the treatment, diagnosis, or prevention of a disease.' For further information, see the FDA Center for Drug Evaluation and Research (CDER) Manual Policies and Procedures, Doc. No. MAPP6 020.3, 22 April 1995.

10 Much of the industry's funding is subsidised by the public sector. The National Institute of Health has a current annual budget of US$31.2 billion per year; see http://www.nih.gov/about/budget.htm (accessed 29 Oct 2010). A lot of the Institute's budget is being spent on the research of medical technologies that are then being taken up by the pharmaceutical industries see Abbott 2005a.

11 For an excellent overview of all health-related TRIPS-plus provisions integrated in international agreements including those other than US-FTAs, see Weissman 2006. This section has benefited greatly from Weissman's report as background material, not only for its content but also for the structure of this section.

12 See, for example, IFARMA 2009a.

13 See IFARMA 2009b.

14 See Kessomboon *et al.* 2010.

15 See   http://www.iprsonline.org/unctadictsd/dialogue/2006-07-31/2006-07-31_docs.htm (accessed 4 April 2011).

16 According to Dutfield and Suthersanen 2008: 96, in 1985 the EPO Enlarged Board of Appeal affirmed the patentability of the second use patents for medicines, as long as they were drafted according to the 'Swiss form of claims', namely that 'a European patent may be granted with claims directed to the use of a substance or composition for the manufacture of a medicament for a specified new and inventive therapeutic application'. See also UNCTAD-ICTSD 2005: 357; Jenkins 2005; Cook *et al.* 1991: 95–7. India, however, included in its revision of its patent law in 2005 a provision (Section 3d) that excludes 'new forms' of 'known substances' from patentability where the new form does not make the drug more effective.

17 New use patents only protect one (or more) specific use(s) rather than the product itself and are difficult to enforce. A use patent cannot prevent a competitor's sale of the product unless the patent holder can demonstrate that the patented use was the goal of the sale. In order to address this problem many inventors try to obtain a product patent in combination with the new use patent by enhancing the old compound through combining it with another compound and through this new combination achieve the protection of the 'enhanced product' and its new application; see Merges and Duffy 2002: 394–6.

18 In US-FTAs with Australia (17.9.1), Bahrain (14.8.2), Morocco (15.9.2), Oman (15.8.1.b). See also Weissman 2006: 45.

19 Art. 4.22, footnote 10.

20 There are different interpretations with respect to this matter. Dutfield and Suthersanen 2008: 14 argue that even though the US term 'useful' could be interpreted as a less demanding requirement than Europe's 'industrial applicability', in practice it may be the other way around. They argue that a product or process that solves a technical problem may not as such have utility and thus fail the US criteria, while satisfying Europe's. For an excellent discussion on the differences between the EU and the US definition of the criteria and the increasing harmonisation between them, see Thambisetty, 2008. A discussion on which patentability criteria is *de facto* higher than another goes beyond the scope of this thesis.

21 35 U.S.C. § 101 and § 112 requires that a patent applicant not only discloses the process of making the invention but also of *using* it. Merges and Duffy 2002: 211.

22 See http://www.uspto.gov/go/og/2001/week05/patutil.htm (accessed 4 April 2011).

23 For example US Court of Appeals in *re Fisher*. See Flattmann *et al.* 2006.

24 Discussing US jurisprudence with respect to the 'utility requirement' goes beyond the scope of this thesis. So does a discussion on what constitutes the difference between basic and applied research in some of the new sciences, such as biotechnology. What matters is that the TRIPS Agreement allowed Member States to develop their own definition of 'industrial application', whereas the language in some US-FTAs denies its negotiating partners this right but seeks to export the US definition of this criteria. For further reading on this topic in the US context, see Merges and Duffy 2002: ch. 3; Chisum *et al.* 2004: ch. 6.

25 In US-FTAs with Chile (17.1), CAFTA (15.9.1), Australia (16.9.11), Morocco (15.9.11.b), Singapore (16.7.1). In the Peru and Colombia FTAs the reinterpretation is not obligatory: 'For the purposes of this Article, a Party may treat the terms "inventive step" and "capable of industrial application" as being synonymous with the terms "non-obvious" and "useful," respectively.' Art. 16.9.1.

26 Discussion surrounding the impact of patenting of research tool on downstream inventions, particularly as it relates to biochemistry is also subject to debate in the US. For a discussion on the matter, see Chisum *et al.* 2004: ch.6. See, for example, FTC 2003: ch.4; Merges and Nelson 1990.

27 In US-FTAs with Chile (17.9.6), Singapore (16.8.7), Jordan (23.a), CAFTA (15.9.6.a), Morocco (15.9.7), Bahrain (14.8.6.a), Peru and Colombia (16.9.6.b), Australia (17.9.8.a), Oman (15.8.6.a).

28 In US-FTAs with Oman (15.8.6.a) and Bahrain (14.8.7).

29 In US-FTAs with Jordan (23.a), Singapore (16.8.4), Chile (17.10.a), Australia (17.9.8.b), Bahrain (14.8.6.b), Morocco (15.10.3), CAFTA (15.9.6.b), Oman (15.8.6.b), original Peru and Colombia (16.9.6.a) (later revised).

30 In US-FTAs with Singapore (16.7.8), Bahrain (14.8.6.b), Oman (15.8.6.b). For footnotes 32–35 see also Weissman 2006: 43.

31 For a more detailed analysis on data exclusivity, see Correa 2004c; Reichman 2004; Pugatch 2005.

32 For a broader legal analysis on this question, see Carvalho 2002.

33 US Public Law 98–417. For a history on the Hatch Waxman Act, see Engelberg 1999.

34 Section 505(j) 21 U.S.C. 355(j).

35 This section is based on Roffe *et al.* 2007.

36 Such as in US-FTAs with Chile (17.10.1), CAFTA (15.10.1.a), Australia (17.10.1a); Jordan (Art. 4.22). (In the case of Jordan the provision on data exclusivity adopts the language of the TRIPS Agreement and does not refer to specific times or terms of protection, apart from footnote 10, which specifically states that NCEs include the protection for new uses for old chemicals for a period of three years.)

37 Such as the FTA with Morocco (15.10.1), Singapore (16.8.1), original Colombia and Peru (16.10.1.a) (later revised).
38 Apart from the FTA with Singapore, which does not refer to a NCE.
39 Such as in the FTAs with Morocco (15.10.1), Oman (15.9.1c), CAFTA (15.10.1.c), Australia (17.10.1.c), Bahrain (14.9.1.c), Colombia and Peru (16.10.1.c). See also Weissman 2006: 27.
40 Such as in the FTA with Chile (17.10.1). See also Weissman 2006.
41 Such as in the FTA with Singapore (16.8.2).
42 Such as in CAFTA (15.10.1.b), Bahrain (14.9.1.b), Australia (17.10.1.c), Morocco (15.10.1 footnote 12), Colombia and Peru (15.10.1.b) (later revised).
43 Such as in the FTA with Bahrain (14.9.2), Australia (17.10.2), Morocco (15.10.2), Oman (14.9.2). See also Weissman 2006: 29.
44 See http://www.cirp.org/library/ethics/helsinki/ (accessed 4 April 2011).
45 For further information on the effects of the 180 days' marketing exclusivity on generating generic competition, see Engelberg 1999: 416.
46 In US-FTAs with Chile (17.10.2.c), Australia (17.10.4), Bahrain (14.9.4), Morocco (15.10.4), CAFTA (15.10.2), Oman (15.9.4), original Peru and Colombia (16.10.3) (later abolished), Jordan (only has to notify 4.23.b). See also Weissman 2006: 35.
47 In some cases the IPRs provisions in US-FTAs go beyond the US level of protection or enforcement. For a discussion, see Abbott 2006.
48 The table is based on Vivas-Eugui and von Braun 2007.
49 For further reading on this, see also Roffe *et al*. 2007.

Notes to Chapter 4

1 In 2009/2010 Uribe tried to amend the Constitution to allow him to run for Presidency for a third term. The amendment was eventually rejected by the Constitutional Court.
2 Alianza Popular Revolucionaria Americana (American Popular Revolutionary Alliance Party).
3 For an extensive overview of the history of Peru's economic policy, see Morón *et al*. 2005.
4 For further background on the FTAA negotiations, see Vivas-Eugui 2003.
5 See http://ustraderep.gov/Document_Library/Letters_to_Congress/2003/Andean_Free_Trade_Agreement.html (accessed 4 April 2011).
6 For further reading on the US-Chile FTA, see Roffe 2004.
7 For further reading on the US-CAFTA-DR, see Roffe *et al*. 2007.
8 See http://www.ustr.gov/tpp (accessed 15 March 2011).
9 The seeking of 'stable and secure' preferential market access over preferential market access under unilateral preference scheme is a key incentive for FTAs in general. The Central American FTA CAFTA is a similar example. For a discussion on this see Shadlen 2008. Furthermore, the locking in of existing trade preferences was also considered essential for attracting long-term investment. It was believed that demonstrating the will to engage in a process of broad economic integration and strengthening of rule of law would increase foreign investment; see Levy 2009.
10 For the text of the G3 treaty, see http://www.usergioarboleda.edu.co/tlc/tlc_G3/index.htm (accessed 4 April 2011).
11 See http://www.comunidadandina.org/normativa/res/r358sg.htm (accessed 4 April 2011).
12 The CAN IP regime includes four key decisions: Decision 486 (Common Regime on IP), Decision 351 (Common Regime on Authors Rights and Related

Rights), Decision 345 (Regime on the Protection of Plant Breeders Rights) and Decision 391 (Common Regime on Access to Genetic Resources).

13 Available at http://intranet.comunidadandina.org/IDocumentos/c_Newdocs.asp? GruDoc=07 (accessed 4 April 2011).

14 See http://www.comunidadandina.org/ingles/normativa/D486e.htm (accessed 4 April 2011).

15 Interview with representative of Colombian law firm.

16 See http://www.medicentro.com.co/CIDMED-BIS-data/Decreto2085de2002. htm (accessed 4 April 2011).

17 See http://www.ustraderep.gov/Document_Library/Reports_Publications/2002/ 2002_Special_301_Report/2002_Special_301_Report_Priority_Watch_List. html (accessed 4 April 2011).

18 See: http://www.mincomercio.gov.co/eContent/documentos/normatividad/decre-tos/2004/decreto2314_2004_EquipoNegociador.pdf (accessed 4 April 2011).

19 The Council is made up of the President, a range of Ministers, the director of the Department of Planning as well as the Head of Banco de Colombia. See http:// www.mincomercio.gov.co/eContent/newsdetail.asp?id=1484&idcompany=1 (accessed 15 March 2011).

20 Constitution of Colombia, Art. 150, para. 1.

21 Interviews with two Colombian Senators. The lack of involvement of Members of Congress in economic diplomacy can partially be explained by the dominance that domestic security issues have on the day-to-day agenda of policy-makers. Furthermore, Congress has also been subjected to frequent scandals, which further reduced confidence in national legislators. According to Llano Angel (2010) 91 of the 2006 elected members in Congress, a majority of which from Uribe's alliance, have been accused of being involved with the Paramilitary.

22 Interviews with Colombian Senators.

23 Interviews with Colombian Senator and former employee of Constitutional Court.

24 See, for example, http://www.tc.gob.pe/jurisprudencia/2007/00036-2007-AI%20 Resolucion.html (accessed 5 July 2011). Some decrees emerging from the FTA in relation to land use for mining and oil production were declared unconstitutional and subsequently revoked by Peru's Congress in 2009, in response to violent clashes with indigenous groups leading to the biggest eruption of violence in the country since the Shining Path insurgence; see Mapstone 2009.

25 The Colombian IP team consisted of representatives from the Ministries of Commerce, Health, Environment, Culture, Justice, Communications, Agricul-ture, and Education, the Treasury, Patent and Copyright Authorities, Drug Regulatory Authorities, different science and research institutes, Department of Planning, the Chancellery, and the Humboldt Institute. Interviews, negotiators and non-governmental experts close to the negotiations.

26 For an overview of the individual negotiators put in charge of the respective negotiation tables, see Semana 2004.

27 Interviews with negotiators.

28 The Minister of Agriculture, Cano, a great critic of the negotiations, was trans-ferred during the negotiations to co-direct Colombia's Banco de la Republica subsequently reducing the number powerful veto-players during the negotia-tions. Interview with negotiator.

29 See, for example, INDECOPI 2005.

30 See, for example, an interview with former Minister of Justice, Baldo Kresalja http://168.96.200.71/gsdl/cgi-bin/library?e=d-000-00---0revagro--00-0-0Date-- 0prompt-10---4------0-1l--1-es-50---20-help---00031-001-1-0utfZz-8-00&a=d &cl=CL1.1&d=HASH0117d6b493dcb317c9a37591.2.6 (accessed 4 April 2011).

31 Roca soon after the negotiations resigned from INDECOPI and went back to teach at Peru's leading Business Administration School ESAN.

32 Interviews with Peruvian negotiators.
33 Interview with representative of Peruvian health-authority.
34 Interview with representative of Peruvian health-authority.
35 See: Cabrera Galvis 2006.
36 Interviews with Peruvian and Colombian negotiators.
37 Interviews with representatives of Colombian negotiation team, non-attributable.
38 Also due to its experiences during the FTAA negotiations where the government was badly prepared for the negotiations. See Alvarez Zarate 2004.
39 Interview with private sector representative.
40 Interview with representative of Colombian Ministry of Commerce.
41 Interview with representative of Peruvian negotiation team.
42 Interviews with Peruvian negotiators.
43 The first impact assessment commissioned by ASINFAR dates back to 1999; see Zuleta Jaramillo and Parra Torado 1999.
44 In the case of Colombia, see Archila *et al*. 2005; in the case of Peru, see Apoyo Consultaria 2005.
45 See also other publications by Mision Salud at: http://mision-salud.org/ (accessed 4 April 2011) and Health Action International, Peru: http://www.aislac.org/index.php?IDInforma=publicaciones/documentos_de_interes/documentos%20_de_interes_1.htm (accessed 4 April 2011).
46 For a good overview over the different studies and respective methodologies, see Fairlie *et al*. 2006.
47 See, for example, the thesis of Patricia Martin (Martin and Ramirez 2004).
48 In Colombia the agricultural sector managed to obtain compensation from the government of 500 billion Colombian Pesos – an equivalent of US$237 million, even before the agreement was finalised. In 2009/2010 this money was subject to substantial corruption allegations against members of Presisdent Uribe's governments.
49 See, for example, Mincetur 2004.
50 Interview with representative of Colombian civil society.
51 See Morena Piraquive (2004), referencing German Holguin.
52 This list of 'lineas rojas' is compiled from a publication of the director of DIGEMID in Peru and an unpublished Colombian document outlining the compromise between the MinComercio and Ministry of Health. The Colombian document is with the author; for the publication from Peru, see Villar Lopez 2005.
53 See, for example, Botero 2005.
54 Interviews with Colombian and Peruvian negotiators.
55 Interviews with Colombian trade negotiator and academic expert, close to the negotiations.
56 http://www.tandemin.com (accessed 5 April 2011).
57 Interviews with Colombian negotiators.
58 Interview with Colombian negotiator.
59 Interviews with Colombian negotiators.
60 Common negotiation objectives among the Andean countries were established during the coordination meetings that took place in between negotiation rounds. In these meetings the outcomes of the last rounds were discussed and strategies for the following established. Eleven such meetings took place, with the last one taking place just before Round 12 of the negotiations. Source: interview with Colombian negotiator.
61 Interviews, with Colombian and Peruvian negotiators.
62 Interview, private sector representative, Colombia.
63 The same side payments were later subject to serious corruption allegations. See Duque Lopez 2009.

64 This included, for example, declaring hospitals duty-free zones, increasing the allocation of funds to the health budget, or strengthening the Drug Regulatory Authority.
65 See: http://www.tlcperu-eeuu.gob.pe/index.php?ncategoria1=101&ncategoria2=104&ncontenido=36 (accessed 5 April 2011)
66 Interviews with Peruvian private sector representatives.
67 Interview with a representative of Peruvian generic industry.
68 Interview with a representative of Peruvian generic industry.
69 Interviews with Colombian civil society organizations and the generic industry.
70 Interviews with Colombian negotiators and generic industry respectively.
71 Interview with representative of Ministry of Commerce in Colombia.
72 Interviews with public health official and representative of generic industry.
73 Interview with representative of Colombian generic industry.
74 Interviews with Colombian negotiators and outside experts.
75 Interviews with representatives of US Chamber of Commerce, Peru, and a law firm representing the international pharmaceutical industry.
76 Interview with representative of health-related civil society organisation, Colombia.
77 Interview with Colombian negotiator.
78 Interview with representative of Peruvian health authority.

Notes to Chapter 5

1 Including: IPRs; rules of origin; market access; safety measures; technical protection measures; sanitary and phytosanitary measures; services (telecom, finance, professionals, construction, software, etc); electronic commerce; government procurement; investment; labour standards; environmental standards; and dispute settlement.
2 Bolivia only observed until the 10th negotiation round, after which they withdrew from the process.
3 Interviews with negotiators, Peru and Colombia.
4 Interview with negotiator, Colombia.
5 Espinosa was exchanged on 20 April 2005 after the impeachment of President Lucio Guttierez.
6 Interview with negotiator in Colombia.
7 Interviews with Peruvian and Colombian negotiators.
8 Interview with negotiators, academics and NGOs in Colombia and Peru.
9 Interview with negotiator, Colombia.
10 Interviews with representative of Colombian generic industry.
11 Interview with member of Colombian negotiation team.
12 Interviews with negotiators in Peru and Colombia.
13 Interview with Peruvian negotiator.
14 Interview with Colombian trade negotiator.
15 Interviews with trade negotiators, Peru and Colombia.
16 Cabrera Galvis 2006.
17 Interview with US negotiator.
18 Interviews with negotiators in Peru and Colombia.
19 Throughout the negotiations further links were made between the FTA and other diplomatic questions, such as coca production and drug trafficking, gas and oil resources, water resources, counter-terrorism and Peru's refusal to accept the US exemption from the jurisdiction of the International Criminal Court; see Campodónico 2004.
20 Interviews with negotiators and representatives of civil society organisations, lawyers, and representatives of international industry.

21 CAFTA was signed at the end of May 2004, just two weeks after the FTA negotiations between the USA, Peru, Colombia and Ecuador were initiated.
22 Interviews with negotiators. For a discussion of the provision with respect to Colombia, see also Zerda Sarmiento 2005a.
23 Interviews with members of Colombian negotiation team.
24 Interviews with negotiators from Peru and Colombia.
25 Interview with Colombian negotiator.
26 For similar statements of Uribe, see also Uribe 2004.
27 Interviews with negotiators, Colombia and Peru.
28 Allan Angell was not the only negotiator that resigned from the Andean negotiation to join the private sector. See Correa C. J. 2007.
29 Interviews with representatives of national health authorities, Colombia.
30 See, for example, Attaran 2004; Attaran and Gillespie-White 2001. Attaran's work was responded to by a counter-publication by Joan Rovira 2004.
31 Interviews with health authorities and negotiators, Colombia.
32 Interviews with Peruvian and Colombian negotiators.
33 Such commitments were often made in social events for the negotiators, organised in parallel to ongoing negotiations. The US promises made during such informal gatherings rarely ended in substantive commitments at the negotiation table. Interview with Colombian negotiator.
34 Interviews with negotiators in Colombia.
35 Based on unpublished summary of meeting by one of the participants. Note is with the author.
36 Interview with Colombian negotiator.
37 Interviews with Peruvian and Colombian negotiators.
38 Interviews with Colombian negotiators and representatives of generic industry.
39 Interviews with negotiators and civil society organisations.
40 Interviews with Peruvian and Colombian negotiators.
41 Confirmed by other interviews with negotiators from Peru and Colombia.
42 Interviews with negotiators, Colombia.
43 The final 'lineas rojas' compromise between the Ministry of Health and Commerce in Colombia included:

  a   a reference to the flexibilities promoted by the Doha Declaration on Public Health in the actual agreement, not in a side letter;
  b   maintenance of all TRIPS flexibilities;
  c   maintenance of old patentability criteria including 'industrial applicability';
  d   linkage provisions should not oblige the drug regulatory authority to inform the patent holder, seek his consent or make marketing approval in any form depend on patent status;
  e   an 18-month maximum grace period between the registration of test data in the originator country and the commencement of the three-year protection period of *undisclosed information* in Peru/Colombia; data protection should be introduced only as of 2014 for Peru, while Colombia maintains Decree 2085 until 2014; specific reference should be made that data protection does not apply to products that are under compulsory licence; all parties should reserve the right to define NCEs domestically;
  f   patent term extension only for commercialised products and if the delays are a result of delays caused by the domestic patent office or drug regulatory authorities. Delay may be considered anything after five years of patent filing, or three years of granting. With respect to delays caused due to inefficient practices of domestic drug regulatory processes, delays are defined as four years after submitting the original data.
      Source: Memorandum of Understanding, unpublished, is with author.

44 Economist Pedro Francke points of no more than 18,147 jobs likely to emerge from the FTA (2004).

45 One of the last trade-offs in the negotiations between Peru and the US was to include an 'Understanding on Biodiversity'. The US team used the watered down Understanding to their advantage making important counter-demands in other fields. It is likely that Peru needed to include biodiversity in the agreement for domestic political purposes and celebrated it as a negotiation success. In spite of its weak nature it is indeed the first of a letter of this kind signed by the US.

46 For further information, see Fairlie *et al.* 2006.

47 Interview with representative of Colombian negotiation team.

48 Interviews with a range of civil society representatives that participated in this meeting.

49 Interview with witness to the USTR meeting.

50 Interviews with Colombian CSO representatives.

51 Even though the agreement was concluded on 27 February 2006, it was only signed more than nine months after on 22 November 2006 in Washington, DC. The initial delay of signature was blamed on translation. However, a little later the US government actually included further changes to meat and poultry provisions in the agricultural chapter. See Robledo 2006.

52 Interview with US negotiator.

53 See also Rodriguez-Franco 2008.

54 Interviews with representatives of CSOs, UN bodies, Ministries of Commerce and Health negotiators.

55 Interviews with negotiators, Colombia.

56 They also indicated necessary changes with respect to the Korea and Panama FTAs.

57 Interviews with Colombian government officials.

58 Peruvian critics included incoming President Alan Garcia, who had run his campaign partially on being critical towards the agreement, threatening to renegotiate if elected into office. Once in office, he reversed his position and he became one of the FTAs most outspoken supporters; see Diez Canseco 2007.

59 Interviews with negotiators and civil society representatives in Peru and Colombia.

60 Interview, Colombian negotiator.

61 Interviews with technical negotiators, Peru and Colombia.

62 At the time of the writing of this study, many of Colombia and Peru's negotiation officials during the US-Andean FTA negotiations had moved away from government, and either joined universities, the private sector or international organisations.

63 Plan Colombia is a programme originally developed by President Pastrana in 1998. It is a multi-billion US$ aid programme that is largely spent on military aid to combat guerrilla and other drug-trafficking groups as well as to destroy coca production.

64 Interview with the Colombian negotiator.

65 Interviews with representatives of Mayor's Office in Bogotá.

66 This includes a study commissioned on the impact of the IPRs chapter on the Health Sector in Bogotá. See Zerda Sarmiento 2005b.

67 This view was also confirmed by previous rulings of the Constitutional Court. For example, Sentence C-517 of 1992, M.P. Ciro Angarita Baron who judged: 'The authorities of the regional entities have certain political rights which in the case of conflict with other interest, have to be taken in consideration to avoid compromising their guarantee for territorial autonomy' (translated by author).

68 Interviews with civil society organisations.

69 Interview with private sector representative, Colombia.
70 See http://www.comunidadandina.org/ingles/normativa/D598e.htm (accessed 4 April 2011).

Notes to Chapter 6

1 See, for example, Destler 2005.
2 Interviews with representatives of USTR and US Chamber of Commerce.
3 The ATPDEA eventually did expire on February 2011 for Colombia and Ecuador. By that time Peru already had implemented its FTA with the US and locked in ATPDEA covered market preferences. ATPDEA extension and FTA approval for Colombia are at the time of writing ongoing.
4 Similar arguments have been made with respect to the other WTO sectors. The lack of willingness of WTO members to increase liberalisation have led to a growing demand for FTAs. See, for example, Crawford and Fiorentino 2005.
5 See US Trade Promotion Authority of 2002 cited below.
6 See chapter 2.
7 For further reading on what is often referred to as the IPRs-ratchet, see, for example, Drahos 2003.
8 For further analysis of the US strategy in setting precedence through FTAs, see also Cameron and Tomlin 2000.
9 Trade aversion also seems to be higher against bilateral trade agreements with developing countries then against multilateral negotiations.
10 The nature of voting on trade-related bills by Democrats and Republicans is in reality more nuanced and highly issue dependent particularly among Democrats. However at the time of the US-Andean negotiations partisan voting on trade was particularly strong, among other because Republicans failed to accommodate the minority party into trade policy-making. See Van Grasstek 2009.
11 Reciprocal Trade Agreement Act of 1934 (GAO 2007b). For a historic overview of 'fast track', see Dam 2004.
12 For a detailed overview over the history of US trade policy-making, see Destler 2005 or Mundo 1999: chs 1, 4. For a fascinating account of the ideas that were behind the institutional shift that led to the 1934 Act, see Goldstein 1993: ch. 4.
13 For the full text of the Trade Act of 1974, see http://www.law.cornell.edu/uscode/19/ch12.html (accessed 7 April 2011).
14 For a fascinating history on the continuous attempts by President Bill Clinton to pass fast track in the mid to late nineties, see Devereaux et al. 2006.
15 For a good historical overview of 'fast track', see Devereaux et al. 2006.
16 Technically, the USTR only needs a TPA for the finalisation, not the negotiation of the agreement. Most of the US-Chile FTA and the US-Singapore FTA and indeed the ongoing negotiations in the WTO Doha Round since 2007 were negotiated in absence of a TPA from Congress. However, towards the end of the negotiations a mandate from Congress is crucial, simply because other negotiating partners will lose confidence in the commitment of the USTR to deliver on its promises of not being able to guarantee an up or down vote from Congress.
17 House, Ways and Means Committee and Senate Finance Committee.
18 Interview with Congressional staffer.
19 For further reading on the challenges of developing countries to implement new IPRs obligations, see Vivas-Eugui and von Braun 2007.
20 Interview, US State Department.
21 This interview took place before the 2006 Congressional elections.
22 Interviews, Congressional staff.

23 Interview, former USTR staff.
24 Interview, former USTR staff.
25 The collaboration of the two committees responsible for trade oversight and the other committees also affected by trade agreements is not always smooth and reflects some of the conflict created through jurisdictional overlap.
26 Interview with Congressional staff.
27 Interviews with Congressional staffers.
28 Interview with former USTR staff.
29 Schattschneider wrote as early as 1935 on the central role of interest groups in the formulation of the infamous Smoot-Hawley Tariff of 1930. See Schattschneider 1935.
30 See 19 U.S.C. §§ 3805(a), 3804 (a); (GAO 2007b).
31 For a full list of members of current ITAC 15 Members, see http://trade.gov/itac/ committees/ipr.asp (accessed 7 April 2011).
32 In light of the expiry of many of the most valuable patents in the coming years this is likely to change. Many research-based companies are currently diversifying their portfolio, including through the increasing production of generics; see IP-Watch 2011a. This is likely to change the unified position within pharmaceutical lobbying groups.
33 For further information on the importance of unity within interest groups, see Mundo 1999: 93-94.
34 Post-employment restrictions of Congressional staff depend on the seniority of the individual held office, but are mostly confined to one year. For further information, see http://ethics.house.gov/Media/PDF/Ethics%20Rules%20Highlights%202011.pdf (accessed 7 April 2011). Interestingly, there are no restrictions on lobbyist moving to Capitol Hill. See *New York Times* 2011.
35 Interviews with pharmaceutical lobbyists.
36 Interviews with representatives of pharmaceutical lobbying and other non-governmental lobbyists.
37 Interviews with Congressional staffers and representative pharmaceutical lobbying association.
38 Interview with pharmaceutical lobbyist.
39 For a historic overview of the strategic placement of industry representatives with a vested interest in strengthening IPRs protection in the US and worldwide in a range of powerful advisory committees, see Sell 2003; Drahos and Braithwaite 2002.
40 In spite of this statement, the power of lobbying groups in the EU should not be underestimated. For further reading, see, for example, Pugatch 2004: ch. 5.
41 In the meantime the US Executive has changed its IP policy-making framework, among other by creating the position of an IP enforcement coordinator at the Office of Management and Budget in 2009. The mandate of this job is to develop a unified approach to IP enforcement in the US and abroad.
42 In 1985 the IIPA submitted its first report 'Piracy of US Copyrighted Works in Ten Selected Countries' on economic data on counterfeighted products to the US Congress. Based on this, USTR began requesting input to support the identification of countries for the Special 301 list; see Drahos and Braithwaite 2002.
43 Interview with form USTR staff.
44 Interview with a representative of pharmaceutical lobby.
45 Interview with a representative of pharmaceutical lobby.
46 Interview with a representative of US Chamber of Commerce.

Notes to Chapter 7

1 For further reading on the political importance of administrative relief for domestic trade policy-making, see Mundo 1999: ch. 6.

2 See bill H.R. 3009, Trade Act of 2002, as passed by both House and Senate: http://www.bilaterals.org/IMG/pdf/TPAA_2002.pdf (accessed 7 April 2011).

3 Amendment No. 3411 to Amendment No. 3401, Hearing on the Andean Trade Preference Expansion Act before the Senate, 107th Congress, S4319, S4345-47, 14 May 2002.

4 The withdrawal of parallel import from the non-negotiable IPRs template is primarily a result of domestic political concern. Members of Congress have repeatedly expressed their fears that including parallel import in FTAs could potentially undermine the possibility of importing cheaper drugs from Canada in the future. Indeed, in 2002 a proposal was passed in the then Democrat-controlled Senate that aimed to clear the way for allowing prescription drug importation from Canada. However, the Bush Administration signalled it would not move the proposal forward. See Pear 2002. Discussions on including parallel imports then re-emerged during the US-Australia FTA negotiations where US Members of Congress expressed concerns over domestic implications of parallel import provisions in FTAs. Of particular prominence was a bill tabled by Representative Northup (R-KY), named 'Protecting Free Trade in Pharmaceuticals Act of 2005'. The Bill suggested an amendment to the TPA that called for the avoidance of provisions in trade agreements that restrict the access of consumers in the United States to pharmaceutical imports. While the Bill was never passed, after the US-Australia FTA and US-Morocco FTA parallel importation was not in the final text of any FTA thereafter (source: interview, former USTR staff). Furthermore, a range of Executive Agencies, including the Treasury, did not support an abolishment for parallel import.

5 Interview with US civil society representatives and members of Colombia negotiation team.

6 Press release no longer available online. For the final report see http://www.gao.gov/new.items/d071198.pdf (accessed 7 April 2011).

7 See Kennedy 2005.

8 Questions related to the integration of social factors into trade policy, above all with respect to labour and environment, were the principal reason why President Clinton never managed to get 'fast track' from Congress. For a detailed analysis on this matter, see Destler 2005.

9 For a more detailed analysis on the nature of Democrat and Republican votes on trade-related bills at the time, see VanGrasstek the 2008a. VanGrasstek shows how the Democrat protectionist position towards trade liberalisation should not be generalised but is often targeted towards FTAs with developing countries and the renewal of a TPA to a Republican Administration. Democrats showed less resistance towards multilateral trade negotiations in Geneva as well as the extention of time-limited preferential market access schemes, such as the CBI. In his view Democrats favour such schemes as it allows them to maintain leverage on negotiation partners with respect to labour and environmental standards.

10 Interview with Congressional staffers, House of Representatives.

11 Interview with Congressional staffers, Republican and Democrat.

12 Other less substantial changes were put forward with respect to port security and investment.

13 Interview with Congressional staffers.

14 Only a few Republicans were included in the development of the new template, resulting in senior Republicans such as Senator Hatch complaining that he had been excluded from the process; see Hennig 2007.

15 For a copy of the document, see http://waysandmeans.house.gov/Media/pdf/110/05%2014%2007/05%2014%2007.pdf (accessed 7 April 2011).

16 See http://www.ustr.gov/Trade_Agreements/Bilateral/Peru_TPA/Final_Texts/Section_Index.html (accessed 7 April 2011).

17 The original Democrat objectives for the IPRs template was to entirely remove all TRIPS-plus provisions such as patent term extension, data exclusivity and linkage from the IPRs template. Interview with Democrat Congressional staff.

18 Interview with Republican Congressional staff.

19 According to the Center for Responsive Politics, the AFL-CIO donated US$1.63 million in 2006. See http://www.opensecrets.org/orgs/summary.asp?ID=D000000088 (accessed 4 April 2011).

20 Legislation that would open the market of generic equivalent to biotechnology drugs, was only passed in 2010 after many years of negotiation under the name 'Patient Protection and Affordable Care Act' and provides 12 years of data protection.

21 Interviews with representatives of pharmaceutical lobbying groups.

22 Interviews with congressional staff.

23 Interviews with industry representatives and Congressional staffers.

24 Interviews with Congressional staff.

25 The Panama FTA stalled as its then newly elected President of the National Assembly, Pedro Gonzalez-Pizon, was sought for murdering a US soldier. US policy-makers demanded that he stepped down before the FTA could move ahead; see Hennig 2008. In Korea the remaining block of US beef imports for fears of mad cow disease constituted a stumbling block for particularly Senator Baucus, of Montana, one of the principal beef exporting states in the US.

26 Interview with US government official.

27 Interview with senator of Liberal Party.

28 As emphasised again in President Bush's State of the Union address at the beginning of 2008. See also *Inside US Trade* 2008a.

29 Interview with pharmaceutical lobbyist.

30 Interview with US government official.

31 Interviews Congressional staffers.

32 H.R. 3688: United States-Peru Trade Promotion Agreement Implementation Act. See http://www.govtrack.us/congress/bill.xpd?bill=h110-3688 (accessed 10 April 2011)

33 Interview with Congressional staffer.

34 See http://keionline.org/sites/default/files/r2h_anand_grover_tpp_22march2011.pdf (accessed 3 April 2011).

35 See http://www.opensecrets.org/industries/recips.asp?Ind=H04&cycle=2008 (accessed 9 April 2011).

36 For a furher discussion on a possible future for the TPA, see Hornbeck and Copper 2011.

Notes to Chapter 8

1 See chapter 1.
2 See chapter 3.
3 See chapter 5.
4 See chapter 4.
5 See chapter 5.
6 See chapter 5.
7 See chapter 4.
8 See chapter 5.

9 See chapter 6.
10 See chapter 7.
11 See chapter 7.
12 See chapter 7.
13 See chapter 2.
14 See chapter 7.
15 See chapter 5.
16 See chapters 6 and 7.
17 See chapter 2.

Bibliography

Abbott, F. (1989), 'Protecting First World Assets in the Third World: Intellectual Property Negotiations in the GATT', *Vanderbilt Journal of Transnational Law* 22(4): 689–745.

Abbott, F. (2003), 'Trade Diplomacy, the Rule of Law and the Problem of Asymmetric Risk' in TRIPS, *'IPRs, Trade and Challenges for Development' Trade and Development Symposium*, Cancun, Mexico, Quaker United Nations Office.

Abbott, F. (2004), 'The Doha Declaration on the TRIPS Agreement and Public Health and the Contradictory Trend in Bilateral and Regional Free Trade Agreements', *QUNO Occasional Paper* (14): http://www.geneva.quno.info/pdf/OP14Abbottfinal.pdf.

Abbott, F. (2005a), 'Toward a New Era of Objective Assessment in the Field of TRIPS and Variable Geometry for the Preservation of Multilateralism', *Journal of International Economic Law* 8(1): 77–100.

Abbott, F. (2005b), 'The WTO Medicines Decision: The Political Economy of World Pharmaceutical Trade and the Protection of Public Health', *The American Journal of International Law* (99): 317–58.

Abbott, F. (2006), *Intellectual Property Provisions of Bilateral and Regional Trade Agreements of the United States in Light of U.S. Federal Law*, Geneva, UNCTAD-ICTSD.

Abdel Latif, A. (2005), 'Developing Country Coordination in International Intellectual Property Standard-Setting', *Trade-Related Agenda, Development and Equity* (24), Geneva, South Centre.

Acosta Medina, A. (2006), *El TLC en Blanco y Negro*, Sociedad Colombiana de Economistas, Bogotá, Colombia.

Acre, M. (2005), *Market Reform in Society – Post-Crisis Politics and Economic Change in Authoritarian Peru*, Pennsylvania, Pennsylvania State University Press.

AFL-CIO (2007), 'Testimony of Thea Mei Lee – Policy Director – American Federation of Labor and Congress of Industrial Organizations (AFL-CIO)', *Hearing of the Senate Finance Committee – On the U.S. – Peru Trade Promotion Agreement*, Washington, DC: www.aflcio.org/issues/jobseconomy/globaleconomy/upload/Lee_Peru_FTA.pdf.

Agencia Peru (2005a), 'Lemor: TLC debe firmarse antes que venza el ATPDEA', *Agencia Peru Online*, 6 September 2005: www.agenciaperu.com/economia/2005/sep/lemor_tlc.htm.

Agencia Peru (2005b), Toledo: 'Sí o sí' significa la voluntad política de mi gobierno', *Agencia Peru Online*, 14 July 2005: www.agenciaperu.com/economia/2005/jul/toledo_tlc.htm.

Albin, C. (2001), *Justice and Fairness in International Negotiation*, Cambridge, Cambridge University Press.

Alcaldía Mayor de Bogotá (2004a), *Bogotá Frente al TLC*, Alcaldía Mayor de Bogotá, Colombia.

Alcaldía Mayor de Bogotá (2004b), *Para Democratizar el TLC*, Alcaldía Mayor de Bogotá, Colombia.

Alcaldía Mayor de Bogotá (2004c), *Recomendaciones de Bogotá para la Negociación de un Tratado de Libre Comercio con Estados Unidos – Asuntos Constitucionales, Institucionales, Solución de Diferencias, Inversión y Competencia*, Alcaldía Mayor de Bogotá, Colombia.

Alvarez Zarate, J. M. (2004), *ALCA y TLC con Estados Unidos: La agenda de negociacion, sus costos y beneficions frente a los intereses nacionales*, Bogotá, Universidad Externado de Colombia.

Anderson, E. C. (2006), 'Chávez: Colombia-US trade pact killed the Andean Community', *El Universal*, 22 April 2006.

Andina (2009), 'US Senate Approved One-year Extension of ATPDEA', *Andina – Agencia Peruana de Noticias*, 23 December 2009.

Angell, M. (2004), *The Truth About The Drug Companies*, New York, Random House.

Apoyo Consultaria (2005), *Impacto de las negociaciones del TLC con EEUU en materia de propiedad intelectual en los mercados de medicamentos y plaguicidas*, Apoyo Consultaría, Lima, Peru.

Arboleda Zapata, J. C. (2004), 'Ley Espejo para frenar una negociación sin límites', *El Pulso*, June 2004: www.periodicoelpulso.com/html/jun04/debate/debate-04.htm.

Archila, E. J., Carrasquilla, G., Melendez, M. and Uribe, J. P. (2005), *Estudio sobre la Propiedad Intelectual en el Sector Farmacéutico Colombiano*, Fedesarrollo, Bogotá, Colombia.

Asif, I. (2005), *Drug Lobby Second to None – How the pharmaceutical industry gets its way in Washington*, The Center for Public Integrity, Washington, DC.

Asif, I. (2007), *Spending on Lobbying Thrives – Drug and health products industries invest $182 million to influence legislation*, The Center for Public Integrity Washington, DC.

Attaran, A. (2004), 'How Do Patents and Economic Policies Affect Access to Essential Medicines in Developing Countries?', *Health Affairs* 23(3): 155–166.

Attaran, A. and Gillespie-White, L. (2001), 'Do Patents for Antiretroviral Drugs Constrain Access to AIDS Treatment in Africa?', *The Journal of the American Medical Association* 286(15): 1886–92.

Baker, D. (2006), 'A Framework for Assessing the Costs and Benefits to Developing Countries of TRIPS-plus Rules in Trade Agreements', *Expert Meeting on Developing a Methodology to Assess the Impact of TRIPS-plus Provisions Affecting Drug Prices*, Geneva, ICTSD, WHO and the World Bank Institute.

Barbosa, D. (2006), 'TRIPs Art. 7 and 8, FTAs and Trademarks', *IP, FTAs, and Sustainable Development*, Washington, DC, American University.

Bayne, N. (2003), 'Economic Diplomacy in Practice', in N. Bayne and S. Woolcock (eds), *The New Economic Diplomacy: Decision-Making and Negotiation in International Economic Relations*, Hampshire, Ashgate pp.63–42.

Bayne, N. and Woolcock, S. (2003a), *The New Economic Diplomacy*, Hampshire, Ashgate.

Bayne, N. and Woolcock, S. (2003b), 'What is Economic Diplomacy?', in N. Bayne and S. Woolcock (eds), *The New Economic Diplomacy: Decision-Making and Negotiation in International Economic Relations*, Hampshire, Ashgate pp. 1–20.

Bayne, N. and Woolcock, S. (2007), 'What is Economic Diplomacy?', in N. Bayne and S. Woolcock (eds), *The New Economic Diplomacy* (2nd edn), Hampshire, Ashgate.

Beecher, H. W. (1859), *Life Thoughts*, Edinburgh, Alexander Strahan and Co.

Bhagwati, J. (1991), *The World Trading System at Risk*, Harvester Wheatsheaf.

Bhagwati, J. (2002), 'Afterword: The Question of Linkage', *The American Journal of International Law* 96(1): 126–34.

Binder, S. A. (2003), *Stalemate: Causes and Consequences of Legislative Gridlock*, Washington, DC, Brookings Institution Press.

Bloomberg (2006), 'Chavez Says Venezuela Plans to Withdraw From G-3 Trade Bloc', *Bloomberg.com*, 7 May 2006.

Blustein, P. and Allen, M. (2005), 'Trade Pact Approved By House', *Washington Post* 28 July 2005.

Bolpress (2005), 'TLC: Renuncia un negociador peruano y destituyen al colombiano responsable de negociar temas de propiedad intelectual – Las ambiciosas propuestas de EE.UU. indisponen a los gobiernos de Perú y Colombia', *BolPress* 28 February 2005.

Botero, J. H. (2004), 'Letter to Members of Congress', in N.P. Gutierrez, C.J. Gonzalez Villa, G.A. Rivera Florez and C.I. Cuervo (eds), Bogotá, Ministerio de Comercio, Industria y Turismo.

Botero, J. H. (2005), Letter to Venus Albeiro Silva, Bogotá, Ministerio de Comercio, Industria y Turismo, 8 March 2005.

Braithwaite, J. and Drahos, P. (2000), *Global Business Regulation*, Cambridge, Cambridge University Press.

Branstetter, L. (2005), 'Do Stronger Patents Induce More Local Innovation?', in K. E. Maskus and J. H. Reichman (eds), *International Public Goods and Transfer of Technology under a Globalized Intellectual Property Regime*, Cambridge, Cambridge University Press.

Bravo, A. (2004), 'La Industria Farmaceutica Nacional Frente a un TLC con los Estados Unidos', *Alcadía Mayor*, Bogotá, Colombia.

Bridges Weekly (2005), 'Concerns Raised Over Access to Medicines Under Trade Treaties', *Bridges Weekly Trade News Digest*, Geneva, ICTSD, 14 July 2004.

Bridges Weekly (2007a), 'Canadian WTO Notification Clears Path for Rwanda to Import Generic HIV/AIDS Drug', *Bridges Weekly Trade News Digest*, 10 October 2007.

Bridges Weekly (2007b), 'US Democrats Unveil Trade Policy, Days Before Key Deadline', *Bridges Weekly Trade News Digest*, Geneva, ICTSD, 28 March 2007.

Bridges Weekly (2011), 'Trade Preference Schemes, FTAs Become Political Footballs in US Congress', *Bridges Weekly Trade News Digest*, Geneva, ICTSD, 10 February 2011.

Brown, S., Evans, L., Defazio, P., Schakowsky, J., Grijalva, R., Mcnulty, M., McGovern, J. P., Pascrell, B., Michaud, M., Lynch, S., Lee, B., Woolsey, L., Payne, D. M., Strickland, T., Delahunt, W. D., Solis, H., Gutierrez, L., Jackson, J. L., Waters, M., Wexler, R., Oberstar, J., Holt, R., Ryan, T. and Sanchez, L. (2005), Letter to Ambassador Portman, US Congress, Washington, DC.

Business Monitor International (2006), *The Colombia Pharmaceuticals and Healthcare Report*: www.businessmonitor.com/pharma/colombia.html.

Caballero Argáez, C. (2004), 'Un palo en la rueda?', *El Tiempo*, 8 May 2004.

Cabrera Galvis, M. (2006), 'Prologo', A. Acosta Medina (ed). *El TLC en Blanco y Negro*, Bogotá, Sociedad Colombia de Economistas.

Callan, E. (2007), 'Go-ahead for US-Peru Free-trade Deal', *Financial Times*, 8 November 2007.

Callan, E. and Guha, K. (2007), 'White House and Democrats Strike Trade Policy Deal', *Financial Times*, 11 May 2007.

Cameron, M. A. and Tomlin, B. W. (2000), 'Negotiating North American Free Trade', *International Negotiation* 5(1): 43–68.

Campodónico, H. (2003), 'Cristal de Mira – G-21, ALCA, TLC y nuestra política de inserción internacional', *La Republica*, 3 October 2003.

Campodónico, H. (2004), 'Balance de la VI Ronda para el TLC en Tucson', *La Republica*, 5 December 2004.

Campodónico, H. (2005) 'Despues de la VII Ronde del TLC: Solo nos queda "minimizar los danos"?', *La Republica*, 27 February 2005.

Campodónico, H. (2006), 'The Andean Free Trade Agreement: now or never?', *Third World Resurgence*, Third World Network: www.twnside.org.sg/title2/resurgence/182-183/Cover08.doc.

Cardenas, M., Junguito, R. and Pachon, M. (2005), 'Political Institutions and Policy Outcomes in Colombia: The Effects of the 1991 Constitution', *Working Papers*, Fedesarollo, Bogotá, Colombia, 30 January 2005.

Carvalho, N. P. D. (2002), *The TRIPS Regime of Patent Rights*, London, The Hague, Tokyo, Kluwer Law International.

Centro Peruano de Estudios Sociales (CEPES) (2004), Dr Baldo Kresalja – TLC, 'No nos dejemos llevar por la etiqueta' *La Revista Agraria* 60(5).

Charnovitz, S. (2004), 'Using Framework Statutes to Facilitate U.S. Treaty Making', *The American Journal of International Law* 98(4): 696–710.

Childs, P. E. (1999), 'The Centenary of Aspirin: Wonder Drug of the Twentieth Century', *Chemistry in Action* (59).

Chisum, D. S., Nard, C. A., Schwartz, H. F., Newman, P. and Kieff, F. S. (2004), *Principles of Patent Law: Cases and Materials* (3rd edn), New York, Foundation Press.

Clark, W. R., Duchesne, E. and Meunier, S. (2000), 'Domestic and International Asymmetries in United States – European Union Trade Negotiations', *International Negotiation* 5(1): 69–95.

Clarkson, S. (2002), *Uncle Sam and Us*, Washington, DC, Woodrow Wilson Center Press.

CNN (2006) 'Peru Approves Free-trade Pact with U.S.', *CNN*, 28 June 2007.

Colombia Hoy (2006), 'La Crisis del Modelo Uribe', *Colombia Hoy*, 27 September 2009.

Commission on Intellectual Property Rights (2002), 'Integrating Intellectual Property Rights and Development Policy', London: www.iprcommission.org/graphic/documents/final_report.htm.

Committee on House Ways and Means (2005), 'Report on Trade Mission to Colombia, Ecuador and Peru', US Congress, Washington, DC: http://waysandmeans.house.gov/media/pdf/109cong/wmcp/wmcp109-6.pdf.

Confessore, N. (2003), 'Welcome to the Machine – How the GOP disciplined K Street and Made Bush Supreme', *Washington Monthly*, July/August: www.washingtonmonthly.com/features/2003/0307.confessore.html.

Conybeare, J. (1987), *Trade Wars: The Theory and Practice of International Commercial Rivalry*, New York, Columbia University Press.

Cook, T. M., Doyle, C. and Jabbari, D. (1991), *Pharmaceuticals, Biotechnology and the Law*, London, Macmillan Publishers Ltd.

Correa C. J. (2005), 'Salud reclama espacio en el TLC', *El Tiempo*, 4 March 2005.

Correa C. J. (2007), 'Otra funcionaria del Gobierno relacionada con TLC renunció para irse a multinacional de medicinas', *El Tiempo*, 17 November 2007.

Correa, C. M. (2004a), 'Bilateral Investment Agreements: Agents of new global standards for the protection of intellectual property rights?', *GRAIN*: http://www.grain.org/briefings_files/correa-bits-august-2004.pdf.

Correa, C. M. (2004b), 'Can the TRIPS Agreement Foster Technology Transfer to Developing Countries?', in J. H. Reichman and K. E. Maskus (eds), *International Public Goods and Transfer of Technology under a Globalized Intellectual Property Regime*, Cambridge, Cambridge University Press.

Correa, C. M. (2004c), 'Protecting Test Data For Pharmaceutical and Agrochemical Products under Free Trade Agreements', *UNCTAD – ICTSD Dialogue on Moving the Pro-Development IP-Agenda Forward: Preserving Public Goods in Health, Education and Learning*, Bellagio, Italy, ICTSD.

Correa, C. M. (2005), 'Can the TRIPS Agreement Foster Technology Transfer to Developing Countries?', in K. Maskus and J. Reichman (eds), *International Public Goods and Transfer of Technology Under a Globalized Intellectual Property Regime*, Cambridge, Cambridge University Press.

Correa, C. M. (2006), 'Implications of Bilateral Free Trade Agreements on Access to Medicines', *Bulletin*, Geneva, World Health Organization 84(5):399–404.

Correa, C. M. (2007), 'Public Health and the Implementation of the TRIPS Agreement in Latin America', in C. Blouin, J. Heymann and N. Drager (2007), *Trade and Health: Seeking Common Ground*, North-South Institute, Ottawa, McGill University.

Cortes Gamba, M. E. (2006), *Intellectual Property in the FTA: Impacts on Pharmaceutical Spending and Access to Medicines in Colombia*, Bogotá, IFARMA/Mision Salud.

Cortes Gamba, M. E., Zerda Sarmiento, A., Sarmiento, D. and de la Hoz Pinzon, G. A. (2004), *Modelo Prospectivo del Impacto de la Protección a la Propiedad Intelectual sobre el Acceso a Medicamentos en Colombia*, Bogotá, PAHO and IFARMA.

Cowhey, P. F. (1993), 'Domestic Institutions and the Credibility of International Commitments: Japan and the United States', *International Organization* 47(2): 299–326.

Crawford, J. A. and Fiorentino, R. V. (2005), 'The Changing Landscape of Regional Trade Agreements', *WTO Discussion Paper* (8).

Crump, L. (2006), 'Global Trade Policy Development in a Two-Track System', *Journal of International Economic Law* 9(2): 487–510.

Cubillos, F. R. and Santamaría, R. (2005), 'Luis Madrid habla de error que le costó retiro en TLC', *La Republica*, 28 February 2005.

Dam, K. (2004), 'Cordell Hull, the Reciprocal Trade Agreement Act, and the WTO', *John M. Olin Law & Economics Working Paper Series* (228), University of Chicago.

de Jonquieres, G. (2002), 'Europe hopes to "hit the White House where it hurts"', *Financial Times*, 26 March 2002.

de la Flor, P. (2010), 'El TLC Perú-Estados Unidos: Riesgos y Oportunidades', in J. R. Perales and E. Morón (eds) (2010), *La Economía Política del Tratado de Libra Comer-cio entre Perú y Estados Unidos*, Woodrow Wilson International Center for Scholars, Washington, DC.

Destler, I. (2005), *American Trade Politics* (4th edn), Washington, DC, Institute for International Economics.

Destler, I. (2007), 'American Trade Politics in 2007: Building Bipartisan Compromise', *Policy Brief*, Washington, DC, Peterson Institute for International Economics, May 2007.

Devereaux, C., Lawrence, R. Z. and Watkins, M. (2006), *Case Studies in U.S. Trade Negotiations*, Washington, DC, Petersen Institute for International Economics.

Diaz, G. (2010), 'Inserción Internacional: ImPactos Previsibles y Agenda Pendiente' in J. R. Perales and E. Morón (eds) (2010), *La Economía Política del Tratado de Libre Comercio entre Perú y Estados Unidos*, Woodrow Wilson International Center for Scholars, Washington, DC.

Diez Canseco, J. (2004), 'TLC: Defender la salud y nuestro patrimonio biogenetico', *La Republica*, 15 August 2004.

Diez Canseco, J. (2007), 'Perú: Los enigmas de García y el TLC', *Servindi*, 2 January 2007.

Drahos, P. (2001a), *Bilateralism in Intellectual Property*, London, Oxfam: http://www.maketradefair.com/en/assets/english/bilateralism.pdf.

Drahos, P. (2001b), 'BITs and BIPs: Bilateralism in Intellectual Property', *Journal for World Intellectual Property* 4(6): 791–808.

Drahos, P. (2003), *Expanding Intellectual Property's Empire: The Role of FTAs*, GRAIN.

Drahos, P. (2004), 'Intellectual Property and Pharmaceutical Markets: A Nodal Governance Approach', *Temple Law Review* 77(2): 401–424.

Drahos, P. and Braithwaite J. (2000), *Global Business Regulations*, Cambridge, Cambridge University Press.

Drahos, P. and Braithwaite, J. (2002), *Information Feudalism – Who owns the knowledge economy?*, New York, New Press.

Drahos, P., Faunce, T., Goddard, M. and Henry, D. (2004), 'The FTA and the PBS: A submission to the Senate Select Committee on the US-Australia FTA', Australian Senate.

Drinkard, J. (2005), 'Drugmakers Go Furthest to Sway Congress', *USA Today*, 25 April 2005: www.usatoday.com/money/industries/health/drugs/2005-04-25-drug-lobby-cover_x.htm.

Duque Lopez, M. V. (2009), 'Seguro: Agro Ingreso Seguro', *Razon Publica*, 5 October 2009: www.razonpublica.com/index.php?option=com_content&view=article&id=124:seguro-agro-ingreso-seguro&catid=21:conflicto-drogas-y-paz&Itemid=30.

Dutfield, G. (2003), *Intellectual Property Rights and the Life Science Industries: A 20th Century History*, Burlington, VT, Ashgate Publishing Co.

Dutfield, G. (2006), 'Protecting Traditional Knowledge: Pathways to the Future', *UNCTAD/ICTSD Issue Papers on IPRs and Sustainable Development* (16).

Dutfield, G. (2008), 'Making TRIPS Work for Developing Countries' in G. Sampson and W. Bradnee Chambers (eds), *Developing Countries and the WTO: Policy Approaches*, United Nations University.

Dutfield, G. and Suthersanen, U. (2008), *Global Intellectual Property Law*, Cheltenham, UK, Edward Elgar.

Econometria (2005), 'Estudio de la politica de precio de medicamentos en Colombia', *Econometria S.A.*, June 2005.

Economist, The (2005), 'From Seed to Harvest', *The Economist*, 19 June 2005.

Edwards, S. (2001), *The Economics and Politics of Transition to an Open Market Economy: Colombia*, OECD, Paris.

El-Said, M. (2005), 'The Road from TRIPS-Minus, to TRIPS, to TRIPS-Plus', *The Journal of World Intellectual Property Rights* 8(1): 53–65.

El Comercio (2005a), 'Renuncio Negociador – Alerta en propiedad intelectual del TLC', *El Comercio*, 26 May 2005.

El Comercio (2005b), 'Salud pide regular mercado de medicinas para afrontar TLC', *El Comercio*, 3 June 2005.

El Comercio (2006), 'Debe aprobar este Congreso el TLC?', *El Comercio*, 23 January 2006.

El Comercio (2007), 'TC declararía inadmisible demanda contra el TLC', *El Comercio*, 13 November 2007.

El Comercio (2008), 'Perú: el Congreso tendrá que revisar diez decretos legislativos por día', *El Comercio*, 7 July 2008.

El Peruano (2005a), 'Garcia garantiza apoyo del APRA a firma de TLC', *El Peruano*, 2 December 2005.

El Peruano (2005b), 'Mincetur: Seria grave postergar TLC con EE.UU', *El Peruano*, 29 January 2005.

El Peruano (2005c), 'Ministra Mazzetti propone sistema de compensacion', *El Peruano*, 19 November 2005.

El Peruano (2005d), 'Peru competirá mejor con China cuando firme TLC', *El Peruano*, 7 February 2005.

El Peruano (2005e), 'Peru gana con TLC', *El Peruano*, 8 December 2005.

El Peruano (2005f), 'Referendum sobre TLC será muy perjudicial para el país', *El Peruano*, 9 February 2005.

El Peruano (2005g), 'Sin TLC próximo gobierno fracasara', *El Peruano*, 1 February 2005.

El Peruano (2005h), 'Subsidios agrícolas de los países ricos terminan en 2013', *El Peruano*, 22 December 2005.

El Peruano (2006), 'Kit de Propiedad Intelectual', *El Peruano*, 21 November 2006.

El Tiempo (2004), 'Colombia inicia la cuenta regresiva para la firma del TLC', *El Tiempo*, 17 May 2004.

El Tiempo (2007), 'Aprobados cambios a TLC en la Cámara', *El Tiempo*, 25 September 2007.

Engelberg, A.B. (1999), 'Special Patent Provisions for Pharmaceuticals: Have they Outlived Their Usefulness – A Political Legislative and Legal History of U.S. Law and Observations for the Future', *IDEA, The Journal of Law and Technology* 39: 389–428.

Epstein, D. and O'Halloran, S. (1995), 'A Theory of Strategic Oversight: Congress, Lobbyists, and the Bureaucracy', *Journal of Law, Economics and Organization* 11(2): 227–55.

Epstein, D. and O'Halloran, S. (1996), 'Divided Government and the Design of Administrative Procedures: A Formal Model and Empirical Test', *The Journal of Politics* 58(2): 373–97.

Evans, P. B. (1993), 'Building an Integrative Approach to International and Domestic Politics – Reflections and Projections', in P. B. Evans, H. K. Jacobson and R. D. Putnam (eds), *Double-Edged Diplomacy – International Bargaining and Domestic Politics*, Berkeley, University of California Press.

Evans, P., Jacobsen, H. and Putnam, R. (eds) (1993), *Double-Edged Diplomacy: International Bargaining and Domestic Politics*, Berkeley, University of California Press.

Evenett, S. J. and Meier, M. (2006), *The U.S. Congressional Elections in 2006: What Implications for U.S. Trade Policy*, Swiss Institute for International Economics and Applied Economic Research, University of St. Gallen.

Fairlie, A. (2005a), 'Intregación Regional y Tratados de Libre Comercio: Algunos escenarios para los Países Andinos', in A. Fairlie (ed), *Paises Andinos Frente al TLC y la Comunidad Sudamericana de Naciones*, Lima, LATN/Friedrich Ebert Stiftung.

Fairlie, A. (2005b), *TLC a ritmo de cueca vs. integración regional*, Lima, Universidad Catolica.

Fairlie, A. (2005c), *Costos y Beneficios del TLC con los Estados Unidos*, Lima, Friedrich Ebert Stiftung.

Fairlie, A., Queija de la Sotta, S. and Rasmussen Albitres, M. (2006), *Tratado de Libre Comercio Peru – EE.UU: Un Balance Critica*, Lima, LATN/CISEPA.

Falke, A. (2006), 'A Reluctant Crusade: Die Aussenhandelspolitik der Vereinigten Staaten und George W. Bush', in J. Hils and J. Witzewski (eds), *Defekte Demokratie – Crusader State? Die Weltpolitik der USA in der Aera Bush*, Trier, Atlantische Texte.

Farnsworth, E. and Hufbauer, G. C. (2007), 'Bullying Latin America' (Op Ed), *Baltimore Sun*, 2 August 2007.

FDA (2006), *Frequently Asked Questions for New Drug Product Exclusivity*, Washington, DC, US Food and Drug Administration.

Fernandez, D. (2003), 'Strategic Balancing of Patent and FDA Approval Processes to Maximize Market Exclusivity', *Modern Practice*, November 2003.

Fink, C. and Reichenmiller, P. (2005), 'Tightening TRIPS: The Intellectual Property Provisions of Recent US Free Trade Agreements', *Trade Note 20*.

Fisher, R. and David, W. (1999), 'Authority of an Agent' in R. H. Mnookin and L. E. Susskind (eds), *Negotiating on Behalf of Others*, London, Sage Publishing.

Fisher, R. and Ury, W. (1982), *Getting to Yes: Negotiating Agreement Without Giving In*, London, Hutchinson Business.

Flattmann, G. J., Loy, J. A. and Schechter, A. J. (2006), '"Fisher" and Beyond: Issues for Patenting Expressed Sequence Tags', *New York Law Journal* 235(119).

Foro Salud (2005), 'No Podemos Aceptar Un TLC Que Ponga En Riesgo La Salud Publica', *La Republica*, 20 November 2005.

Foro Salud, Red GlobaL, Conveagro, CCP and CGTP (2005), 'Antes de la septima ronda del TLC con EE.UU: No ceder por apuro innecesario y antidemocratico', *La Republica*, 6 February 2005.

Francke, P. (2004), 'TLC con EE.UU no disminuirá estado de pobreza en el Perú', *La Republica*, 21 November 2004.

Francke, P. (2005), 'TLC: Sin Colombia y Ecuador?', *La Republica*, 20 November 2005.

FTC (2003), *To Promote Innovation: The Proper Balance of Competition and Patent Law and Policy*, Washington, DC, Federal Trade Commission.

GAO (2007a), *Intellectual Property – U.S. Trade Policy Guidance on WTO Declaration on Access to Medicines May Need Clarification*, Government Accountability Office, GAO: http://www.gao.gov/new.items/d071198.pdf.

GAO (2007b), *International Trade: An Analysis of Free Trade Agreements and Congressional and Private Sector Consultations under Trade Promotion Authority*, Washington, DC, Government Accountability Office: www.gao.gov/new.items/d0859.pdf.

Garcia, L. A. (2006), *Un Nuevo Tratado de Libre Comercio en la Region – Algunas consideraciones relativas a propriedad intelectual en le TLC – Peru-Estados Unidos*, Lima, Sociedad Peruana de Derecho Ambiental.

Garcia Orjuela, C. (2005), 'Competencias del Congreso de la Republica en Materia de Tratados Internacionales Procedimiento y Caracteristicas de la Aprobacion de Tratados Internationales en el Ordenamiento Juridico Colombiano', *Colombia Internacional* (61) Universidad de los Andes.

Gerhart, P. M. (2007), 'The Tragedy of TRIPS', *Michigan State Law Review* 143: 143–83.

Gervais, D. (2003), *The TRIPS Agreement: Drafting History and Analysis* (2nd edn), London, Sweet & Maxwell.

Gervais, D. (ed) (2007), *Intellectual Property, Trade and Development – Strategies to Optimize Economic Development in a TRIPS-Plus Era*, Oxford, Oxford University Press.

Gestion (2007), 'Avanza ratificación del TLC en Congreso de EE.UU', *Gestion* 11 May 2007.

Gilpin, R. (2001), *Global Political Economy – Understanding the International Economic Order*, Princeton and Oxford, Princeton University Press.

Goldstein, J. (1993), *Ideas, Interests, and American Trade Policy*, Ithaca, New York, Cornell University Press.

Goodin, R. E. (1996a), 'Institutions and Their Design', in R. E. Goodin (ed), *The Theory of Institutional Design*, Cambridge, Cambridge University Press.

Goodin, R. E. (1996b), *The Theory of Institutional Design*, Cambridge, Cambridge University Press.

Gowa, J. (1983), *Closing the Gold Window: Domestic Politics and the End of Bretton Woods*, Ithaca, New York, Cornell University Press.

Grieco, J. (1988), 'Anarchy and the Limits of Cooperation: A Realist Critique of the Newest Liberal Institutionalism', *International Organization* 42(3): 485–507.

Grossmann, G.M. and Helpman, E. (1994), 'Protection for Sale', *The American Economic Review* 84(4): 833–50.

Haas, E.B. (1958), *The Uniting of Europe: Political, Social and Economic Forces, 1950–1957*, Stanford, Stanford University Press.

Haas, E.B. (1980), 'Why Collaborate? Issue-Linkage and International Regimes', *World Politics* 32(3): 357–405.

Haight Farley, C. (2006), 'Trademark Issues in Current Negotiations', Presentation at Workshop on *IP, FTAs, and Sustainable Development*, Washington, DC, American University: http://www.ciel.org/Tae/IP_CIELandAU_28Feb06.html.

Health Action International (2006), *TLC Aprobado en Base a Medias Verdades e Ignorancia*, June 2006, HAI Peru, Lima.

Helfer, L. R. (2004), 'Regime Shifting: The TRIPs Agreement and New Dynamics of International Intellectual Property Lawmaking', *Yale Journal of International Law* 29(1).

Hennig, J. (2007), 'Peru FTA Supporters Fear Tight Vote, Democrats Discuss Trade', *Inside US Trade*, 25 May 2007.

Hennig, J. (2008), 'House, Senate Leadership Cool to FTAs After State of the Union', *Inside US Trade*, 1 February 2008.

Hepburn, J. (2004), *Patents, Trade and Food: How Strong Patent and Plant Variety Protection Affect Food Security*, Geneva, Quaker United Nations Office.

Hestermeyer, H. (2007), *Human Rights and the WTO – The Case of Patents and Access to Medicines*, Oxford, Oxford University Press.

Hockin, T. A. (2003), *The American Nightmare – Politics and the Fragile World Trade Organization*, Oxford, Lexington Books.

Holguin Zamorano, G. (2007), *TLC y Salud*, Bogotá, Mision Salud.

Hornbeck, J. F. and Copper, W. H. (2011), *Trade Promotion Authority (TPA) and the Role of Congress in Trade Policy*, Congressional Research Service, Washington, DC.

Huenemann, J. E. (2002), 'On the Trade Policy-Making Process in the United States', in IADB (ed), *The Trade Policy Making Process – Level One of the Two Level Game: Country Studies in the Western Hemisphere*, Washington, DC, Inter-American Development Bank.

Hulse, C. (2008), 'House Votes to Put off Trade Deal Bush Sought', *New York Times*, 11 April 2008.

ICTSD (2005), 'WIPO Members Fail to Reach Agreement at Patent Harmonisation Meeting', *Bridges Weekly Trade News Digest*, 8 June 2005.

ICTSD (2008), 'US Democrats Vote to Indefinitely Suspend Action on Colombia FTA', *Bridges Weekly Trade News Digest* (12).

IFAC-3 (2004), 'The U.S.-Central American Free Trade Agreement (FTA) – The Intellectual Property Provisions – 12 March 2004', Industry Functional Advisory Committee on Intellectual Property Rights for Trade Policy Matters (IFAC-3), Washington DC, USTR.

IFARMA (2009), 'Impact of the EU-Andean Trade Agreement on Access to Medicines in Peru, Bogotá, Colombia', IFARMA.

ILD (2009), *'International Lawyers' Delegation to Colombia*, Follow-up Report, 31st January 2009. Available at: http:// www.unison.org.uk/acrobat/B44 64.pdf.

IIPA (2003), *Public Comments on the Caribbean Basin Economic Recovery Act (CBERA)*, Washington, DC, International Intellectual Property Alliance: http://www.iipa.com/rbi/2003_Sep30_CBERA_TPSC-rev.pdf.

IIPA (2005), *Letter to the International Trade Commission: Annual Report on the Impact of the Caribbean Basin Economic Recovery Act on U.S. Industries, Consumers and Beneficiary Countries*, Washington, DC, International Intellectual Property Alliance: http://www.iipa.com/pdf/IIPA%20CBERA%20CAFTA%20filing%20to%20USITC%2009062005.pdf.

IIPA (2007), *US Trade Tools – Caribbean and Central America*, Washington, DC, International Intellectual Property Alliance: http://www.iipa.com/cbera_cbtpa.html.

IMS (2003), *U.S. Pharmaceutical Market: Trends, Issues, Forecasts*, Powerpoint Presentation, IMS Health.

INDECOPI (2005), *Análisis del Impacto Económico de un Régimen de Protección de Datos de Prueba en el Mercado Farmacéutico Peruano*, Lima, INDECOPI.

INDECOPI (2006), *El Acuerdo de Promoción Comercial con Estados Unidos: Alcances e Implicancias en Competencia, Propiedad Intelectual, Obstáculos Técnicos al Comercio y Defensa Comercial*, Lima, INDECOPI.

Inside US Trade (2006), 'Hopes for Swiss FTA Dwindle after Portman-Deiss Meeting', *Inside US Trade*, Washington, DC, 27 January 2006.

Inside US Trade (2007a), 'Brand-Name Drug Industry Alarmed at IPR Precedent Of FTA Template', *Inside US Trade*, Washington, DC, 18 May 2007.

Inside US Trade (2007b), 'Hoyer Says House Consideration of Peru may be Possible in July', *Inside US Trade*, Washington, DC, 29 June 2007.

Inside US Trade (2007c), 'Peru IPR Text Reflects FTA Template, Shows Reduced PhRMA Sway', *Inside US Trade*, Washington, DC, 6 July 2007.

Inside US Trade (2007d), 'PhRMA Will Not Back Latin FTAs, to Lobby for Korea Pact Only', *Inside US Trade*, Washington, DC, 24 August 2007.

Inside US Trade (2008a), 'Administration to Launch "Relentless" Campaign for Colombia FTA', *Inside US Trade*, Washington, DC, 11 January 2008.

Inside US Trade (2008b), 'Rice Leads Delegation to Colombia with CAFTA, Peru FTA Supporters', *Inside US Trade*, Washington, DC, 25 January 2008.

Intellectual Property Watch (2005), 'Japan Proposes New IP Enforcement Treaty', *Intellectual Property Watch*, Geneva, 15 November 2005.

Intellectual Property Watch (2007), 'Rwanda Pioneers Use of WTO Patent Flexibility for HIV/AIDS Medicine', *Intellectual Property Watch*, Geneva, 20 July 2007.

Intellectual Property Watch (2011a), 'The 2011 Drug Patent "Cliff!" and the Evolution of IP Valuation', *Intellectual Property Watch*, Geneva, 11 January 2011.

Intellectual Property Watch (2011b), 'Pharma Backs Calls for Extension of TRIPS Deadline for Least-Developed Countries', *Intellectual Property Watch*, Geneva, 10 February 2011.

Intellectual Property Watch (2011c), 'Pharma Industry Seeks to Bring a Fresh Face to Public Health Policy', *Intellectual Property Watch*, Geneva, 23 March 2011.

International Lawyers Delegation (2009), *International Lawyers Delegation Fellow-Up Report to Colombia 2009*, UNISON: http://www.unison.org.uk/acrobat/B4464.pdf.

ITAC-15 (2006), *The U.S.-Colombia Trade Promotion Agreement (TPA): The Intellectual Property Provisions*, Industry Trade Advisory Committee on Intellectual Property Rights (ITAC-15), Washington, DC, USTR.

Jackson, J. H. (2002), 'Afterword: The Linkage Problem – Comments on Five Texts', *The American Journal of International Law* 96(1): 118–25.

Jenkins, N. (2005), 'Pharmaceuticals: First and Second Medical Use Claims', in Judge Q. Fysh, A. Roughton, T.M. Cook and M. Spence (eds), *The Modern Law of Patents*, London, Reed Elsevier.

Jones, B. (2001), *Politics and Architecture of Choice*, Chicago, University of Chicago Press.

Jorge, M. F. (2007a), 'New US Trade Policy: A Turning Point?', *Journal of Generic Medicines – The business journal for the generic medicines sector* 5(1): 5–8.

Jorge, M. F. (2007b), 'Trade Agreements and Public Health: Are US Trade Negotiators Building an Intellectual Property Platform Against the Generic Industry? Are they Raising the Standards to go Beyond the US Law?', *Journal of Generic Medicines – The business journal for the generic medicines sector* 4(3): 169–79.

Katzenstein, P. J. (1976), 'International Relations and Domestic Structures: Foreign Economic Policies of Advanced Industrial States', *International Organization* 30(1): 1–45.

Katzenstein, P. J. (1977a), 'Conclusion: Domestic Structures and Strategies of Foreign Economic Policy', *International Organization* 31(4): 879–920.

Katzenstein, P. J. (1977b), 'Introduction: Domestic and International Forces and Strategies of Foreign Economic Policy', *International Organization* 31: 587–606.

Kennedy, E. (2005), 'The Doha Declaration and the Trade Promotion Authority of 2002', Congressional Record – Senate.

Keohane, R. and NYE, R. (1977), *Power and Interdependence – World Politics in Transition*, New York, Little Brown.

Kessomboon, N., Limpananout, J., Kulsomboon, V., Maleewong, U., Eksaengsri, A. and Paothong, P. (2010), 'Impact on Access to Medicines from TRIPS-Plus: A Case Study of Thai-US FTA', *Southeast Asian Journal of Tropical Medicine and Public Health* 41(3): 667–77.

King, N. J. (2007), 'Baucus Criticizes U.S.-Korea Trade Pact', *Wall Street Journal*, 2 April 2007: http://blogs.wsj.com/washwire/2007/04/02/baucus-criticizes-us-korea-trade-pact.

Krasner, S. D. (1983), *International Regimes*, Ithaca, NY, Cornell University Press.

Krasner, S. D. (1977), 'US Commercial and Monetary Policy: Unravelling the Paradox of External Strength and Internal Weakness', *International Organization* 31(4): 635–71.

Krauss, E. S. (1993), 'U.S.-Japan Negotiations on Construction and Semiconductors, 1985–1988', in P. B. Evans, H. K. Jacobson and R. D. Putnam (eds), *Double-Edged*

Diplomacy – International Bargaining and Domestic Politics, Berkeley, Los Angeles, London, University of California Press.

La Republica (2004a), 'Nueva presión de funcionario norteamericano', *La Republica*, 3 December 2004.

La Republica (2004b), 'Peru debe prepararse para enfrentar costos de un TLC', *La Republica*, 11 April 2004.

La Republica (2007), 'Rangel me dijo: El TLC is your baby', *La Republica*, 13 May 2007.

Lall, S. (2003), *Indicators of the Relative Importance of IPRs in Developing Countries*, Geneva, UNCTAD-ICTSD.

Landau, A. (2000), 'Analyzing International Economic Negotiations: Towards a Synthesis of Approaches', *International Negotiation* 5(1): 1–19.

Lax, D. and Sebenius, J. (1986), *The Manager as Negotiator: Bargaining for Cooperation and Competitive Gain*, New York and London, The Free Press.

Lax, D. A. and Sebenius, J. K. (2006), *3-D Negotiation – Powerful Tools to Change the Game in Your Most Important Deals*, Boston, Harvard Business School Press.

Lee, M. (2007), *Putting Health on the Fast Track: Compliance with the Doha Declaration on Public Health as a Principal Negotiating Objective for Trade Promotion Authority*, Geneva, CIEL: http://www.ciel.org/Publications/Lee_DohaUSTR_25July07.pdf.

Levin, S. (2007), *Prescription Medicines: Changes to Peru and Panama FTA Represent Democratic Priorities and Real Progress*, House of Representatives, Washington, DC, US Congress.

Levy, P. I. (2009), 'The United States–Peru Trade Promotion Agreement: What Did You Expect?', *Working Paper Series on Development Policy*; No.1, October 2009, The American Enterprise Institute.

Llano Angel, H. (2010), 'Álvaro Uribe Vélez: Un Presidente Paradójico. Corporación Viva La Ciudanía', Bogotá, Colombia.

Lohmann, S. (1997), 'Linkage Politics', *The Journal of Conflict Resolution* 41(1): 38–67

Lohmann, S. and O'Halloran, S. (1994), 'Divided Government and U.S. Trade Policy: Theory and Evidence', *International Organization* 48(4): 595–632.

Lopez, C. (2007), 'Ponencia para primer debate al proyecto de ley numero 178 de 2006 Senado, 200 de 2007 Camara 'pro medio del cual se aprueba el Acuerdo de Promocion Comercial Entre la Republica de Colombia y Los Estados Unidos de America, sus Cartas Adjuntas y su Entendimientos, suscrito en Washington el 22 de Noviembre de 2006', Bogotá, Senate of Colombia.

Lustig, N., Bosworth, B. P. and Lawrence, R. Z. (eds), (1992), *North American Free Trade – Assessing the Impact*, Washington, DC, Brookings Institution.

Machlup, F. and Penrose, E. (1950), 'The Patent Controversy in the Nineteenth Century', *The Journal of Economic History* 10(1): 1–29.

Mansfield, E. (1994), 'Intellectual Property Protection, Foreign Direct Investment, and Technology Transfer', *Discussion Paper* (19), Washington, DC, International Finance Corporation.

Mapstone, N. (2009), 'Peru to suspend land laws after violence', *Financial Times*, 11 June 2009.

Martin, C. P. and Ramirez, J. M. (2004), 'El Impacto Económico de un Acuerdo Parcial de Libre Comercio entre Colombia y Estados Unidos', *Borradores de la Economía* (326), Banco de La Republica Colombiana: http://ideas.repec.org/p/bdr/borrec/326.html.

Marulanda Lopez, F. (2007), *Hacia un TLC mas justo*, Conferencia Episcopal De Colombia, Secretary General.

Maskus, K. E. (2003), 'Transfer of Technology and Technological Capacity Building', *ICTSD-UNCTAD Dialogue, 2nd Bellagio Series on Development and Intellectual Property*, Bellagio, Italy, UNCTAD-ICTSD.

Maskus, K. E. (2004), 'Encouraging International Technology Transfer', *UNCTAD-ICTSD Issue Papers in Intellectual Property Rights and Sustainable Development* (7).

Maskus, K. E. (2006), 'Drug Pricing Under Generic Competition: A Review of the Economics Literature', *Expert Meeting on Developing a Methodology to Assess the Impact of TRIPS-plus Provisions Affecting Drug Prices*, Geneva, ICTSD, WHO and the World Bank Institute.

Maskus, K. E. and Reichman, J. H. (eds), (2005) *International Public Goods and Transfer of Technology Under a Globalized Intellectual Property Regime*, Cambridge, Cambridge University Press.

Matthews, D. (2002), *Globalising Intellectual Property Rights*, London, Routledge.

Matthews, D. (2006), *NGOs, Intellectual Property Rights and Multilateral Institutions: Report of the IP-NGOs Research Project*, London, Queen Mary College, University of London.

May, C. (2000), *A Global Economy of Intellectual Property Rights: The New Enclosures*, London, Routledge.

May, C. (2007a), *The World Intellectual Property Organization – Resurgence and the Development Agenda*, London, Routledge.

May, C. (2007b), 'The Hypocrisy of Forgetfulness: The Contemporary Significance of Early Innovations in Intellectual Property', *Review of International Political Economy* (14)1: 1–25.

May, C. and Sell, S. K. (2006), *Intellectual Property Rights – A Critical History*, Boulder and London, Lynne Rienner Publishers.

McCall Smith, J. (2006), 'Compliance Bargaining in the WTO', in J. Odell (ed), *Negotiating Trade: Developing Countries in the WTO and NAFTA*, Cambridge, Cambridge University Press.

McDermott, J. (2007), *Access to Life-Saving Medicines: Real Change in the Peru FTA*, House of Representatives, Washington, DC, US Congress.

Merges, R. P. and Duffy, J. F. (2002), *Patent Law and Policy: Cases and Materials* (3rd edn), LexisNexis.

Merges, R. P. and Nelson, R. (1990), 'On the Complex Economics of Patent Scope', *Columbia Law Review* (90): http://cyber.law.harvard.edu/IPCoop/90merg2.html.

Merino Roman, M. (2003), 'Congreso debatirá si conviene al Perú retirarse del G-21', *La Republica*, 5 October 2003.

Meunier, S. (2005), *Trading Voices: The European Union in International Commercial Negotiations*, Princeton, Princeton University Press.

Milner, H. V. (1988), *Resisting Protectionism*, Princeton, Princeton University Press.

Milner, H. V. (1993), 'The Interaction of Domestic and International Politics – The Anglo-American Oil Negotiations and the International Civil Aviation Negotiations, 1943–1947', in P. B. Evans, H. K. Jacobson and R.D. Putnam (eds), *Double-Edged Diplomacy – International Bargaining and Domestic Politics*, Berkley, University of California Press.

Milner, H. V. (1997), *Interests, Institutions, and Information: Domestic Politics and International Relations*, Princeton, Princeton University Press.

Milner, H. V. (1998), 'Rationalizing Politics: The Emerging Synthesis of International, American, and Comparative Politics', *International Organization* 52: 759–786.

Milner, H. V. and P. B. Rosendorff (1997), 'Democratic Politics and International Trade Negotiations: Elections and Divided Government as Constraints on Trade Liberalization', *Journal of Conflict Resolution* 41(1): 117–46.

Mincetur (2004), 'Lo que dicen las cifras – TLC y crecimniento exportador', in Mincetur (ed), *TLC – Por un Peru exportador*, Lima, Ministerio de Comercio Exterior, Industria y Turismo.

Mincetur (2005), *Preguntas & Respuestas sobre el TLC Peru – EE.UU*, Lima, Ministerio de Comercio Industria y Turismo.

Mincomercio (2004), *TLC: Línea Política Presidencial*, Bogotá, Ministerio de Comercio Industria y Turismo.

Mincomercio (2006), *Ayuda de Memoria de la Reunión Sostenida en la Oficina del Representante Comercial de Estados Unidos (USTR) sobre Propiedad Intelectual el Dia 16 de Febrero de 2006*, Ministerio de Comercio, Industria y Turismo, Bogotá, Colombia.

Mincomercio (2007), *Cuestionario del Partido Liberal Colombiano sobre el texto del acuerdo del TLC firmado por Colombia y los Estados Unidos*, Ministerio de Comercio, Industria y Turismo, Bogotá, Colombia.

Ministerio de Salud (2006), *Potenciales Efectos del Tratado de Libre Comercio Con Estados Unidos en el Acceso a Medicamentos*, Ministerio de Salud, Peru.

Mo, J. (1995), 'Domestic Institutions and International Bargaining: The Role of Agent Veto in Two-Level Games', *The American Political Science Review* 89(4): 914–24.

Mohme Llona, G. (2004), Editorial – 'Inaceptables presiones norteamericanas', *La Republica*, 10 October 2004.

Moravczik, A. (1993), 'Integrating International and Domestic Theories of International Bargaining', in P. B. Evans, H. K. Jacobsen and R. D. Putnam (eds), *Double-Edged Diplomacy – International Bargaining and Domestic Politics*, Berkeley, University of California Press.

Morgenthau, H. (1949), *Politics Among Nations: The Struggle for Power and Peace*, New York, Knopf.

Morici, P. (1991), 'Lessons From the Canada–U.S. Free Trade Agreement', *Regulation* 14(1).

Morón, E., Bernedo, M., Chávez, J. F., Cusato, A., Winkelried, D. (2005), *Tratado de Libre Comercio con los EEUU: Una Oportunidad para Crecer Sostenidamente*, Universidad del Pacífico and Instituto Peruano de Economía, Lima, Peru.

Morón, E., Sanborn, C. (2006), *The Pitfalls of Policymaking in Peru: Actors, Institutions and Rules of the Game*, Interamerican Development Bank, Washington, DC, April.

MSF (2005), *Untangling the Web of Price Reductions* (8th edn), MSF.

MSF (2008), *Untangling the Web of Antiretroviral Price Reductions* (11th edn), MSF.

Mundo, P. A. (1999), *National Politics in a Global Economy*, Georgetown University Press.

Musungu, S. and Oh, C. (2006), *The Use of Flexibilities in TRIPS by Developing Countries: Can they Promote Access to Medicine?*, Geneva, South Centre.

Neale, M. A. and Bazerman, M. (1991), *Cognition and Rationality in Negotiation*, New York, Free Press.

New York Times (2011), 'Cutting Out the Middleman', *New York Times*, 2 April 2011.

Nicolaidis, K. (1999), 'Minimizing Agency Costs in Two-Level Games', in R. H. Mnookin and L. E. Susskind (eds), *Negotiating on Behalf of Others*, London, Sage Publishing.

O'Halloran, S. (1994), *Politics, Process, and American Trade Policy*, Ann Arbor, University of Michigan Press.

Odell, J. (1993), 'International Threats and Internal Politics – Brazil, the European Community and the United States, 1985–1987', in P. B. Evans, H. K. Jacobson and R. D. Putnam (eds), *Double-Edged Diplomacy – International Bargaining and Domestic Politics*, Berkeley, University of California Press.

Odell, J. (2000), *Negotiating the World Economy*, Ithaca, Cornell University Press.

Odell, J. (2002), 'Creating Data on International Negotiation Strategies', *International Negotiation* (7): 39–52.

Odell, J. (2003), 'Making and Breaking Impasses in International Regimes: The WTO, Seattle and Doha', *EUI Working Papers*, 2003/1.

Odell, J. (2006), 'Introduction', in J. Odell (ed), *Negotiating Trade: Developing Countries in the WTO and NAFTA*, Cambridge, Cambridge University Press.

Odell, J. and Sell, S. K. (2006), 'Reframing the Issue: The WTO Coalition on Intellectual Property and Public Health, 2001', in J. Odell (ed), *Negotiating Trade: Developing Countries in the WTO and NAFTA*, Cambridge, Cambridge University Press.

OECD (2007), *Compendium of Patent Statistics*, Paris, OECD.

Office of Rep Levin (2008), Press Release: 'Administration Must Adopt New China Trade Strategy', Office of Rep Sander Levin, Washington, DC: http://www.house.gov/apps/list/press/mi12_levin/PR032708.shtml.

Office of Senator Kennedy (2006), 'Sen. Kennedy and Rep. Waxman Call for Investigation of U.S. Trade Agreements and International Health', Office of Senator Kennedy, Washington, DC.

Okediji, R. L. (2004), 'Back to Bilateralism? Pendulum Swings in International Intellectual Property Protection', *University of Ottawa Law and Technology Journal* (1) 125–147.

Okediji, R. L. (2006), *The International Copyright System: Limitations, Exceptions and Public Interest Considerations for Developing Countries*, Geneva, UNCTAD-ICTSD.

Ortiz, M. (2004a), 'Con sabor amargo culmina la tercera ronda negociadora del TLC con Lima', *La Republica*, 1 August 2004.

Ortiz, M. (2004b), 'Negociadores agrarios volvieron de la V ronda de TLC con las manos vacias', *La Republica*, 31 October 2004.

Ortiz, M. (2004c), 'Negociadores andinos defraudados por pretensiones de Estados Unidos', *La Republica*, 27 October 2004.

Ortiz, M. (2004d), 'Negociaran medidas de protección al agro en la sexta ronda del TLC', *La Republica*, 29 October 2004.

Ortiz, M. (2004e), 'TLC: Laboratorios piden excluir medicinas de las negociaciones', *La Republica*, 22 October 2004.

Ortiz, M. (2004f), 'Un puñado de congresistas de EEUU quiere excluir a Perú y Ecuador del TLC', *La Republica*, 10 October 2004.

Ortiz, M. (2005a), 'Negociaciones para el TLC avanzaron poco en Cartagena', *La Republica*, 13 February 2005.

Ortiz, M. (2005b), 'Ronda del TLC será decisiva para agro y medicamentos', *La Republica*, 6 February 2005.

Ostergard Jr, R. L. (2007), *Economic Growth and Intellectual Property Rights Protection: A Reassessment of the Conventional Wisdom*, in D. Gervais (ed), *Intellectual Property, Trade and Development – Strategies to Optimize Ecnomic Development in a TRIPS-Plus Era*, Oxford, Oxford University Press.

Outterson, K. and Smith, R. (2006), 'Counterfeit Drugs: The Good, the Bad and the Ugly', *Albany Journal of Science & Technology* (15).

Pahre, R. (1997), 'Endogenous Domestic Institutions in Two-Level Games and Parliamentary Oversight of the European Union', *The Journal of Conflict Resolution* 41(1) 147–74.

Paredes, R. (2010), 'Los Retos de la Implementación del APC en el Peru', in J. R. Perales and E. Morón (eds) (2010), *La Economía Política del Tratado de Libre Comercio entre Perú y Estados Unidos*, Woodrow Wilson International Center for Scholars, Washington, DC.

Park W. G. and Lippoldt, D. (2003), *The Impact of Trade-related Intellectual Property Rights on Trade and Foreign Direct Investment in Developing Countries*, OECD Trade Directorate.

Pastor, R. A. (1993), 'The United States and Central America – Interlocking Debates', in P. B. Evans, H. K. Jacobson and R. D. Putnam (eds), *Double-Edged Diplomacy – International Bargaining and Domestic Politics*, Berkeley, University of California Press.

Pear, R. (2002), 'Plan to Import Drugs From Canada Passes in Senate, but Bush Declines to Carry it Out', *The New York Times*, 18 July 2002.

Pear, R. and Oppel, R. A. J. (2002), 'Results of Elections Give Pharmaceutical Industry New Influence in Congress', *The New York Times*, 21 November 2002.

Pempel, T. J. (1977), 'Japanese Foreign Economic Policy: The Domestic Bases for International Behavior', *International Organization* 31(4): 723–74.

Perales, J. R., Morón, E. (eds) (2010), *La Economía Política del Tratado de Libre Comercio entre Perú y Estados Unidos*, Woodrow Wilson International Center for Scholars, Washington, DC.

Perales, J. R. (2010), 'La Política comercial del Perú en el contexto regional', in J. R. Perales and E. Morón (eds) (2010), *La Economía Política del Tratado de Libre Comercio entre Perú y Estados Unidos*, Woodrow Wilson International Center for Scholars, Washington, DC.

Pereira, E. (2006), 'Salida del representante comercial de E.U. le pone acelerador al Tratado de Libre Comercio', *Portafolio*, 1 February 2006.

Peruvian Times (2008), 'Bolivia stonewalls Peru's proposed amendment to Andean Community intellectual property rules', *Peruvian Times*, 18 June 2008.

Peters, B. G. (2005), *Institutional Theory in Political Science: The 'New Institutionalism'*, London, Continuum.

Pfetsch, F. R. and A. Landau (2000), 'Symmetry and Asymmetry in International Negotiations', *International Negotiation* 5(1): 21–42.

PhRMA (2006), 'Special 301 Report 2006 – Peru', Washington, DC, PhARMA.

Pichihua Serna, J. (2006), 'The FTA and Access to Medicines in Peru: The Economic Impact of Intellectual Property', *Expert Meeting on Developing a Methodology to Assess the Impact of TRIPS-plus Provisions Affecting Drug Prices*, Geneva, ICTSD, WHO and World Bank Institute.

Pollack, M. A. (1997), 'Delegation, Agency, and Agenda Setting in the European Community', *International Organization* 51(1): 99–134.

Portafolio (2006), 'Se destapa crisis en el equipo negociador de medicamentos de Colombia en el TLC', *Portafolio*, 1 February 2006.

Primo Braga, C. A. (1989), 'The Economics of Intellectual Property Rights and the GATT: A View From the South', *Vanderbilt Journal of Transnational Law* 22: 243–64.

Puentes, C. (2007), *Alianza público – privada: Alianza público – privada: fundamento del TLC en Colombia*, Presentation held on 20 June 2007, CEPAL.

Pugatch, M. P. (2004), *The International Political Economy of Intellectual Property Rights*, Cheltenham, Edward Elgar Publishing Ltd.

Pugatch, M. P. (2005), 'Intellectual Property and Pharmaceutical Data Exclusivity in the Context of Innovation and Market Access', in D. Vivas-Eugui, G. Tansey and P. Roffe (eds), *Negotiating Health*, London, Earthscan.

Pulecio, J. R. (2004), 'Bogotá Frente Al TLC: Consideraciones Desde Una Perspectiva Institucional', *Bogotá frente al TLC*, Bogotá.

Pulecio, J. R. (2005), 'La estrategia Uribe de negociación del TLC', *Colombia International* (61) 12–32, Bogotá, Universidad de los Andes.

Putnam, R. (1988), 'Diplomacy and Domestic Politics: The Logic of Two-Level Games', *International Organization* 41(3): 427–460.

Rahm, E. (2007), 'Generic Pharmaceutical Alliance says Peru FTA Strikes Right Balance on Medicines, House of Representatives', Washington, DC, US Congress.

Raiffa, H. (1987), *The Art and Science of Negotiations*, Cambridge, Harvard University Press.

Rangel, C. and Levin, S. (2007), 'Letter to Ambassador Schwab re FTA with Colombia', in S. Schwab (ed), Washington, DC, US Congress.

Reichman, J. H. (2004), 'Undisclosed Clinical Trial Data Under the TRIPS Agreement and its Progeny: A Broader Perspective', *UNCTAD-ICTSD Dialogue on Moving the pro Development IP Agenda Forward: Preserving Goods in Health, Education and Learning*, Bellagio, UNCTAD-ICTSD.

Rens, A., Prabhala, A. and Kawooya, D. (2006), 'Intellectual Property, Education and Access to Knowledge in Southern Africa', UNCTAD, ICTSD, tralac.

Restrepo Velez, L. G. (2005), *Carta Abierta*, 2 December 2005.

Restrepo Velez, L. G. (2007), 'Reforma de la Salud, TLC y Medicamentos', in *El Signo Vital* (1).

Reuters (2008), Congress Extends Andean Trade Benefits 10 Months, *Reuters.com*, 28 February 2008: http://www.reuters.com/article/politicsNews/idUSN28600421 20080228.

Robledo, J. E. (2006), *El TLC Recoloniza a Colombia*, Bogotá, TC Ediciones.

Rodriguez-Franco, D. (2008), *Globalizing Intellectual Property Rights: The Politics of Law and Public Health*, Center for the Study of Law, Justice and Society, Bogotá, Colombia.

Roffe, P. (2004), 'Bilateral Agreements and a TRIPS-plus World: The Chile-USA Free Trade Agreement', *TRIPS Issue Papers* (4), Ottawa, Quaker International Affairs Programme.

Roffe, P. and Vivas-Eugui, D. (2007), 'A Shift in Intellectual Property Policy in US FTAs?', *Bridges Monthly*, Geneva, ICTSD.

Roffe, P., Spennemann, C. and von Braun, J. (2005), 'From Paris to Doha: The WTO Doha Declaration on the TRIPS Agreement and Public Health – A Historical Analysis', in P. Roffe, D. Vivas-Eugui and G. Tansey (eds), *Negotiating Health: Intellectual Property and Access to Essential Medicines*, London, EarthScan.

Roffe, P., von Braun, J. and Vivas-Eugui, D. (2007), 'A New Generation of Regional and Bilateral Trade Agreements: Lessons from the US-CAFTA-DR', in C. Blouin, J. Heymann and N. Drager (eds), *Trade and Health, Seeking Common Ground: Integrating health objectives and international trade policies*, Montreal, Canada, McGill, Queen's University Press.

Rogan, J. (2002), 'Pointed View', *Forbes.com*, 10 July 2002.

Rosenau, J. (1969), *Linkage Politics: Essays on the Convergence of National and International Systems: Linkage Politics Revisited*, New York, Free Press.

Rossi Buenaventura, F. (2006), *Salvamos los Genericos?*, Bogotá, Fundación Misión Salud.

Rovira, J. (2004), *Los efectos de la patentes sobre el acceso a los medicamentos en los países en desarrollo: resumen de la problemática actual y comentario a un reciente articulo sobre el tema*, GeoSalud: http://geosalud.com/tlc/patentes.htm.

Rovira, J. (2005), *Guia para estimar el impacto sobre el accesso a los medicamentos de cambio en los derechos de propiedad intelectual DPI*, WHO/PAHO, 2005.

Ryan, M. P. (1998), *Knowledge Diplomacy: Global Competition and the Politics of Intellectual Property*, Washington, DC, Brookings Institution Press.

Sanchez, J. (2008), '750,000 lost jobs? The dodgy digits behind the war on piracy' *Ars Technica*, 7 October 2008: http://arstechnica.com/tech-policy/news/2008/10/dodgy-digits-behind-the-war-on-piracy.ars.

Santa Cruz, M. (2007), 'Intellectual Property Provisions in European Union Trade Agreements – Implications for Developing Countries', *Issue Paper 20*, Geneva, ICTSD.

Sarmiento, E. (2005), 'Por Qué No Firmar el TLC', *Colombia International* (61) 136–145, Universidad de los Andes.

Schattschneider, E. E. (1935), *Politics, Pressure, and the Tariff*, New York, Prentice Hall.

Schelling, T. C. (1960), *The Strategy of Conflict*, Cambridge, Harvard University Press.

Schifferes, S. (2003), *US Names 'Coalition of the Willing'*, BBC, 18 March 2003.

Schott, J. J. (ed) (2003), *Free Trade Agreements, US Strategies and Priorities*, Washington, DC, Institute for International Economics.

Schwab, S. (2007), 'Statement by USTR Schwab on House Passage of the U.S.-Peru Trade Promotion Agreement', Washington, DC, USTR.

Sebenius, J. K. (1983), 'Negotiation Arithmetic: Adding and Subtracting Issues and Parties', *International Organization* 37(2): 281–316.

Sek, L. (2005), *Andean-U.S. Free Trade Agreement Negotiations*, Washington, DC, Congressional Research Service, The Library of Congress: http://digital.library.unt.edu/govdocs/crs/data/2005/meta-crs-7286.tkl.

Sell, S. K. (1998), *Power and Ideas: North-South Politics of Intellectual Property and Antitrust*, Albany, State University of New York Press.

Sell, S. K. (2003), *Private Power, Public Law: The Globalization of Intellectual Property Rights*, Cambridge, Cambridge University Press.

Sell, S. K. (2005), 'The Quest For Global Governance in Intellectual Property and Public Health: Structural, Discursive, and Institutional Dimensions', *Temple Law Review* (77) 363–400.

Sell, S. K. (2006), 'Books, Drugs and Seeds: the Politics of Access', *Transatlantic Consumer Dialogue, 'The Politics and Ideology of Intellectual Property'*, Brussels.

Sell, S. K. (2010), 'Business and Democracy? Pharmaceutical Firms, Intellectual Property and Developing Countries', in T. Porter and K. Ronit (eds), *The Challenges of Global Business Authority: Democratic Renewal, Stalemate or Decay?*, New York, SUNY Press.

Semana (2004), 'Los negociadores – Una selección de 11 jugadores tienen la responsabilidad histórica de negociar con celeridad y firmeza el Tratado de Libre Comercio con Estados Unidos "Están preparados"', *La Semana* (28).

Shadlen K. C. (2005), 'Exchanging development for market access? Deep integration under multilateral and regional-bilateral trade agreements, *Review of International Political Economy* 12(5): 750–75.

Shaffer, G. C. (2003), *Defending Interests: Public-Private Partnership in WTO Litigation*, Washington, DC, Brookings Institution.

Shepsle, K. (2005), 'Rational Choice Institutionalism', in S. A. Binder, R. Rhodes and B. Rockman (eds), *Oxford Handbook of Political Institutions*, Oxford, Oxford University Press.

Silva Solano, L. C. (2007), 'El Proceso de Negociacion del TLC entre Colombia y Estados', in *Colombia Internacional* (65), Universidad de los Andes, Bogotá, Colombia.

Simon, H. A. (1995), 'Rationality in Political Behavior', *Political Psychology* 16(1): 45–61.

Smith, M. (1993), 'The North American Free Trade Agreement: Global Impacts', in K. Anderson and R. Blackhurst (eds), *Regional Integration and the Global Trading System*, Hertfortshire, Harvester Wheatsheaf.

Sociedad Peruana de Derecho Ambiental (SPDA) (2006), *Un Nuevo Tratado de Libre Comercia en la Region – Algunas Consideraciones Relativas a Propiedad Intelectual en el TLC Peru-Estados Unidos*, SPDA, Lima.

Spector, B. (1978), 'Negotiation as a Psychological Process', in I. W. Zartman (ed), *The Negotiation Process – Theories and Applications*, Beverly Hills, Sage Publications.

Steinberg, R. H. (1997), 'Trade-Environment Negotiations in the EU, NAFTA, and WTO: Regional Trajectories of Rule Development', *The American Journal of International Law* 91(2): 231–67.

Steinberg, R. H. (2002), 'In the Shadow of Law or Power? Consensus-Based Bargaining and Outcomes in the GATT/WTO', *International Organization* 56(2): 339–74.

Stephan, P. B. (1995), 'Barbarians Inside the Gate: Public Choice Theory and International Economic Law', *American University Journal of International Law and Policy* 10(2): 745–67.

Stewart, T. P. (ed), (1999), *The GATT Uruguay Round: A Negotiating History – Volume IV: The Endgame*, Kluwer Law.

Strawbridge, J. (2007), 'Bush Sends Final Peru FTA Bill to Congress; Pelosi Links FTA To TAA', *Inside US Trade*, 28 September 2007.

Suárez Montoya, A. (2006), 'Colombia: Negociando de rodillas, firmando de rodillas y . . . renegociando de rodillas', *aporrea.org*.

Tangarife Torres, M. (2004) *El Tratado de Libre Comercio con Estados Unidos: Fundamentos Jurídicos para la negociación*, Camara de Comercio de Bogotá.

Tansey, G. (2002), *Food Security, Biotechnology and Intellectual Property: Unpacking some Issues around TRIPS*, Geneva, Quaker United Nations Office.

Tansey, G. and Rajotte, T. (2008), *The Future Control of Food – A Guide to International Negotiations and Rules on Intellectual Property, Biodiversity and Food Security*, London, Earthscan, IDRC.

Tarar, A. (2001), 'International Bargaining with Two-Sided Domestic Constraints', *Journal of Conflict Resolution* 45(3): 320–40.

Thambisetty, S. (2008), 'Legal Transplants in Patent Law: Why Utility is the New Industrial Applicability', *LSE: Law, Society, Economy – Working Papers* (6).

Tello, M. (2005), 'Es necesaria la firma del TLC Perú-EEUU', *Economía y Sociedad* (58), CIES, December 2005.

Toledo, A. (2004), 'TLC: Compartiendo un sueno', in Mincetur (ed), *TLC: Por un Peru exportador*, Lima, Ministerio de Comercio Exterior, Industria y Turismo.

Tollison, R. D. and Willett, D. (1979), 'An Economic Theory of Mutually Advantageous Issue Linkages in International Negotiations', *International Organization* 33(4): 425–49.

Trosow, S. E. (2003), 'Fast-Track Trade Authority and the Free Trade Agreements: Implications for Copyright Law', *Canadian Journal of Law & Technology* 2(2): 135–149.

Tsebelis, G. (1995), 'Decision Making in Political Systems: Veto Players in Presidentialism, Parliamentarism, Multicameralism and Multipartyism', *British Journal of Political Science* 25(3): 289–325.

Tsebelis, G. (2002), *Veto Players: How Political Institutions Work*, Princeton, Princeton University Press.

Tully, D. (2003), 'Prospects for Progress: The TRIPS Agreement and Developing Countries After the Doha Conference', *Boston College International & Comparative Law Review* 26(1): 129–44.

UNCTAD-ICTSD (2003), *Intellectual Property Rights – Implications for Development*, Geneva, UNCTAD-ICTSD.

UNCTAD-ICTSD (2005), *Resource Book on TRIPS and Development*, Cambridge, Cambridge University Press.

Uribe, A. (2004), 'Palabras del Presidente Uribe', *Foro de El Tiempo y Union Fenosa sobre el TLC*, Bogotá: http://www.presidencia.gov.co/sne/2004/septiembre/23/19232004.htm.

Uribe, A. (2005), 'Palabras del Presidente Uribe', *Cámara de Comercio Colombo-Americana*: http://oacp.presidencia.gov.co/snerss/detalleNota1.aspx?id=4406.

US Congress (2007), *Peru and Panama FTA Changes*, US Congress.

US House of Representatives (1989), 'Trade Legislation Enacted into Public Law – 1981 through 1988', Committee on Ways and Means, Washington, DC, US House of Representatives.

US International Trade Commission (2003), *The Impact of Trade Agreements: Effects of the Tokyo Round, U.S.–Israel FTA, U.S.–Canada FTA, NAFTA and the Uruguay Round for the U.S. Economy*, Washington, DC, US ITC.

US International Trade Commission (2005), *Andean Trade Preference Act: Impact on U.S. Industries and Consumers and on Drug Crop Eradication and Crop Substitution, 2005 Eleventh Report*, Washington, DC, US ITC.

US International Trade Commission (2006), *US-Peru Trade Promotion Agreement: Potential Economy Wide and Selected Sectoral Effects*, Washington, DC, US ITC.

US International Trade Commission (2010), *Andean Trade Preference Act: Impact on U.S. Industries and Consumers and on Drug Crop Eradication and Crop Substitution, 2009, Fourteenth Report*, Washington, DC, US ITC.

USTR (2004), *2004 Special 301 Report*, Washington, DC, USTR.

USTR (2005a), *Administration Requests Extension of Trade Promotion Authority*, Washington, DC, USTR.

USTR (2005b), *Foreign Trade Barriers – Colombia*, Washington, DC, USTR.

USTR (2007), *Trade Facts – The Case of the US-Peru Trade Promotion Agreement (PTPA)*, Washington, DC, USTR.

Valladares Alcalde, G. (2005), 'Propiedad Intelectual y medicamentos en el Peru – Los derechos de quien?', *Anuario Andino de Derechos Intelectuales* (2).

Valladares Alcalde, G., Cruzado Ubillus, R., Seclen Palacin, J. and Pichihua Serna, J. (2005), *Evaluación de los Potenciales Efectos sobre Acceso a Medicamentos del Tratado de Libre Comercio que se Negocia con los Estados Unidos de América*, Lima, Ministerio de Salud.

Valladares Alcalde, G., Cruzado Ubillus, R., Seclen Palacin, J. and Pichihua Serna, J. (2006), *Potenciales Efectos del Tratado de Libre Comercio con Estados Unidos en el Acceso a Medicamentos*, Lima, Ministerio de Salud.

Velásquez, F. E. (2006), *Le Descentralización: una Apuesta Política de Futuro para Colombia*, Paper presented at Seminar: '20 años de la descentralización en Colombia: presente y futuro'.

VanGrasstek, C. (2008a), *U.S. Trade Policy and Developing Countries: Free Trade Agreements, Trade Preferences, and the Doha Round*, ICTSD, Geneva. http://www.ceim.uqam.ca/IMG/pdf/VanGrasstek.pdf.

VanGrasstek, C. (2008b), 'The Colombia Free Trade Agreement, the Twenty-year Itch and the Doha Round', in *Bridges Monthly* 12(3), May, ICTSD, Geneva: http://ictsd.org/i/news/bridges/12122.

Villar Lopez, R. A. (2005), 'Foro Nacional – TLC y Medicamentos – Su impacto en la salud publica', in I.Y.D. Direccion General de Medicamentos (ed), *Foro Nacional – TLC y Medicamentos*, Lima, Dirección General de Medicamentos, Insumos y Drogas.

Villarreal, M. A. (2007), 'U.S.-Peru Economic Relations and the U.S.-Peru Trade Promotion Agreement', *CRS Report for Congress*, 27 July: www.fas.org/sgp/crs/row/RL34108.pdf.

Vivas-Eugui, D. (2003), 'Regional and Bilateral Agreements and a TRIPS-plus World: The Free Trade Area of the Americas (FTAA)', *QUNO TRIPS Issues Paper* (1).

Vivas-Eugui, D. and Spennemann, C. (2006), 'The Treatment of Geographical Indications in Recent Regional and Bilateral Free Trade Agreements', *Diálogo Regional sobre Propiedad Intelectual, Innovación y Desarrollo Sostenible*, Costa Rica, ICTSD.

Vivas-Eugui, D. and von Braun, J. (2007), 'Beyond FTA Negotiations – Implementing the New Generation of Intellectual Property Obligations', in P. Yu (ed), *Intellectual Property and Information Wealth: Issues and Practices in the Digital Age*, Connecticut, Praeger Publishers.

von Braun, J. and Pugatch, M.P. (2005), 'The Changing Face of the Pharmaceutical Industry and Intellectual Property Rights', *Journal for World Intellectual Property* 8(5): 599–623.

Waltz, K. (1979), *Theory of International Politics*, Reading, Addison-Wesley Publishing Co.

Wasson, E. (2008), 'Rangel Sees No Role in Benchmarks for Advancing Colombia FTA', *Inside US Trade*, 15 February.

Watal, J. (2000), *Intellectual Property Rights in the World Trade Organization: The Way Forward for Developing Countries*, London, Kluwer Law International.

Waxman, H. (2005), *Trade Agreements and Access to Medications under the Bush Administration. Committee on Government Reform*, Washington, DC, Minority Staff Special Investigation Division, US House of Representatives.

Waxman, H. (2007), *Peru FTA: A Step in the Right Direction for Access to Medicines*, House of Representatives, Washington, DC, US House of Representatives.

Waxman, H., Mcdermott, J., Allen, T., Doggett, L., Schakowsky, J. D., Stark, P., Degette, D., van Hollen, C., Lee, B., Blumenauer, E., Lewis, J. and Emanuel, R. (2007), *Letter to Ambassador Schwab*, Washington, DC, US Congress.

Weissman, R. (2006), 'Public Health and TRIPs Plus Provisions in FTAs', Washington, DC, Essential Action.

Welsh, W. (2004), 'Tauzin Switches Sides from Drug Industry Overseer to Lobbyist', *USA Today*, 15 December.

Whalley, J. and Hamilton, C. (1996), *The Trading System After The Uruguay Round*, Washington, DC, Institute for International Economics.

WHO (2006), 'WHO/TCM Strategy for Technical Cooperation 2006–2008: Access to Medicines in the Context of Intellectual Property Rights and Trade Agreements', in WHO/TCM (ed), Geneva, WHO.

Wiener, R. (2004), 'Colaboracion Peru-Colombia-EEUU: Sí o Sí, y Recontrasí colaboradores', *El Correo*, 3 September: http://www.elcorreo.eu.org/esp/article. php3?id_article=5602.

Wilkinson, J. and Castelli, P. (2000), *The Internationalisation of Brazil's Seed Industry: Biotechnology, Patents and Biodiversity*, Rio de Janeiro, ActionAid Brasil.

Wing, L. K. (2004), 'Beat the Clock: With Elections Around the Corner, Peru's Toledo Needs Big Trade Deals—and Growth—Now', *Latin Trade*, March.

Woolcock, S. (2003a), 'State and Non-State Actors', in N. Bayne and S. Woolcock (eds), *The New Economic Diplomacy: Decision-Making and Negotiation in International Economic Relations*, Hampshire, Ashgate 63–76.

Woolcock, S. (2003b), 'Theoretical Analysis of Economic Diplomacy', in N. Bayne and S. Woolcock (eds), *The New Economic Diplomacy: Decision-Making and Negotiations in International Economic Relations*, Hampshire, Ashgate.

Woolcock, S. (ed) (2006), *Trade and Investment Rule-making: The Role of Regional and Bilateral Agreements*, Tokyo, United Nations University Press.

World Bank (2000), 'Trade Blocs and the World Trading System', in World Bank (ed), *Trade Blocs*, Washington, DC, World Bank.

World Bank (2002), *Global Economic Prospects – and the Developing Countries*, Washington, DC, World Bank.

World Bank (2004), *Global Economic Perspectives, Trade, Regionalism, and Development*, Washington, DC, World Bank.

World Bank (2005), *World Development Indicators 2005*, Washington, DC, World Bank.

World Bank (2009), *World Development Indicators 2009*, Washington, DC, World Bank.

Yu, P. (2006), 'Anticircumvention and Anti-anticircumvention', *Denver University Law Review* (84) 13–77.

Zartman, I. W. and Berman, M. R. (1982), *The Practical Negotiator*, New Haven, Yale University Press.

Zartman, I. W. and Rubin, J. Z. (2000), 'The Study of Power and the Practice of Negotiation', in Zartman, I. W. and Rubin, J. Z. (eds), *Power and Negotiation*, Michigan, University of Michigan.

Zerda Sarmiento, A. (2004), *Negociacion del TLC – Sindrome de la Metologia*, Bogotá, Universidad Nacional de Colombia.

Zerda Sarmiento, A. (2005a), 'Impacto de las Provisiones TRIPs-Plus Contempladas en el TLC Colombia – Estados Unidos', *LATN – Working Papers* (41).

Zerda Sarmiento, A. (2005b), *Impactos del Tratado de Libre Commercio Colombia-Estados Unidos en el Sector Salud del Distrito Federal*, Universidad Nacional de Colombia, Bogotá.

Zoellick, R. (2003), 'America Will Not Wait for the Won't-do Countries', *Financial Times*, 22 September.

Zuleta Jaramillo, L. A. and Parra Torado, M. L. (1999), 'Incidencia del Régime de Patentes de la Industria Farmacéutica Sobre la Economía de Colombia', Bogotá, Fedesarollo.

Index

For Product Safety Concerns and Information please contact our EU representative GPSR@taylorandfrancis.com Taylor & Francis Verlag GmbH, Kaufingerstraße 24, 80331 München, Germany

Printed and bound by CPI Group (UK) Ltd, Croydon, CR0 4YY
08/05/2025
01864374-0001

1